TAROT REVELATIONS

JOSEPH CAMPBELL

RICHARD ROBERTS

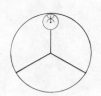

VERNAL EQUINOX PRESS
BOX 581
SAN ANSELMO, CA 94960

Third Edition, 1987

Library of Congress Cataloging in Publication Data
Campbell, Joseph, 1904–
    Tarot revelations
    Bibliography
    1. Tarot I. Richard Roberts
II. Title
Bf 1879.T2C28   1982   133.3'2424   81–86684
ISBN 0-942380-00-2   AACR 2

COVER BY JO GILL

VERNAL EQUINOX PRESS
BOX 581
SAN ANSELMO, CA 94960

TAROT REVELATIONS

The selections and illustrations from the works listed below and others acknowledged in the author's reference notes are reprinted by permission of the holders of copyright and publication rights. Especially grateful thanks to Princeton University Press for permission to use extensive quotations from the works of C. G. Jung.

Princeton University Press: *Psychology and Alchemy, Mysterium Conjunctionis,* and *Alchemical Studies,* by C. G. Jung, translated by R. F. C. Hull. Copyright 1968, 1970 and 1967 by Princeton University Press.

Spiritual Disciplines: Eranos Yearbooks, Vol. 4. Edited by Joseph Campbell. Copyright 1960 by Princeton University Press.

Aurora Consurgens, Edited by M. L. Von Franz. Copyright 1966 by Princeton University Press.

The Mysteries: Eranos Yearbooks, Vol. 2. Edited by Joseph Campbell. Copyright 1955 by Princeton University Press.

Man and Time: Eranos Yearbooks, Vol. 3. Edited by Joseph Campbell. Copyright 1957 by Princeton University Press.

Note: All Princeton excerpts require written permission.

Penguin Books, Inc.: *Alchemy: Science of the Cosmos, Science of the Soul,* by Titus Burckhardt. Copyright 1971. *The Game of Wizards, Psyche, Science, and Symbol in the Occult,* by Charles Poncé. Copyright 1975. Reprinted by permission of Penguin Books.

Harper & Row: *Beyond Stonehenge,* by Gerald Hawkins. Copyright 1973.

Viking Press: *The Masks of God, Occidental Mythology,* by Joseph Campbell. Copyright 1964.

Bantam Books: *The Spear of Destiny,* by Trevor Ravenscroft. Copyright 1974.

Dedication
by
Richard Roberts

Poems
by
Richard Roberts

This book is dedicated to my two fathers
To Joseph Campbell
father of my spiritual birth
To Stanley Byron Roberts
father of my material birth

"OUR FATHER"

Stanley Byron Roberts was a great singer and a hybridizer of new varieties of roses, among which were Vanity Fair and Copper Lustre. It is said that in the next life, one goes to what one has created on earth; hence, in this poem, written at his deathbed, a world of singing flowers awaits him which he himself created here on earth.

My father was trying to be born again.
In his soul's wandering,
He came at last to an immense wall
In which there were no gateways or openings.
Looking over the wall,
He saw a field of flowers extending for eternity.
The flowers emitted a joyous glow of the One
    White Light,
Within which were all the colors of all the rainbows,
In all the universes of the One.
The Light shimmered, danced, and knew him.
And all the flowers sang a welcome to him.
"Here is Our Father," they chorused in joy.
"Here is Our Creator."
And he knew them too.
They were all the seeds he had sown,
Born again themselves and transfigured in the Light.
He left his body at the wall.
His spirit was like a field of shimmering flowers
    of light,
Each flower a mouth that sang the glory of liberation
    and union.

CAMPBELL'S CLOSET

In every man's unconscious there is an eternal image of the hero, the Self. In the closet of Joseph Campbell there is a photo, archetypal in human drama, of his winning a half-mile footrace in a time within two-fifths of a second of the world's record.

> Beyond the daylit, measured threshold,
> Where consciousness can rarely enter,
> Past the discarded apparel of other eras,
> Raiment, vesture, guise, *personae*
> Of how many previous lives?
> Past flint, and bone, and antler knives,
> When you were dawn's paleolithic hunter,
> Beyond clay calendars and orange amphorae,
> When you were noon's neolithic planter,
> Beyond snakeskins and unguents of shamans,
> Crucible and chalice of alchemist and priest,
> Returning step by ancient step,
> Through strange subliminal zones,
> You gain again the midnight room,
> Kernel of the dark world's cradle.
> Here the Hero attains ever the hardwon laurel
>   of divinity.

IN MEMORIAM
JOSEPH CAMPBELL 1904-1987

Und so lang du das nicht hast,
Dieses: stirb und werde,
Bist du nur ein trüber Gast
Auf der dunkeln Erde.

— Goethe

And as long as you do not have
This: die and become,
You are only a troubled sojourner
Upon the dark earth.

The above literal translation leaves the poetry behind; however, the "Dieses" to which Goethe refers is the truth of death and rebirth, the highest human aspiration to transform oneself, always and evermore, so that one's spiritual potential remains unfettered during the lifetime by considerations of personal weal or woe. In so living, one's death is not feared but anticipated as a further rebirth to an unknown but nevertheless welcome dimension. Life lived as adventure! An enhanced awareness of this truth is what Joseph Campbell brought to us during his lifetime, in his books and lectures, and in his personal company.

And we all loved him, because the gift of this truth he gave us, made all of us feel so free, so heroic. We were like forgotten prisoners living in the dank dungeons of nihilism liberated to dance in the sunlight.

I, myself, was just such a troubled sojourner as Goethe mentions, never at home with myself or others, without a spiritual center, until a book came into my life which began the change of Becoming, a future contained within my present, a secret map of heroic potential. That book was

Joseph Campbell's *The Hero With a Thousand Faces*. But my story has been repeated many thousand-fold, for many others had found the path of personal individuation in that same book, which first appeared about the middle of this century, when little light—if any—shone on the philosophical scene. Nihilism and Existentialism ruled the day: Man was alone in a dark world bereft of spiritual value.

Joe's book did not look to the academics for truth, but searched out the literature of the people: mythology. In the stories of those *common* men who experienced a relation to the divine, thereby becoming *un*common men—heroes, Joe discovered a universal pattern that had meaning for Everyman. One had only to read his book to discover where one was in relation to the pattern, the path of self-unfoldment, and then—once discovered—prepare for the next inevitable adventure; for he had written, "every failure to cope with a life situation must be laid, in the end, to a restriction of consciousness." Thus his book "spoke" to me, and to so many others.

I believe it was twenty years ago, 1967, when I first met Joseph Campbell. At that time I often carried with me wherever I went, *The Hero With a Thousand Faces*. My greatest delight was body-surfing, riding the waves without a board. But when not in the water, my time on the beach was spent reading, and *The Hero* always went with me. One day my friend Alan Watts told me that he knew the author of the book, and would give me a letter of introduction when I next went to New York.

Joe said he was about to run at the New York Athletic Club indoor track when I called him, and he invited me to join him. He was then 63 years old. After our workout we adjourned to the N.Y.A.C. bar, and we began the first of hundreds of "fond evenings of ale and good conversation," as—years later—he was to sign one of his books for me.

Our friendship became the most important relationship in my life. He was inspirational, of course, to any creative person, but he also led me to Jung's works, which became the psychic center around which would revolve all of my subsequent writing. But beyond that, he became my mentor, and "the father of my spiritual birth," as I said at the front of this book in the dedication of my poem to him. It sounds like a serious business, but almost all of my time with him was great fun. Eventually he was to sign my old dog-eared copy of *The Hero With a Thousand Faces* that had seen me through so many dark hours, "To Dick Roberts, for his own shining adventure."

When Michael Murphy and Dick Price opened the Esalen Institute in Big Sur, California, their concept was that one would be able to spend a weekend or week with someone whose books had been influential or inspiring for them. One of the first persons that they contacted to lead such seminars was Joseph Campbell, and Esalen was to become Joe's favorite place to visit.

As the concepts of *The Hero With a Thousand Faces* began to be embraced by the human potential movement, his books began to sell quite well, and the demand for him as a lecturer spread all over the country. And what a talk he could give! I remember him telling me that preparing for a lecture was just like getting ready to run a race, so that when the gun went off one knew exactly what to do and where to go. His writing is the perfect blend of profound, soul-stirring inspirations presented with the most apt expression, yet when his dynamic personality broke out of the old lecture-hall "talk" mode by innovating large projections of color slides, then the feeling and sensation functions of the audience, which had largely been neglected heretofore, now responded with cries of "oooh's" and "aaah's" as, for example, when the Minoan snake goddess was projected on the screen. He became the most popular lecturer of his time. I remember the pride he took in the collection of slides he was amassing, shot with his own camera. Later, in the mid-1970's when we began to collaborate as lecturer in my Third Model of the Universe seminars, he presented me with my own slide projector as a birthday present.

Often the demand for his talent exceeded the space of the hall allotted for the lecture. One weekend the University of California had to move the lecture to the Grand Ballroom of the St. Francis Hotel in San Francisco.

During these years he was visiting the San Francisco Bay Area as often as four times a year, and his seminars would take him in many directions. On these trips I was his wheel-man, picking him up at the airport, generally in the early afternoon. Then I would drive him to my house, where I was sure to see that he rested with a nap before dinner. At night we drank Younger's Double-Century ale from Scotland and conversed. Next day I drove him to his seminar, staying to listen in or participate as his guest. Sometimes—particularly at Esalen—these seminars might last a weekend, or even a week. Then it was back to my house, a nap and dinner, and another "fond evening of ale and good conversation." Next day I would drive him to the airport, where he would catch an early flight for New York.

In 1971, I think it was, we began a mutual birthday celebration, since he was born on March 27, and I on March 21. Each year more and more people would learn of the celebration and ask to come, so that we finally had to move the parties to the upper floor of that grand Scottish pub The Edinburgh Castle. One year we even did a seminar there entitled "An Evening of Celtic Lore," with Joe reading from *Finnegan's Wake*, and a group called The Celtic Tradition playing.

When I went to Westport, Connecticut to visit my parents, I would always stop in New York to have dinner one or two nights with Joe and his wife Jean Erdman, who performed the most fantastic production I have ever seen, "The Coach with the Six Insides," a dance version of *Finnegan's Wake*. Jean had been a student of Joe's when he began teaching at Sarah Lawrence. Their marriage was right out of a storybook, and as I used to tell him—not without a tinge of jealousy—"Not everyone can meet and marry The Goddess." Although I saw many groupies go after Joe over the years, he never wavered in his devotion to Jean. Their creative cross-pollination in one another's company was a beautiful thing to watch.

In retrospect I am grateful for the synchronicity that enabled me to have Joseph Campbell for a friend. How marvelous to have so much time with one of the great men of all time. How fortunate to co-author a book with him.

I think I have conveyed something of what the life and works of Joseph Campbell have meant to me personally, but in the larger literary pantheon of great books I recall once telling him that of the ten most important books written since the mid-century, two of them would have to be his: *The Hero With a Thousand Faces,* and *The Masks of God;* volume 4: *Creative Mythology.* I think perhaps that these two were his favorites as well.

Then there is that most exalted judgment of a writer's life—the advancement of human consciousness. In this century, Jung and Campbell, more than any others, taught us the truth of death and rebirth, and the infinite vistas of the human spirit. In his time, Joseph Campbell bestowed many spiritual gifts on all who would listen. I owe him many debts over many karmas, but knowing him, in the next life he will not ask me to repay, but invite me once more to share an ale and one more good conversation.

TAROT REVELATIONS

PART I.
"EXOTERIC TAROT"
JOSEPH CAMPBELL: FORWARD
JOSEPH CAMPBELL: "SYMBOLISM OF THE MARSEILLES DECK"

PART II.
"ESOTERIC TAROT"
COLIN WILSON: INTRODUCTION
RICHARD ROBERTS: "SYMBOLISM OF THE WAITE/RIDER DECK"

1

TAROT REVELATIONS

PART I

"EXOTERIC TAROT"

BY

JOSEPH CAMPBELL

FOREWORD

by
Joseph Campbell

My introduction to Tarot dates from an informal talk on the symbolism of playing cards delivered in 1943, in Maud Oakes' New York apartment, by my extraordinary friend, Heinrich Zimmer, who then — to the shock of all who knew him — passed away hardly two weeks later. When the notes of his university lectures on Hinduism and Buddhism were subsequently turned over to me for editing and publication, I found among them nothing on playing cards; and since, for the next twenty-odd years, my time was engaged entirely in the dual task of bringing forth, not only my own works, but also those of my departed friend, all thought of Tarot faded until, in 1967, while lecturing at the Esalen Institute in Big Sur, California, I was asked by a member of my group for an interpretation of the "Waite" deck. Examining this pack that evening in my room, I recalled that Zimmer had spoken of the four suits (Swords, Cups, Coins, and Staves) as corresponding to the four medieval estates (Nobles, Clergy, Villains, and Serfs), and of the twenty-two atouts as suggesting grades of initiation. These two clues sufficed; and in the morning I was able to propose what seemed to me, at least, to be a tolerable reply to the gentleman's question.

But the subject had now captured my imagination and, on returning to San Francisco on my way back to New York, I spoke to Richard Roberts about it, who immediately proposed a reading of my fortune, the result of which is published in his book, *Tarot and You*. This confirmed my interest, and, on arriving in New York, I bought in my favorite bookstore three decks: a Marseilles, a Waite, and "The Great Italian"; after which, spreading all three before me, I sat for some three hours, gazing and rearranging, until, abruptly, the Marseilles atouts 6 to 9 and 14 to 17 spoke to me, and the whole pack fell into place.

I wrote to Roberts of my finding and he, in reply, proposed a collaboration in which I should write of the Marseilles deck, with its medieval associations, and he, of the Waite and its formation out of the late nineteenth-century esotericism of its author, Arthur Edward Waite. I concurred; and during his next visit to New York, we two set out together on pilgrimage (by subway) to the home and fabulous playing-card collection (the largest, I am told, in the world) of Albert G. Field, who hospitably opened to us all those portions of his treasury that he and Roberts thought could be relevant to our project. And what I beheld, that afternoon, let me know why my long departed friend, Heinrich Zimmer, had been interested in playing cards. There were sets from India of such circular cards as I recalled having seen him toss onto the table, sets from the Far East and from the Near East; and with a pang I realized that in the course of that forgotten talk I must have been introduced to much of the history of these games.

However, my chief concern while viewing the marvelous collection was in the European sets; for what in the Marseilles deck had most excited my imagination had been its reflection of what I thought I recognized as a tradition expounded by Dante in his *Convito*. In fact, it had been my recollection specifically of Chapters 23 and 28 of "The Fourth Treatise" of that philosophical work that first opened to me, that evening in Big Sur, the message of the four Marseilles atouts, 6 to 9. Whereupon the sequence of cards 14 to 17 appeared to me to match the order of the poet's four major works, *La Vita Nuova, Inferno, Purgatorio,* and *Paradiso.* Highly significant in this connection (I have now found) is the fact that our earliest evidences for the existence in Europe of Tarot packs date exactly from Dante's time,* while the first set of which we have tangible, visible evidence (that prepared by the artist Jacquemin Gringon-

---

*See Catherine Perry Hargrave, *A History of Playing Cards* (New York: Dover Publications, 1966), pp. 31-39.

neur for Charles VI of France, seventeen atouts of which are preserved in Paris in the Bibliothèque Nationale) appeared only seventy-one years after Dante's death, namely in 1392. A single philosophical strain, it seemed to me, could be recognized as supporting, on one hand, the mighty edifice of Dante Alighieri's *Divine Comedy* and, on the other, the enigmatic imagery of a contemporary pack of cards.

Whereas the imagery of the Waite deck is of a strikingly different style and source. Prepared under the close supervision of its author, Arthur Edward Waite, by Pamela Colman Smith — a young American artist then at work with the Abbey Theater, helping Yeats with the scenery of his plays — it is a product of the mystical thinking of Yeats' Order of the Golden Dawn, of which both Waite and Miss Smith were members. The initiates of this arcane company conceived the deities of Celtic, Classical, Oriental and primitive myth to be veritable manifestations of aspects of the life-structuring force that Yeats in his poems calls *Anima Mundi*; and as F.A.C. Wilson has noted in a recent study of Yeats' iconography,* there was in this manner of thought something anticipatory of C. G. Jung's psychological theory of the Collective Unconscious and its Archetypes.

Richard Roberts, accordingly, has pointed, in his analysis of the symbolism of the Waite-Smith deck, not only to its background in esoteric astrological, gnostic, and alchemical traditions, but also, by anticipation, forward to the archetypology of Jung — who, in developing his insights, was significantly influenced (as he everywhere lets us know) by the same gnostic and alchemical texts from which the members of the Order of the Golden Dawn drew inspiration. The crucial difference, I would say, between their understanding and Jung's, rests in his interpretation of the archetypes as psychological, whereas Yeats and the rest believed literally in the objectivity, not only of the mythic personifications, but also of incarnate "secret masters," much in the way of

---

*F. A. C. Wilson, *Yeats' Iconography* (New York: The Macmillan Company, 1960), p. 169.

Theosophists. This trend infected their thinking, and equally their writing, with all sorts of mystifications, references to hidden books unknown to modern libraries, and to mysteries and teachings which it would be death for initiates to reveal. As we read, for example, in a passage from Waite's chapter on "The Doctrine Behind the Veil":

> "There is a Secret Tradition concerning the Tarot, as well as a Secret Doctrine contained therein; I have followed some part of it without exceeding the limits which are drawn about matters of this kind and belong to the laws of honor."*

But now — and here, it seems to me, is a point of the greatest interest — there can be recognized in Dante's work and in the mystical lore of his century direct influences from many of same alchemical, gnostic, and astrological works that were drawn upon both by Jung and by the members of the Golden Dawn. An extremely prolific and influential Spanish school of translators, laboring in Toledo under King Alfonso the Wise of León and Castile (r. 1252-1284), had been for some time rendering out of Arabic into Latin fundamental texts, both of Moslem and of ancient Classical thinkers: Aristotle, for example, as well as Ibnu'l-'Arabi; and one of Dante's honored masters, Brunetto Latini (1210-1294), whom the poet greets with the greatest respect in the seventh circle of his Hell, had visited Toledo shortly before his death. Moreover, in the Sicily of those years, in the favorite court of the Holy Roman Emperor Frederick II (r. 1220-1250), there were masters of philosophy both of Moslem and of the various Christian schools, alchemy and astrology being basic to all their thought, no less than to that of Yeats' Golden Dawn.

So that in our separate examinations of the Waite-Smith and Marseilles Tarot decks, Richard Roberts and I have found ourselves continually breaking into areas of much greater expanse and richness than either of us had anticipated when we started. And what we have learned to

---

*Arthur Edward Waite, *The Pictorial Key to the Tarot* (University Books, 1960) p. 68.

recognize thereby has been the influence through centuries of an order of thought little treated in our academic histories. Frances A. Yates' *Giordano Bruno and the Hermetic Tradition* (University of Chicago Press, 1964) is about as clear and sound an introduction to the subject as I have discovered anywhere, and for anyone wishing to continue in these studies, that would be an excellent work from which to take one's start. Meanwhile, for entertainment and learning, there is this little game of Tarot, in two very different, yet related, transformations. It has been for us a truly fascinating adventure, leading sometimes through baffling mazes of verbosity, with references to mystic volumes known to the inward eyes alone of initiates meditating (as Joyce remarks in *Ulysses*) with "pineal glands aglow":

"Yogibogeybox in Dawson chambers. *Isis Unveiled*. Their Pali book we tried to pawn. Crosslegged under an umbrel umbershoot he thrones an Aztec logos, functioning on astral levels, their oversoul, mahamahatma. The faithful hermetists await the light, ripe for chelaship, ringroundabout him." (p. 189)

But in the end, always, we have come to revelations of a grandiose poetic vision of Universal Man that has been for centuries the inspiration both of saints and of sinners, sages and fools, in kaleidoscopic transformations. It is our hope and expectation that our readers, too, may be carried through the picture play of these two enigmatic card packs, through the magic of THE MAGICIAN's wand and guidance of THE PROPHETESS, to insights such as may lead, in the end, to the joy in wisdom of THE FOOL.

"THE MARSEILLES TAROT"

SYMBOLISM OF THE
MARSEILLES DECK

by
Joseph Campbell

The earliest set of Tarot cards of which actual examples survive was prepared in 1392 for King Charles VI of France by the painter Jacquemin Gringonneur. Seventeen of their number are preserved in Paris in the Bibliothèque Nationale, and the imagery resembles that of the Marseilles deck. The date, furthermore, is of the close of Dante's fourteenth century, who was born in 1265 and died in 1321. Moreover, it is from the beginning of that century, 1330, 1340, or so, that we begin to hear of complaints from the clergy about members of their flocks making use of playing cards. Thus it appears that the medieval Tarot must have begun to become popular in Europe exactly in Dante's time; and this gives me reason to believe that the analogies with Dante's thought that I recognized when, as told in my Introduction, I first laid out a set of the cards on my table, there at Esalen, cannot be incidental, but are of the essence.

Richard Roberts, in his chapters on the nineteenth-century Waite deck, points out that Tarot packs are composed of two contrasting sets. The first is of four suits of fourteen cards each, Swords, Cups, Coins, and Staves, fifty-six cards in all, while the second, known as the Major Arcane, Honors, or Atouts, is a packet of twenty-one numbered picture cards, plus one, unnumbered, called The Fool.

What the set of four suits represents are the four estates, or classes, of the medieval social order. The Swords signify the nobility; the Cups, suggesting the chalice of the Catholic Mass, are for the clergy; the Coins, for the merchants, or "third estate," the townsmen, the burghers; while the

Staves, Clubs, or Batons, stand for the "churls," the peasantry and servants. Each suit consists of ten numbered cards, followed by four face cards (not three, as in our packs): first the Knave, then the Knight, on whom the Knave would be attendant, next the Queen, and finally the King. And what each of these sequences would have represented in a medieval context would have been a scale of mounting spiritual, as well as social, power. Only in that of the Coins would the power have been economic, as it is generally in our day. Among the nobility and clergy, for example, the power scale would have been of rank, and among the "churls," also, of a kind of rank based on age, prestige in the village, or position in service. Card Two of the Coin series carries the advertisement of the publisher of the pack, which is, of course, natural and proper for a merchant and his wares.

But is it not strange and interesting, that each of the four suits should culminate in face cards representing figures of the nobility? Knave, Knight, Queen, and King! This would seem to me to suggest (if it is not merely an unconsidered convention) that ascent along any of the lines may lead to *spiritual* realizations of equivalent value and importance; such values being represented in figures of the nobility, since the cards were the playthings rather of the nobles than of priests. Our first known set was prepared, as already remarked, for a king, while our first evidence of the existence of such cards in Europe at all comes from the sermons against them of the clergy.

In any case, the cards, as we know them, date from the end of the fourteenth century, and the dominant religion of that time was of the medieval Catholic Church; whereas, when we turn to any one of our own decks of playing cards, the symbolism that we open to is of the Protestant seventeenth century. The Swords have become Spades, all of the various late-medieval words for "sword" having been derived from the Latin *spatha* (Greek *spathē*): Italian *spada,* Provençal *espaza,* Spanish and Portugese *espada,* and Old French *espée.* The Cups, which formerly represented the chalice of the Catholic mass, have become Hearts; for in Protestant thinking it was not in the rituals and dogmas of

10

the Roman clergy but in one's own heart, one's conscience, that spiritual guidance was to be found. The Coins have become Diamonds, and the Clubs have remained Clubs, though differently pictured. Thus, together with the new theology, there has come an erasure of explicit class references in the symbology of our cards. The Spades look more like shovels than swords, and the Clubs are like nothing at all. Both the nobles and the clergy having lost power to the merchant class in the new society that was coming into being, there was to be one power only, namely money.

But to return, now, from our own day and its order of values to that very different one of the closing Middle Ages, and bearing in mind the importance of the principle of birth, as then interpreted, with no mobility possible from class to class, upward or downward, as today through the acquisition or loss of money, we may understand how and why it should have been that such advances in power as were represented in the fifty-six cards of the four Tarot suits would have had to have been interpreted rather in spiritual kingship along any of the ways of the four suits through virtuous living in whatever the class and station of one's birth might have been. And in the series of the higher set, the Trumps, Honors, or Atouts, this accent on the spiritual life is emphatic.

We notice, first, that the opening card, The Magician, is of a juggler manipulating miniatures of the signs of all four suits: Swords in the form of knives, small cups for the Cups or Chalices, dice and coins for the Coins, and for the Staves or Clubs a wand. He is in control, that is to say, of the symbols of all four social estates, able to play or conjure with them, and so, represents a position common to, or uniting, them all, while leading — as we shall very soon see — beyond their highest grades. Twenty numbered picture cards follow, which have been arranged here in five ascending rows of four cards each, to suggest the graded stages of an ideal life, lived virtuously according to the knightly codes of the Middle Ages. And then, beyond and outside of this numbered series, comes The Fool, whose card, like our Joker Wild, is unnumbered. I have placed him outside and at the end of the set, to signify his freedom to roam as a vagabond, beyond as well as through all of the numbered stations, trumping them all.

So let us proceed to a review of the stages by which the young juggler of the beginning of this Honors series advances to the fulfilled and final estate of this ageless wandering Fool.

1. **The Magician.** As noticed, he is young, yet in control of the symbols of all four suits, which suggests that the course which he initiates can be followed in the ways of any or all of the four social estates; i.e., that any path of life well followed may lead to an opening of the spiritual door, of which he is the guardian.

2. **The High Priestess.** She, too, is young, and in my arrangement appears directly beneath the card of The Lovers; for young people of the sort that become engaged in spiritual adventures of the kind symbolized in this Honors series experience love as something sacred; and the maiden of noble character is then its priestess. Schopenhauer writes beautifully, in his essay "On the Will in Nature," of the first meeting of the eyes of a young woman and young man. A deeply motivated, instinctive measuring is implicit, of complementarities, implied children, and projects into the future of imagined lives together. In terms of Carl G. Jung's archetypology, the figures of these first two Honors cards might be read as representing, respectively, the Animus and the Anima, complementary images of the ideal male in the psyche of the female and female in the psyche of the male. When objectified, such images have a compulsive, profoundly moving, inspirational effect; as in Dante's case, for example, whose experience of the beauty of his *femme inspiratrice* was such that it bore him, in visionary transport, through Hell, Purgatory, and the circles of Paradise, to a beatific vision of the glory of God. Beatrice was thus the "High Priestess," indeed, of his exaltation. Moreover, already in the twelfth and thirteenth centuries of the Troubadours and Minnesingers, ennobling love had been poetically celebrated as an experience of no less than divine import, with the idealized Lady as its priestess. The appearance, therefore, of this ecclesiastically crowned "High

Priestess" at the opening of the Marseilles Honors sequence accords nicely with the medieval European tradition of the ennobling spirituality of Love.

3. **The Empress.** In rank and power transcending the Queens of the minor suits, she is their "Queen of Queens." She appears in this arrangement below the knightly chariot driver of the two powerful steeds, the blue and the red, the sensual and the spiritual. Plato, in his *Phaedrus,* in his famous image of the chariot drawn by two steeds, "one of them noble and good, and of good stock, while the other is of opposite character, and his stock opposite" (*Phaedrus* 246b), writes of the necessity to control and coordinate the two; while Dante's Virgil, at the fourth stage of the *Purgatorio,* delivers a lecture on the two effects of love, the one exalting, the other degrading. The knightly chariot driver represented in the Tarot deck in the prime of life and in control of the joined pair of his steeds, the red one of the soul (to use Plato's term), and the blue of the body, would thus be (as was Lancelot to Guinevere) the proper lover of the Queen of Queens; for as the wholly spiritual High Priestess of Column One typifies the virtue of love in its dawning, so The Empress of Column Two, its maturity.

4. **The Emperor.** From Column Two to Column Three we pass from Maturity to Age. The Emperor is white-bearded, and, as "King of Kings," appears enthroned beneath the Honors card named Justice: the virtue which, according to Dante, is the cardinal virtue of age (*Convivio* IV. 27), and more especially, of all rulers enthroned, scepter in hand, on seats of judgment and authority. *Diligite iustitiam, qui iudicatis terram,* we read in Canto XVIII of his *Paradise,* "Love justice, you that be judges of the earth."

5. **The Pope.** Passing now from Column Three to Column Four, we have moved from Age into that final stage of life which Dante has termed Decrepitude. The mind is to be directed here from secular to purely spiritual concerns, and in the Europe of the Middle Ages the institution representative of this turn was the Roman Catholic Church with the Pope as its visible head.

Thus in our first sequence of four cards, following Card One, of The Magician, we have found represented in two female and two male symbolizations, four transformations of consciousness through the archetypal stages of a human lifetime; and directly above, in the second range, are to be seen representations of the accordant virtues, as follows:

6. **The Lovers.** Dante, in the *Convivio,* assigns to the period of the body's growth the years from birth to twenty-five. His term for the whole period is Adolescence, and the virtues that he assigns to it are Obedience and a Sense of Shame, Comeliness of Appearance, and Sweetness of Conduct (*Convivio* IV. 24-25). In this Tarot card, on the other hand, the represented virtue is, rather, Love, which is that celebrated in the poet's telling of his own youth in *La Vita Nuova.* For, indeed, Love is the proper concern, the actual and inevitable concern, of youth.

7. **The Chariot.** Dante's period of "Maturity," as he terms it, extends from twenty-five to forty-five, with the crisis of mid-life at or about the thirty-fifth year. In his own lifetime that was the year of his visionary journey through Hell, Purgatory, and Paradise, when he passed in consciousness from a state of sin, or attachment to the senses, to salvation, by virtue of the guiding influence of Love. The two cardinal virtues proper to this period of life, in his view, are Temperance and Courage, to which were to be added, Love, Loyalty, and Courtesy (*ib.,* IV. 26), in the spirit of the Virgilian and medieval knightly ideal. I have already made note of the two contrary horses of the chariot of this card, as representing Plato's image in the *Phaedrus,* symbolizing the composite structure of soul and body in Man. "Whence the task of our charioteer," as he has said, "is difficult and troublesome." "It is hard," he states again, "by reason of the heaviness of the steed of wickedness, which pulls down his driver with his weight, except that driver have schooled him well (*Phaedrus* 247b).

8. **Justice.** This, as already remarked, is the prime cardinal virtue of Age, the period that, in Dante's view, extends from forty-five to seventy, and to which the second cardinal virtue assigned is Wisdom. Wisdom, Justice, Generosity, and Affability: these are the qualities proper to this time of life (*Convivio* IV. 27); "for," we read in Dante's words, "as Aristotle says, 'man is a civic animal,' wherefore he is re-

quired not only to be useful to himself but also to others. . . .
Wherefore, after our own proper perfection, which is acquired in manhood, that perfection should also come which
enlightens not only ourselves but others, and man should
open out like a rose that can no longer keep closed, and
should spread abroad the perfume which has been
generated within; and this should come about in that third
period of life with which we are dealing." After which there
remains to be experienced and interpreted only the terminal
stage of "Decrepitude," as in our next card:

9. **The Hermit.** Holding high his lamp, colored red, of
the spirit, he matches Dante's understanding of the virtues
proper to whatever years of life may remain beyond our
assigned three score and ten; in the poet's image: the soul
returns to God, as to the port whence it departed when it
came to enter upon the sea of this life, and it looks back
with a blessing upon the voyage that has been made,
because it has been straight and good and without the bit-
terness of a tempest. "And here be it known," he continues,
"that, as Tully says in his writing *Of Old Age,* 'natural death
is as it were our port and rest from our long voyage.' And
even as the good sailor, when he draws near to the port,
lowers his sails, and gently with mild impulse enters into it,
so ought we to lower the sails of our worldly activities and
turn to God with all our purpose and heart; so that we may
come to that port with all sweetness and with all peace"
(*Convivio* IV. 28). The virtues of the hermit, turning from
the goods of this life to God, are obviously proper, also, to
the life style of a pope, whose duty it is to direct his Church
and its flock toward their Heavenly end.

And so it is that in the nine cards of the first two rows of
our Honors arrangement, 1-5 and 6-9, we have found two
planes or levels of symbolization, illustrating in two modes
the four inevitable stages of a human lifetime: below, the
social aspects of the long course, and above, their informing
virtues. We move, next, to a third or middle range, which is
of a testing and transition to higher, visionary spheres of
understanding and fulfillment; and here, too, the imagery
falls naturally into a lifetime-sequence of four stages.

10. **The Wheel of Fortune.** This is an image well known to the lore of the Middle Ages, as represented, for example, in our Figure 1 (from Singleton, *Inferno 2,* facing p. 32: *Imago Mundi,* Miniaturem Corpus Christi College, Cambridge, MS 66, Fol. 66. P: Courtauld Institute of Art), where, on the left, stands Fortune, pointing to the rim, and on the right, Sapience, pointing to the center of the wheel. For on the rim there is always someone going down, someone at the bottom, someone going up, and someone at the top. Dante, in his Fourth Circle of Hell, of the Avaricious and the Prodigal — who with great howls are rolling weighty rocks around in circles — is taught by Virgil of both the folly and the wisdom of this wheel. Wisdom and virtue lie in not regarding the rim. Hence the couple vows in the Catholic marriage ceremony to take each other, to have and to hold, "for better, for worse, for richer, for poorer, in sickness and in health, till death . . ." and much the same must be the focal line of dedication, also, to a vocation. On the Tarot card those fixed to the rim, whether rising, descending, or crowned at the top, are represented as monkeys. The card appears in our arrangement in Column One, above that of youth, The Lovers; the lesson being perfectly clear, namely, that those who in the shaping of their lives allow themselves to be governed, not by love and a central impulse, but by fears and hopes for the accidents of Fortune, are but monkeys and will end their lives in Circle Four of Dante's Hell (*Inferno,* Canto VII), pushing rocks around in circles for evermore. And this, then, is the great test of youth on entering either marriage or a life career.

11. **Force.** The figure is of a woman tearing open the mouth of a lion. Spiritual force, that is to say, not physical, is what is truly great. The card appears in our arrangement over The Chariot with its two steeds, the charioteer being at the apogee of his powers. And again the lesson is clear, as representing the great test that is faced in maturity. The lion is the noble King of Beasts in medieval fable, the supreme representative of physical animal strength. Accordingly, a "lion of a man" would be one of the greatest physical strength — like, say, Achilles in the *Iliad.* Hector, however, is represented in that epic as the more noble of the

two, even though he is slain by Achilles. Spiritual force above the pride and strength of the physical, at the moment of the body's greatest gifts: that is the lesson of this card; the red horse over the blue, to whose pace the blue is to be held in accord.

12. **The Hanged Man.** There has been a great deal of high and fancy talk displayed in the interpretations of this card, and yet its basic reference is both simple and well known. In the south of France and in Italy to this day, to be hung up this way in public is a sign of social disgrace. For instance, when Mussolini was assassinated, his body was hung up this way, with that of his leading general, also upside down, at his right, and that of his mistress, likewise, at his left. The card appears in our arrangement above that of the figure of Justice; for the Emperor administering Justice cannot and must not be concerned with popular opinion, praise or disgrace: he must have died to public opinion, to live under the sign only of Justice. And this would perhaps explain why our own Democratic system of government has become so worm-eaten with rottenness: officials voting with attention fixed not on Justice but on their own fates in the next election are hardly fit to serve the implacable goddess of the equal scales. Dante, writing of this third period of life, points out not only that it should flower and open out "like a rose," but also that, inevitably, this period of life "carries a shade of authority, whereby it seems that men hearken more to it than to any earlier age." Its wisdom is to be shared, not with an eye to personal advantage or reputation, but as a light and law to others, for the general good. "The noble soul in age," in Dante's words, "is wise, is just, is open-handed, and rejoices to tell of the goodness and excellence of others, and to hear of it; that is to say is affable; and truly these four virtues are most fitting to this age. After which we proceed to

13. **Death.** For as the Emperor, serving Justice, must have died to social opinion, so the Hermit and teacher of the spiritual life must have died to the fear of death. Moreover, only one who has thus already died can enter with equanimity into his period of "Decrepitude." And so, at the conclusion of our study of this middle range of the Honors cards,

we may look back and recognize a consistent of principle displayed throughout, symbolized in keys that lead through each of the four stages of life, beyond bondage in the accidents of this world, to a nobler order of realizations: indifference in youth to the turns of the wheel of fortune; in maturity, submission of one's animal to one's spiritual force; in age, wisdom and justice in the dispensation of advice, indifferent to personal advantage; and when approaching death, indifference to the Reaper's scythe. What is required is the finding of that Immovable Point within one's self, which is not shaken by any of those tempests which the Buddhists call "the eight karmic winds": fear of pain, desire for pleasure; fear of loss, desire for gain; fear of blame, desire for praise; fear of disgrace, desire for fame. Or, as we read in the Upanishad:

> He who has the understanding of a chariot-
> driver,
> A man who reins in his mind —
> He reaches the end of the journey,
> That highest place of The Lord.
> (*Katha Up.* 3.8.)

The next range is the first of the supernatural series and opens appropriately with the card:

14. **Temperance.** A winged female is pouring water from a blue vessel into a red, from a vessel of the physical to that of the spiritual life. The image that comes to mind is of the opening of Dante's *La Vita Nuova*, "The New Life," where he tells of his first sight of Beatrice.

> "She appeared to me clothed in a most noble color, a modest and becoming crimson, and she was girt and adorned in such wise as befitted her very youthful age. At that instant, I say truly that the spirit of life, which dwells in the most secret chamber of the heart, began to tremble with such violence that it appeared fearfully in the least pulses, and, trembling, said these words: *Ecce deus fortior me, qui veniens dominabitur mihi* ("Behold a god stronger than I, who coming shall rule over me").

"At that instant the spirit of the soul, which dwells in the high chamber to which all the spirits of the senses carry their perceptions, began to marvel greatly, and, speaking to the spirit of the sight, said these words: *Apparuit jam beatitudo vestra* ("Now has appeared your bliss").

"At that instant the natural spirit, which dwells in that part where our nourishment is supplied, began to weep, and, weeping, said these words: *Heu miser! quia frequenter impeditus ero deinceps* ("Woe is me, wretched! because often from this time forth shall I be hindered").*

This is the first winged figure of the series. Appearing in Column One, above The Wheel of Fortune and The Lovers, she represents the import of the virtue of Love implied in the figure of The High Priestess. Her card, furthermore, is Number 14, matching the position of the Kings as the culminating fourteenth cards of the lower suits; i.e., we have come to the end of the guidance of the merely social, earthly, morally testing orders of experience to a passage to the supernatural. The term "Temperance" is appropriate to the spiritual charge of this moment. Applied to the physical vessel of the body, what it suggests is control of the appetites. Applied on the spiritual side, it suggests the virtue of humility in control of the pride of spiritual inflation, which is the great temptation of the mystical life — as represented, for example, in the last temptation of Jesus, when the devil, as we read in Luke 4:9-12, "took him to Jerusalem, and set him on the pinnacle of the temple, and said to him, 'If you are the Son of God, throw yourself down from here, for it is written, "He will give his angels charge of you, to guard you," and "On their hands they will bear you up, lest you strike your foot against a stone." And Jesus answered him, 'It is said, "You shall not tempt the Lord your God." ' "

---

*Translation, Charles Eliot Norton, *The New Life of Dante Alighieri* (Boston and New York: Houghton Mifflin Company, 1867), p. 2.

15. **The Devil.** Dante's *Inferno* supplies the key to the interpretation of this card. The visionary, under the guidance of Virgil, who has been urged by the spirit of Beatrice to rescue her poet from the occasions of sin, is conducted through the pits of Hell, where he reviews from the prospect of Eternity and The New Life the loathsomeness of lives lived in sensuality and pride. The card here appears in Column Two, above the figure of Force, spiritual Force; for the ultimate sin is pride in one's own spirituality. Such, in fact, was the sin of Lucifer, who in Heaven was the most luminous of the angelic host. He refused to humble himself to God's will. And Dante saw pride as a prime danger to his own conscience. Indeed, generally, this is the prime danger of man's years of maturity, when our powers are at their full. Protected, however, by the virtue of humility, implied in the title of the preceding card, Temperance, the spiritual voyager passes through the reeking pits to the next phase of his course, as shown by the following card:

16. **The Tower of Destruction.** The tower of Pride is here destroyed by the lightning bolt of God's Judgment. Appropriately, the card appears in Column Three, above those of The Hanged Man, Justice, and The Emperor. Its key is to be found in Dante's *Purgatorio,* where the penances corrective of the faults of Hell are displayed.

James Joyce, whose chief literary model was Dante, in both *Ulysses* and *Finnegans Wake*, lets the sound of a great thunderclap represent the moment of the humbling of his heroes' pride. In *Ulysses* it occurs precisely in the middle of the book, where Stephen, the novel's hero, is terrified by such a clap, right after a session of blasphemous boasting:

> "A black crack of noise in the street here, alack, bawled, back. Loud on left Thor thundered: in anger awful the hammerhurler . . . . And he that had erst challenged to bo so doughty waxed pale as they might all mark and shrank together and his pitch that was before so haught uplift was now of a sudden quite plucked down and his heart shook within the cage of his breast as he heard the rumor of that storm" (p. 388).

In *Finnegans Wake,* the fall from his ladder of Finnegan, the great builder of cities and towers, is to the sound of a hundred-lettered word composed of thunder syllables from many tongues: bababadalgharaghtakamminarronnkonn bronntonnerronntthunntrobarrhounawnskawntoohoohoor denenthurnuk!" Giambattista Vico wrote of the voice of thunder as the noise that first woke in brutal primitive man the fear of God and moved him to reform his ways. And in the Bible, of course, the great lesson of the humbling of man's pride is taught in the legend of the Tower of Babel. Actually, the historic model of that tower, namely the great ziggurat of Babylon, had been built as an image of the axial mountain of the universe, up which ascent should be made, rather in worship than in pride, to the seat of the Lord of Light. Dante's image of the axial mountain of Purgatory, up which ascent is made penitentially to the Earthly Paradise, is one of the same basic form and sense. The crucial question, as rendered in the Bible, is whether one mounts the tower in impudence or in penance. In our card the tower is of pride, uncrowned, and, like Joyce's Finnegan from his ladder, the smitten occupants fall to the ground.

17. **The Star.** After Purgatory comes Paradise; for the function of God's chastisement is to prepare the soul for its Heaven-journey. Accordingly, this card now appears, with its picture of the bird of the soul perched, ready for flight, on the top of a little tree. From two red vessels the waters of life are being poured out to the world below, and the figure is nude, signifying innocence; this being the first unclothed figure of the series. So was man before the fall; moreover, the soul, returned through Purgatory to its pristine state, comes naked before its God. Continuing the Dantean image, we are about to mount from here to the first heavenly sphere of The Moon, of which supernal ascent, the poet, when about to rise with Beatrice from their meeting place in the Earthly Paradise, delivers to his reader a warning:

"O you who in a little bark, desirous to listen, have followed behind my craft that singing passes on, turn to see again your shores; put not out upon the deep; for haply, losing me, you would remain astray. The water

which I take was never crossed. Minerva breathes and guides me, and nine Muses point out to me the Bears."
(*Paradiso* II. 1-9)

The stars of this picture card are perhaps intended to refer, in this way, to the Pole Star and the Guiding Bears. In any case, they conduct us to the next and topmost range of this Tarot Honors series, where the highest revelations appear of those ultimate spiritual forces of which the figures of the lower ranges have been the graded reflections. And they are as follows:

18. **The Moon.** As we all surely know, the influence of this sphere governs lovers and all the tides of life, whether of the womb or of the seas. Dogs bark at the moon at its full, and crabs, I have heard, then come out of their holes and dance at night on the beaches. All of life is moved to increase by The Moon, whose rhythmical waxing and waning tell of life's power to cast off the shadow of death through tireless rounds of rebirths in unending cycles of time.

From The Star, as the guiding first revelation of the ultimate Light, to The Moon, its shadowed, increasing reflection, we come, next, to card

19. **The Sun.** The unshadowed revelation of a light of which that of The Moon is but a reflection under the sign of time. Here the twins, male and female, who in Card 15 were in The Devil's keep, stand released, fulfilled, as Adam and Eve before the fall, in the full light of God's presence.

20. **Judgment.** The moment represented is of the blowing of Gabriel's horn, the end of the world and resurrection of the body. This Gabriel is the second winged figure of the series. The resurrected trio seem to me to represent a pious lay couple and their pastor (compare the cardinal's hat of Card 5). The appearance of such an apocalyptic scene at the summit of Column Three accords perfectly with the whole statement of that vertical series: 4. The Emperor, 8. Justice, 12. The Hanged Man, and 16. The Tower of Destruction.

But when, we might ask, is this Day of Judgment to occur? It is usually interpreted as foretold in Mark 14, as an event to be expected in the uncertain future. However, there is another, more distinctly spiritual, less concretely historical way of interpreting the promise, which has been characteristic, from as early as the second and third centuries, of the Gnostic and Hermetic strains of Christian thinking, in striking evidence of which we have now the recently recovered and translated *Gospel According to Thomas,* "a work," as we are told by the learned company of translators, "the primitive text of which must have been produced in Greek about 140 A.D., and which was based on even more ancient sources."* There we find the following remarkable exchange:

"His disciples said to him: When will the Kingdom come?"

"Jesus said: It will not come by expectation; they will not say: 'See, here,' or 'See, there.' But the Kingdom of the Father is spread upon the earth and men do not see it."

In so many words, the reference is not to a future, general, historical end of the world, but to an individual, spiritual — or, as we might say today, psychological — alteration of vision, here and now, so that through all things in this world the radiance of the Kingdom should be recognized as present, forever, world without end. And that this, finally, is the message, forever, world without end. And that this, finally, is the message, also, of the Marseilles deck is made evident in the final numbered card of the Atouts, namely:

21. **The World.** In the beautiful, twelfth-century West Portal of Chartres Cathedral, Christ of the Second Coming appears in the symbolic frame of a mandorla, surrounded by the four signs of Ezekial's vision, which in the Christian tradition are read as referring to the four evangelists: Luke, the bull; Mark, the lion; John, the eagle; and Matthew, the anthropomorphic angel. These same signs in the third and fourth millenniums B.C., however, were read as zodiacal references to the four points of the equinoxes and solstices: Taurus, the Bull, the spring equinox; Leon, the Lion, summer solstice; the Eagle (now Scorpio), the autumnal

---

*A Guilaumont, H.-Ch. Puech, G. Quispel, W. Till, and Yassah 'abd al Misih, *The Gospel According to Thomas* (New York: Harper and Brothers, 1959), p. vi.

equinox; and Aquarius, the Water-carrier, the winter solstice. Moreover, the form of the mandorla is traditionally interpreted as a reference to the female organ of birth, the vulva, as though the cosmic mother-goddess of all space-time were here to be seen giving birth to the Christ of the Second Coming, and thereby to the Kingdom of the Father, which is within us.

In our Tarot card, on the other hand, the revealed vision in the mandorla is not of Christ of the Apocalypse, but The World, in the form of the dancing female androgyne of the alchemists. In her left hand is a wand, symbolic of the male, in her right a conch shell, of the female principle. Compare Figure 10, from the seventeenth-century *Rosarium Philosophorum*. In a twelfth-century hermetic text known as *The Book of the Twenty-four Philosophers* there is a relevant statement that has been quoted, through the centuries, by a number of Christian thinkers* — among others, Alan of Lille (1128-1202), Nicholas Cusanus (1401-1464), Rabelais (1490?-1553), Giordano Bruno (1548-1600), and Pascal (1632-1662), as well as Voltaire (1694-1778); to wit:

> *God is an intelligible sphere, whose center*
> *is everywhere and circumference nowhere.*

Compare the Indian Upanishad:

> Though hidden in all things,
> The World Soul shines not forth;
> Yet is seen by subtle seers
> Of superior, subtle intellect.
> (*Katha Up.* 3.12)

"By discerning that," one reads again, "one is liberated from the mouth of death" (*ib.*, 3.15).

And so we are brought to the condition (universally ranging, careless of the bites of this world, everywhere and yet nowhere at home) of *The Fool,* the wandering mendicant saint or sage, known to himself as that intelligible sphere

---

**Liber XXIV Philosophorum*, Proposition II; Clemens Bäumler, "Das pseudo-hermetische 'Buch der vierundzwanzig Meister,' (*Liber XXIV philosophorum*)," in *Abhandlungen aus dem Gebiete der Philosophie und ihrer Geschichte*. Festgabe zum 70 Geburtstag Georg Freiherrn von Hartling (Freiburg im Breisgau: Herdersche Verlagshandlung, 1913), p. 31.

whose center is everywhere and circumference nowhere.

One more point of interest: turn Card 12, *The Hanged Man,* upside down and the legs will be seen to be in the same position as those of the dancing figure of *The World.* The implied idea is of each of us as an inverted reflection, clothed in the garments of temporality, of the noumenal or "Real." For it was at the station of Card 12, death to the rumors of society, that our first irreversible step was taken away from engagement in the forms of time. Whether upside down or rightside up, their verdicts are indifferent. And we passed, then, through death-to-the-fear-of-death; whereupon the portal opened of the way to the knowledge of that mystery which, in theological terms, would be known as the Image of God within us. Plato recognized the sensible world as a reflex of the intelligible. What is known as above is thus here below, and what is not here is nowhere.

But have we not noticed, also, that The Magician is holding in his left hand the same wand that the World Dancer holds in hers, while in his right, instead of the conch, there is a coin — of philosophical gold? Little wonder if the clergy of those days were at pains to warn their flocks against the unauthorized lesson lurking in these cards!

TAROT REVELATIONS

PART II

INTRODUCTION

BY

COLIN WILSON

INTRODUCTION

by

Colin Wilson

It must have been in the 1960s that I met the author of the present book in San Francisco. I had been lecturing at Grace Cathedral, expanding on some of the themes of my book *The Outsider.* The cheerful, round-faced young man who came and introduced himself to me after the lecture did not look in the least like an Outsider: he looked altogether too sane and normal. But, as we drank a beer later in the Edinburgh Castle, I began to find him increasingly intriguing, particularly the range of his reading — from Conrad and Joyce to Jung and Maslow. In fact, it was soon perfectly clear that his "oddness" lay in the fact that he was so much like myself. That is, he had preferred to work at a manual job because it left his mind free to pursue his real interests — psychology and the paranormal. The quality of his mind had obviously struck other writers whom he had met, and some of these — like Joseph Campbell and Alan Watts — had become close friends.

It would not, perhaps, be perfectly true to say I owe my own increasing interest in the paranormal to Dick Roberts; for I had been fascinated by ghosts and "survival" since childhood, and had plunged into a fairly serious study of magic and witchcraft in the early 1950s, when I had also discovered the *I Ching* with Jung's introduction. But I regarded it as one of my less serious interests — like my curiosity about the Loch Ness monster and the identity of Jack the Ripper. It was Dick who first talked to me seriously about Jung and his notion of "archetypes," and convinced me that "magic" could, in effect, be a completely different, non-intellectual knowledge system. On a subsequent stay with me at my home in Cornwall, he told me the extraordinary story of Jack Schwarz and his strangely circumstantial story of "space contacts," which I later included in *The Occult.**

The truth is that, although I did not at first recognize him as such, Dick Roberts is part of that "Outsider" tradition that runs from Goethe and Rousseau to Hesse and Camus. That is to say, he woke up early to the fact that he had been born into a civilization in which he felt himself to be a stranger. I think it significant that he discovered the work of H. P. Lovecraft in his early teens — long before Lovecraft's name became fashionable with the younger generation — and instantly recognized the hermit of Providence as a fellow spirit. (He tells me he used to spend most of his allowance money at the bookshop of "Bob the Werewolf" in Verona, PA.) He also bought copies of the *Journal* of the Society for Physical Research, and became fascinated by the problem of survival after death. and the baffling difficulties that seem to lie in the way of concrete proof.

But at least fate was kinder to him than to Lovecraft. If he felt total lack of sympathy for the commercial and political

---

*"The Jack Schwarz Story" has become an embarrassment to me (Richard Roberts) because at the time I wrote that he was "un-guru-like"; however, now he is very much a guru, with tours, television appearances, and mail solicitations for money "tithes" for his foundation Aletheia.

The second source of embarrassment is that I no longer believe the "story," although I did at the time that I presented it to Colin Wilson. This is not to say that Jack Schwarz was not telling the truth. He may have been the victim of an elaborate hoax. For readers who have not read Colin Wilson's *The Occult,* the gist of the story is that Schwarz was contacted by Linus from Venus and informed that he was instructing the Venusians nightly on the astral plane because he was from a higher plane than theirs, had crash-landed in a flying saucer from Pluto, had been chosen to the steering council of the New Age, which would take the saucer back to Pluto, and, finally, (!) was "El, Su, Shei-la," in saucer parlance "God's vehicle to bring the truth that is meant to be."

In retrospect, this "story" seems to be a classic example of what the psychologists call "psychic inflation," but I must bear some blame for disseminating the story through *The Occult,* and also "for being too prone to search for the truth in others rather than looking within myself." This from Jane Roberts' Seth, during a conversation in 1973. *Tarot Revelations* is, in part, the result of turning within myself to find Tarot's truth.

ideals of western civilization, at least he was able to take advantage of its educational system to create for himself a relatively comfortable way of life that enabled him to spend all his spare time exploring the world of the subjective and the paranormal. My own first book, *The Outsider,* played a part in his development — he says that it made him aware that his own sense of not-belonging was not necessarily a disadvantage, and that the important thing was not to allow himself to be destroyed by his feeling of alienation, as so many others had.

It was soon after this that he came across Joseph Campbell's *The Hero With a Thousand Faces,* and was taken an important step beyond the old Lovecraftian dilemma of "not belonging." Campbell is basically concerned with the need of the human spirit to achieve maturity, to turn away from misery and self-pity. He speaks, for example, of a rite among the aboriginals of Australia, in which the growing boy is told "The Great Father Snake smells your foreskin; he is calling for it." The child is understandably terrified and takes refuge with his mother. She — and the other women — wail over him ceremonially, no doubt making him feel worse than ever. Then the men take him away, and the rite of circumcision is performed, initiating him into the society of the men. He *has* to be terrified, and to leave behind the desire to take refuge in his mother.

But the most interesting part of Campbell's story is still to come. He tells a story of one of Jung's patients, who dreamed that a snake shot out of a cave and bit him in the genitals. The dream occurred at the point when the patient was becoming convinced of the truth of the analysis, and was learning to free himself from his mother complex. So the image of the snake biting off the foreskin appeared spontaneously in the dreams of a modern European. *This* is what Jung means by an archetype — an "archaic psychic component" that somehow finds its way into the mind out of some collective unconscious.

The "Outsider" finds himself confronted by the same problem. In most cases, he feels himself to be a social misfit because he is more intelligent or sensitive than the people around him. Proust is an obvious example, Lovecraft another. He may take refuge in illness, or in a world of imagination. If, like Proust, he is lucky enough to have an independent income, he may be able to cocoon himself in an artificial security; but that is no solution. Sooner or later, he has to stop being mistrustful and defensive, and prepare himself to "face the snake." The real solution is to change his attitude towards himself: to recognize that the "outsiders" are supposed to be the spearhead of civilization, its leaders, not its rejects.

I had said as much in *The Outsider,* and had rejected the basically pessimistic solutions that appealed to so many of the romantics — from Hoffman to Camus. But I made no attempt to describe precisely how the "outsider" should try to "face the snake." Which explains why the discovery of Jung's archetypes came to Dick Roberts as a revelation. Up until this point, Dick had seen the "two worlds" — let us say, of Lovecraft and Henry Ford — as irreconcilable, confronting one another in basic contradiction. But if Jung was correct, then the romantics were not mere escapists and dreamers, taking shelter from the world of "real life." Lovecraft's "Ancient Old Ones" were a profound intuition of a real truth about the human psyche.

If Lovecraft had understood this, he might have survived, instead of dying of discouragement and undernourishment. Of course, he often asserted the fundamental "reality" of his visions; but he didn't really believe it. He suspected they were lies, and that Henry Ford was right, and that therefore he found himself in a world to which he did not wish to belong. If he had known that he was right, and that Ford was not wrong but simply ignorant, he might have regarded modern civilization with a kindly tolerance, and addressed himself to the task of dispelling some of its stupidity and ignorance.

This, I think, is why Dick Roberts found Jung so revelatory. The discovery imbued him with such a sense of new intellectual orientation that he began to regard some of his earlier interest in 'occultism' with a sterner eye. Astrology struck him as a typical example of this kind of negative wishful thinking, with its implied denial of free will (and therefore of the hero's ability to progress); he decided that

he might make a beginning on 'facing the snake' by trying
to disprove astrology. It looked relatively easy, with its
nonsense about sun signs and the moon in the fifth house
bringing emotional upsets. But when he turned from the
predictions in the newspapers to the books by real astrologers, he recognized instantly that he was back in the
strange world of the archetypes. For some absurd reason,
real astrology works. The planets *do* seem to exert an influence on the temperaments of human individuals, and to do
this in a more-or-less predictable way. Again, Dick Roberts
had a sense of being in touch with a body of half-forgotten
but perfectly down-to-earth ancient knowledge. Moreover,
if astrology "worked," then a person's individual archetypes ought to be visible in his natal chart — that is, a
"map" of the heavens at the precise moment he was born.
He describes his increasing conviction that this *was* so as
one of his most exciting discoveries.*

Now astrology is all very well, because even the most
skeptical materialism can understand how the planets *could*
exert an influence on human affairs; we know that the moon
not only influences the tides, but the emotional states of
human beings. But such matters as the *I Ching* and the
Tarot cards are surely in a different category? Where ancient Chinese divination was concerned, Jung was inclined
to agree that it contradicted the obvious laws of physics,
and this recognition led him to formulate the notion of "synchronicity," an a-causal principle of "connectedness." Yet
Jung's explanation of synchronicity was never entirely
satisfactory. After all, if the world is *all* matter, then it must
obey purely material laws. If it is not all matter, but also
something called 'spirit,' then presumably it also obeys
spiritual laws. But for Jung, synchronicity was not exactly
anything to do with spirit, or mind-over-matter; it was just
an a-causal principle that explains "coincidences that are
not coincidences."

Dick Roberts faced up to this evasion, and concluded
that, if synchronicity is to be accepted, then we also have to

---

*This correlation of archetypes (shadow, animus and anima) and also per-
sona, self, and collective unconscious is copyrighted 1975 with The
Library of Congress as *Archetypal Astrology*.

accept that, in some weird way, our minds can somehow influence and, indeed, create events. He has written: "My life goal is to prove the truth of the Hermetic arts (astrology, Tarot, palmistry, — all divination) by means of Jungian psychology, as a demonstration that the inner psyche influences and brings about the *outer* events." Which is, in fact, an admirable summary of the aim of the present work — as well as of his earlier book *Tarot and You.*

For the reader who finds the whole idea preposterous — or at least, mind-boggling — I can only suggest that he reserve judgment until he has read at least the opening chapter of this book. Let me, in the meantime, offer my own explanation of why I find this strange proposition acceptable.

In an autobiography called *Voyage to a Beginning,* I expressed my own basic intuition about the human situation in the sentence, "Man is the planet of a double star." The external world exerts its enormous gravitational force, and its sheer size negates us. Yet in moods of intensity, we also recognize the existence of an inner world, a realm of "power, meaning and purpose" in which we feel completely at home. This is what Kierkegaard meant by "Truth is subjectivity." And "I" spend my time being torn between the force of these two worlds. In theory, I would like to land on the inner world and live there; in practice, the outer world always pulls me back. This is the basic outsider problem — the feeling that truth somehow lies inside us, and that if we could only find a method of descending into our own depths — perhaps through Shaw's "seventh degree of concentration" — we could achieve a degree of intensity of which the external world would be incapable of robbing us.

Now the discovery — by Sperry, Ornstein and others — that man has a "double brain," throws an interesting light on this problem. This discovery was made — as everyone now knows — as a result of severing the bridge of nerve fibre that connects the two halves of the cerebral hemispheres. For some odd reason, the right side of the brain controls the left side of the body, and vice versa. The first thing Sperry noticed was that if a patient knocked into something with his left side, he didn't notice. Moreover, if a split brain patient is shown an apple in the right visual field and an orange in the left, and asked what he has just been shown, he replies "An apple." If asked to write what he has just seen, with his left hand, he writes "An orange." Asked what he has just written, he replies "Apple." It seems that the person we call "I" lives in the left side of the brain, and that an inch away, there is another "I," who feels he is also the legitimate occupant of the head.

It had, in fact, been known for a long time that the left brain controls language and rational thought, while the right seems to be in charge of pattern-recognition and intuition. In other words, the left is a scientist, the right an artist.

Now I had been puzzled for a long time by the riddle of poltergeist phenomena. We know that "noisy ghosts" are caused by disturbed children or teenagers; the odd thing is that the teenager himself is totally unaware of it. Now I saw how this could be possible. The person who causes objects to fly around the room lives in the right brain, and has somehow become disassociated from the left-brain ego, just as in a split-brain operation. The energy involved, I suspect, comes from the earth — the same energy that causes a dowsing rod to twist in the diviner's hands.

A greal deal of thought about this problem has convinced me of another implication — so far unverified in the laboratory: that the function of the left brain is to look *outward* to the external world, to be the 'front man,' the guard. The function of the right is to look inward, to our internal functions, and to supply us with energy. Those states of relaxation that William James called "melting moods" are states in which we withdraw into this right brain consciousness. If we are nervous or tense, the left brain declines to permit this withdrawal; it keeps crying "Wolf" and shattering the mood.

This obviously explains the actual mechanisms of the "double star" effect. Every time we try to withdraw into that inner sanctum, the shop-bell sounds and drags us out again. Drugs and alcohol muffle the bell. Neurosis arises from this conflict — and not, as Freud believed, from sexual hang-ups.

The interesting thing is this: that during the course of a lifetime, we accumulate a vast library of all kinds of information inside us. Everything we have ever seen or read or thought or felt is in there, as fresh as when it happened; so are a thousand things we only *half* saw or heard, and registered unconsciously.

But this inner world is also the world of insight and intuition. When I can withdraw quietly into myself, I suddenly see the *connection* between two things whose relationship had not struck me earlier. Or rather, it is as if my inner self managed to bring the connection to my attention — as if it already knew about it.

This is an interesting idea: that the "you" who lives in that silent hemisphere of your brain *knows* a vast amount more than the rational "you," who wastes far too much of his time peering at things through a magnifying glass and cannot see the wood for the trees.

The problem is that the "silent" you has the greatest difficulty conveying its knowledge to the rational ego. For the left-brain you is like an overworked housewife who is too busy to take anything in; she says "Yes dear," and thinks about something else. Experiments have shown that the right brain *can* convey knowledge to the left — even in split brain patients — but it has to be simple. For example, red and green lights are flashed alternately in the right visual field, and "you" are asked which color you have just seen. "You" don't know, of course, so the result should be completely random. Sperry discovered this was not so. The patient would guess "Red," then start (as if nudged in the ribs) and correct himself: "No, green." The right brain had almost literally kicked him under the table. And it often warns us when we are about to do something stupid or dangerous by giving us an odd feeling of discomfort. But it cannot convey complex insights. To get these, "you" — the left brain ego — have to make the effort to enter that non-verbal area. (This is the aim of meditation.)

And now, I think, it should be possible to grasp Dick Roberts' basic assumption that "divination" can actually work. What we are assuming is that the left-brain ego is offering that other "you" a *code* through which it can signal its messages. Astrology, I hasten to add, is not such a code; I suspect that it will one day be understood quite simply as an interaction of cosmic forces (the planets and the earth) with the psyche. But the Tarot *is* such a code; so is the *I Ching*. In short, if the right-brain ego wants to convey a piece of information, then by shuffling a Tarot pack or throwing down three coins, you can offer it the means of indicating what it wishes to say. (Dowsers also know that a short pendulum can be equally effective.) That sounds hard to believe, until we recognize that even the left brain ego can perform apparently miraculous feats. Someone who was astonishing me with card tricks the other day told me that the most brilliant card-magician he had ever met was the comedian Milton Berle, who could actually memorize the position of every card in the pack. And if Milton Berle's left brain ego can perform such a feat, I find it easy to accept that his right brain could perform apparent miracles. Or yours. Or mine. Provided we give it the chance, and try to listen to what it is saying.

For two centuries now, the human spirit has been in revolt against the world of the Gradgrinds, and their obsession with "facts, hard facts." The Romanticism of the 19th century was one long shout of defiance. But it may be worth bearing in mind that Dickens' Gradgrind was not a villain; on the contrary, he was a kindly, generous, idealistic human being, blinded by his own dogmatism. Even Henry Ford once apologized for saying "History is bunk," explaining that he only meant he had no time to read it. The Romantics exaggerated the problem out of weakness and a sense of vulnerability. And people like Dick Roberts and Joseph Campbell are restoring it to perspective, and bringing about a reconciliation that is based on insight and strength. If they succeed, the intellectual perspective of the 21st century could be more exciting than anything we can imagine.

TAROT REVELATIONS

PART II

"ESOTERIC TAROT: SYMBOLISM OF THE WAITE/RIDER DECK"

BY

RICHARD ROBERTS

PREFACE

In the following pages I shall demonstrate:

1. That the Keys of the Tarot Major Arcana depict numerical archetypes, which stand as the pre-formative powers behind material manifestation.

2. That the pictures on each Key are geometrical reflections of the numerical archetype of each Key.

3. That the Magic Nine layout of Keys reveals the way in which the numerical archetypes interact with one another, and, hence, presents the most profound interpretation of the Major Arcana.

4. That Tarot is an alchemical revelation, revealing the descent and ascent of Hermes/Mercurius/Thoth.

5. That the path of this descent/ascent follows the traditional Ladder of Souls, or Stairway of Planets, disguised as seven triads of Keys, Zero (The Fool) transcending the sequence of 21 Keys.

6. That since the Stairway of Planets was the path of the descending and ascending soul of man, the Tarot Major Arcana constitute a western Book of the Dead.

7. That if the spiral of serpent or caduceus is followed through the Major Arcana, alternately regenerating and returning to unity, like the expanding and contracting rhythm of the cosmos, further revelations appear in which we may read the monomyth of the world's religions, the Monad's descent from Above to Below, and the consequent ascent to Above.

8. That this descent from Above represents spirit's incarnation into the elemental world, from the mineral kingdom to man, demonstrated by the correspondence of the four suits to the four Grail hallows and the four fixed signs of the zodiac.

9. That in addition to the alchemical conjunction or sacred marriage of King Sun and Queen Moon, the Major Arcana reveal an astrological correspondence to the conjunction of Sun (Leo) and Moon (Cancer) at the summer solstice of 2,000 B.C.

I am interested in hearing from readers who wish to write me at Box 581, San Anselmo, California 94960.

CHAPTER I

THE GREAT MYTH

1. Exoteric and Esoteric Tarot

The common attitude towards Tarot, prototype of modern playing cards, is that Tarot is fortune-telling, and, therefore, utterly bereft of value. However, in *Tarot and You* I noted that "Tarot is above all a symbolic system of self-transformation"[1] comparable to what Jung terms the "individuation process." Indeed, the purpose of that book was to remove Tarot from the fortune-telling field and through actual readings which I gave with the cards, to demonstrate that Tarot could be a valuable psychological tool, when the free-association technique was utilized rather than traditional occult interpretation. Moreover, *Tarot and You* set forth certain correlations between the cards and the archetypes of the collective unconscious. Proceeding on that, I created the Jungian Spread, which reads initially the archetypal level of an individual so that the connection may be seen between inner formative factors and outer life events. This procedure is valid not only from the point of view of Jungian psychology, but also from that represented in the *Emerald Tablet,* an eighth-century touchstone of Hermetic wisdom, in which we read, "As Above, so Below"; or, from the psychological standpoint, "As within, so without."

When, in 1969, Joseph Campbell and his wife visited me in San Francisco, the fog being in and there being nowhere to go, we "fooled" with our first Tarot reading and found the stations of the hero's journey turning up, as in Campbell's book, *The Hero With a Thousand Faces.* Subsequently, we developed independently two different layouts of the cards, each feeling that his own best revealed the mysteries of the Major Arcana (the 22 cards). The two systems are presented herein. Campbell treats of the Marseilles Tarot, and his approach is exoteric, dealing with the relation of this deck to late medieval symbols. My intention, rather, is to delineate the esoteric elements in A.E. Waite's turn-of-the-century Tarot. Waite alters the earlier Tarot, and his creation depicts Hermetic and alchemical elements which may be either out of the mainstream or restorations of earlier elements lost by the time (1392) of the earliest-known Tarot deck. His deck cannot be authenticated as true to Tarot tradition, since that earliest-known deck is exoteric. However, his Golden Dawn Society was heir to the Hermetic wisdom of earlier ages, and being Hermetic, its members were secretive regarding the changes which they made in the order and character of the cards, believing that mysteries revealed are profaned. Consequently, their esoteric Tarot is now, by and large, unintelligible to the world.

The value of the present book may be that for the first time both sides of the coin are made clear to the reader. We have heard for so long that Tarot is "The Book of Thoth" that Tarot's true origins are shrouded in specious mystery. Again, we must remember that it comes to us circa 1392, and for this reason Joseph Campbell's identification of the images of the Major Arcana with that era is particularly valuable in placing Tarot in proper historical perspective. Commensurate with our varied approaches to Tarot, Campbell's treatment will be scholarly and objective, whereas mine will be personal and at times hugely subjective, because the Hermetic approach to art and life depends upon the synchronicity (correspondence) of inner (psychic) and outer (mundane) events. Thus, the Great Work (*Opus*) of the alchemist was done on himself, his life the work of art, "artistic creation within a sacred tradition . . . an inward process whose goal is the ripening, transmutation, or rebirth of the soul of the artist himself."[2] In Hermetic philosophy, the work and the life merge, the artist or alchemist being part of — and inseparable from — the process. As William Butler Yeats has put it another way, "How to tell the dancer from the dance?"

Secondly, the Hermetic tradition has a strong element of divination. To "divine" means to communicate with one's god, but in Hermeticism we must remember that god is within. Since astrology and Tarot are forms of divination, they lead inexorably to the god (Jungian "Self") within the psyche of each of us, and to the spiritual revelations that are true for all. Science as we know it is based upon empirical experience. Contrarily, Hermetic science possesses a heritage of traditional symbols which are present in the collective unconscious of everyman, and which derive not from outer experience but from inner revelation. ". . . the knowledge of nature which a man obtains from such an insight cannot be of a purely rational or discursive kind. For him the world has now become as if transparent: in its appearance he sees the reflection of eternal 'prototypes.' And even when this insight is not immediately present, the symbols which spring from it nevertheless arouse the memory or 'recollection' of these prototypes. Such is the Hermetic view of nature."[3]

Hermeticism has often been linked to Gnosticism, which flourished contemporaneously in the last centuries B.C. and first A.D. Both systems taught liberation of the soul through acquisition of secret knowledge (*gnosis*) of the world and its creator. I believe this wisdom is contained in microcosm within the Major Arcana of the Waite/Rider Tarot. Both Gnosticism and Hermeticism have specific astrological elements, which I shall discuss subsequently, and this astrological system surfaced again in medieval Europe — in a kind of code form — as alchemy. This same astrological system is present in Tarot, as in the parallel alchemical sequence linking planets and metals; hence, I think it not unreasonable to suggest that the appearance in Europe of alchemy and Tarot *at the same time* was not accidental. Both were esoteric forms of earlier wisdom systems that became secret out of the necessity of preserving the lives of those to whom the philosophy had been communicated; for pain of death at the hands of the zealous Christian Church awaited heretics.

The question arises, "What are the origins of Tarot? What race or people created it?" Aleister Crowley calls Tarot "The Book of Thoth," but there is no evidence of this. Since "The Book of Thoth" is not in existence now, Crowley could not make any direct textual correlations. It is not as important to link Tarot with a particular country or people, however, as it is to place it in the proper tradition, that is, Hermeticism. The alchemical and astrological correspondences in Tarot definitely link it to the Hermetic arts.

2. Tarot as a Book of the Dead

The roots of Hermeticism are deep indeed. A great part of the Egyptian tradition is Hermetic, and there are definite parallels between Thoth and Hermes. I propose to demonstrate that in the meaning and sequence of the Major Arcana, Tarot is traditionally Hermetic and, what is most fascinating of all, a kind of Western Book of the Dead. This is not readily apparent, the secretive Hermetic tendency disguising the form in an elaborate symbolical system. To my knowledge, no one has put forth this theory on Tarot; yet certain magical and secret societies have inherited the Hermetic legacy, one of these having been the Society of the Golden Dawn, which numbered among its early 20th-century members Arthur Edward Waite, A. E. (George Russell), Crowley, and William Butler Yeats. Waite was a great scholar of alchemy, interpreting in the light of its symbols many important Renaissance texts. Under his guidance the Golden Dawn created a modern (1910) deck of Tarot which lent itself easily to divination, since the Minor Arcana (56 cards—four suits, in sequence from deuce to ace) were given pictorial representations. For example, rather than showing simply ten swords, in the card of that name there is a man with ten swords piercing his prostrate body. Naturally, all sorts of dire associations leap to mind, facilitating divination.

There is a progression (in the 22 Keys of the Major Arcana) of the soul's initiation into higher consciousness. There are the classic Hermetic/Gnostic elements of descent from the spiritual light to the darkness of the abyss, followed by an ascent to reunion with the light, followed by the resolution of opposites: dark and light, good and evil, masculine and feminine, etc. In this Great Work, Hermes is often the spiritual principle, himself the Logos as well as the guide and "pointer of the way" for the souls of men who would follow after him.

Traditionally, intercourse between the divine and human planes is represented as proceeding in two ways. Most frequently, the divine descends to earth from a higher plane of consciousness, generally symbolized as an elevated spiritual or physical plane, such as heaven or a mountain top (Olympus). But a human being may ascend in vision to the divine plane and then return to earth to teach the revelation of his breakthrough in consciousness, as in shamanism, Buddhism, and the legend of Moses on Mount Sinai.

The passage of a god from the cosmic plane to the mundane, or of either a god or mortal from the mundane plane to that of some order of immortals (the Land of the Ever-Young, an Earthly or Celestial Paradise, etc.), I shall treat in the following pages as the Great Myth, and its rendering in the form of Tarot is to be my subject. The twenty-two Key cards of the Tarot Major Arcana depict in essence the stages of this Great Myth. As consistently symbolic of what have been traditionally known as the "Greater Mysteries," their deciphering will be the whole concern of my section of this volume. Just how the Great Myth came to be preserved in cards that evolved into our modern playing cards remains, however, an even Greater Mystery than the Major Arcana.

CHAPTER II

THE INFINITE LADDER

> From the highest to the lowest,
> everything rises by intermediate steps
> on the infinite ladder.
> —*The Emerald Tablet*

1. *Mercurius, The Magician*

Modern playing cards evolved from the 14th-century Tarot cards, which had even earlier origins. The principal difference between cards of today and Tarot is Tarot's addition of 26 cards, to total 78 instead of 52. Four of those added are Knights, in each of the four suits, the suits being known as Swords, Cups, Coins (Dishes or Pentacles), and Wands (or Staves) — from which our own four suits of Spades, Hearts, Diamonds, and Clubs have evolved. In the sequence of each of these, the Knights follow the Pages (our present day Jacks) and are themselves followed by the Queens and Kings. The remaining 22 additional cards are of the so-called Major Arcana, Keys 0-22, and it will be to these that our whole argument will be devoted.

Card games were already well established in the East and Near East long before the appearance of Tarot about the period of the beginning of the Renaissance in Italy. We are told, for example, by the chronicler Covelluzo that in 1379 "There were encamped about Viterbo paid troops of the opposing factions of Clement VII and Urban VI, who did commit depredations of all kinds, and robberies in the Roman states. In this year of such great tribulations the game of cards was introduced into Viterbo, which came from the Saracens and was called Naib."⁴ In the eighteenth century, before the discovery of the Rosetta Stone (1790), when the hieroglyphs of the Egyptians were still indecipherable to European man, Court de Gebelin advanced a theory of the supposed Egyptian origins of Tarot. Unfortunately, in occult matters, bizarre ideas tend to become fashionable, and this is one that has persisted: witness the popular "Book of Thoth" deck, composed by Aleister Crowley. A few years after Court de Gebelin's publication, but still pre-Rosetta Stone, a Parisian wigmaker named Alliette, who took a fancy to the notion, reversed the spelling of his own name and in the character of Etteilla, stepped forward as the high priest of occult science. After these two, there followed in the nineteenth century Papus and Eliphas Levi to perpetuate the fashion of Egyptian attributions.

As to any possible link of Tarot to Egypt, I think that we may say only this: that Thoth is the Egyptian equivalent to Hermes/Mercury, and that there *are* Hermetic elements in Tarot. In *A History of Playing Cards,* Catherine Hargrave has noted that "the Italian suit signs are the four symbols sacred to Hermes, forging another link connecting playing cards with fortune-telling. Those who sought help from Hermes' oracle in the old days first made an offering of silver to the temple priests, and the crossing of a gypsy's palm with silver is a survival of that ancient rite. Of the atouts," she continues (the "atouts" are the cards of the Major Arcana), "Le Bateleur and Le Fou are both said to have originally signified Mercury."⁵ Le Bateleur is The Juggler, Key I, and Le Fou, The Fool, Key Zero. Presently we shall explore in detail the qualities and functions of Hermes/Mercury/Thoth, but for a beginning we may note that one interesting feature of the god's role in classical mythology is his appearance frequently as trickster. As the "Peck's Bad Boy" of the gods, Hermes/Mercury is the most volatile and unpredictable — even as is the mercurial metal quicksilver. One cannot catch it (the god's fleetness); it is deucedly elusive. At once fluid and solid, it suggests an amalgam of opposites — all opposites: good and evil, dark and light, masculine and feminine; and in this sense, in alchemical lore, it is represented as anticipating and effecting the marriage, the *hierosgamos,* of sun and moon. In A. E. Waite's Hermetically inspired deck, Key I, The Juggler, has evolved into The Magician, who gestures, "As above, so below," suggesting in the way of the *Emerald Tablet* a mystical marriage of the divine and human planes. For magicians, not unlike jugglers, can instruct us in the illusory nature of appearances. Nature's laws seem to be contravened as the juggler's balls stay in the air, and in the works of the magician, one element may hide in another for a time, perhaps assuming another form, while the elusive pea of reality is never found under the apparent shell. The higher lesson to be read in all this is the Hermetic mystery of self-transformation.

Now, Mercury is a metal; Mercury also is a planet; and even to the novice, astrological elements are apparent in the Marseilles as well as the Waite version of the Major Arcana. Keys 18 and 19, for example, are both entitled "The Moon" and "The Sun." Astrology is an Hermetic art, and finding depictions of two of the planets gives one a hint that Tarot as a whole may be Hermetic as well. Of extreme importance is the Major Arcana's positioning of Moon and Sun together; for this is one way of representing the traditional *hierosgamos,* or mystical marriage, which in alchemy is most frequently symbolized by a Queen Moon and King Sun. The Waite/Rider pack, proceeding on the assumption, I suppose, that the traditional placement of Sun and Moon together — as if in "marriage" — was not accidental but denoted something of great import, has added specific alchemical symbols to the Major Arcana. Waite himself, in his book *The Pictorial Key to the Tarot,* has not called attention to these alchemical elements; indeed, throughout the volume he is more intent upon preserving than unveiling secrets. He was following, evidently, the motto of Rosencreutz's *Chymical Wedding,* "Mysteries profaned and made public fade and lose their grace. Therefore, cast not pearls before swine, nor spread roses for the ass." For example, in relation to his switching of Keys 8 and 11 he states simply: "As the variation carries nothing with it which will signify to the reader, there is no cause for explanation."[6] There is, nevertheless, a way of laying out the Major Arcana — as we shall see — that reveals the esoteric meaning of each card and gives support to Waite's (and the Golden Dawn's) switching of these two cards.

There is a further correlation of astrology and Tarot to be noted in Key 10, The Wheel of Fortune. In *The Secret Books of the Egyptian Gnostics,* Doresse notes: "All the pagan religions of the Near East and the Mediterranean had adapted their creeds to the great myths of astrology, which was accorded the status of a science, and according to which man was subject to the planets and constellations from before birth until death, shackled to the Wheel of Fate.'" To astrologers the planet Jupiter is regarded as the greater benefic, and what good fortune may come one's way is often attributed to influences of that sphere; hence, Jupiter can be properly associated with Key 10, The Wheel of Fortune.

Three more manifest relations of a planet to the cards can be readily recognized in Key 13, Death, Key 14, Temperance, and Key 15, The Devil, all suggesting Saturn to an astrologer. In medieval Europe, Death and the Devil often appear to be almost synonymous, as in Dürer's "Knight, Death, and the Devil"; while in the guise of the grim reaper, carrying hourglass and sickle, Saturn is both time and death, the end of time and process.

Now let us examine the relation of the metals in alchemy to the planets, where their names are used interchangeably, and proceed from there to an interpretation of a symbol of great importance to the Great Myth: that of the Stairway of the Seven Planets.

Let us begin with an examination of the *solificatio* from Apuleius' *The Golden Ass* (2nd century A.D.). "I approached the confines of death, and having trod on the threshold of Proserpine, I returned from it, being carried through all the elements. At midnight I saw the sun shining with a splendid light; and I manifestly drew near to the gods beneath, and the gods above, and proximately adored them." Lucius, who had been transformed into an ass, is redeemed as a man after the intervention of Isis. He participates in a mystery rite, and what is of interest to us here is that the procession has an equivalence to the Tarot, with Hermes/ Mercury/Thoth leading the participants. The uninitiated is of course the lowest of the low, until redeemed by the rite and judged worthy (Key 20, Judgment).

Just so, the alchemical process may be seen as a rite of initiation for matter and man to become spirit or, symbolically, gold of the sun (Key 19). Lucius as ass (lead) is "carried through all the elements." As we shall see, there is a relation between ideas in Gnosticism and alchemy. Germane to Lucius' initiation is the fact that in Origen's description of the Ophite *Diagramma*[8] the seventh, or last, Archon is "ass-shaped" Onoel or Thartharaoth. The first Archon is lion-shaped. The correspondence is to the zodiacal sign of Leo, and its ruler the Sun, whereas the ass corresponds to Capricorn, the goat, and its metal is lead. Both goat and ass are linked symbolically to the devil, in that Capricorn is the sign of the winter solstice, the abyss of the zodiac, and also in that both ass and goat are unregenerate "trickster" animals. One does not turn one's back on either because they cannot be trusted. In psychological terms, therefore, they represent the same shadowy elements as does the devil, the unadapted unconscious contents. The Sun-god Osiris was a synonym for lead, and his tomb the emblem of alchemy; for that tomb was the place of resurrection as well as of death. So, too, Helios (Sun) is inherent in lead, indeed, it is there known alchemically as "the dark sun." And man is inherent in ass, that is to say, the divine soul, in descending through the Archons or planetary spheres, has taken on a material form that may appear to be antithetical to the divine spark of its origin. In *A Dictionary of Symbols,*[9] J. E. Cirlot defines the ass as "an attribute of Saturn, in his capacity as the 'second sun.' It is always in heat, and hated by Isis. The significance of the mock crucifix, with an ass's head, from the Palatine, must be related to the equation of Yahve (Jehovah) with Saturn, although it may be that it is related to the jester-symbol." Actually it is related to both fool (Saklas) and Saturn.

In *Psychology and Alchemy,* Jung defines the ass as "daemon triunus, a chthonic trinity, which is portrayed in Latin alchemy as a three-headed monster and identified with Mercurius, salt, and sulphur."[10] In the latter are all the alchemical elements necessary to the process (passive salt, active sulphur, and the catalyst Mercury). Thus the correspondence to alchemy of the mystery procession in which Lucius (ass, Saturn, lead, trickster/devil) is transformed and "crowned as Helios."[11]

2. The Stairways of Planets

In his book *Hidden Symbolism of Alchemy and the Occult Arts,* Dr. Herbert Silberer has this to say:

> The idea of the ladder set up to heaven, of steps, etc., is universal in religions. . . . Most significant is the connection of the 7 steps of development with the infusion of the nature myth in the alchemistic theories of 'rotations.' For the perfection of the Stone, rotations (i.e., cycles) are required by many authors, in which the materia (and so the soul) pass through the spheres of all the planets. They leave to be subjected successively to the domination (the regimen) of all seven planets. This is related to the ideas of those neoplatonists and gnostics according to which the soul must, on its way (anodos) to its heavenly home, i.e., to its celestial goal, pass through all the planetary spheres and through the animal cycle. . . . Also, in the life of the world, if it is completely lived, man passes through, according to the ideas of the old mystery teachings, the domination of the seven planets.[12]

It is in this sense of an *anodos* that the Tarot symbols constitute a Western Book of the Dead. How the twenty-two Major Arcana can be compared to the seven steps of the Stairway of Planets, I shall discuss momentarily, but first let us observe another author's ideas on the symbology of steps. According to Cirlot:

> ". . . this is a symbol which is very common in iconography all over the world. It embraces the following essential ideas: ascension, gradation, and communication between different, vertical levels. In the Egyptian system of hieroglyphs, steps constitute a determinative sign which defines the act of ascending; it forms part of one of the appellations of Osiris, who is invoked as 'he who stands at the top of the steps.' Ascending, then, can be understood both in a material and in an evolutive and spiritual sense. Usually, the number of steps involved in the symbol is of symbolic significance. . . . In Mithraism, the ceremonial steps were seven in number, each step being made of a different metal (as was each different plane of the ziggurat in a figurative sense). According to Celsus, the first step was of lead (corresponding to Saturn). The general correspondence with the planets is self-evident. Now, this idea of gradual ascent was taken up particularly by the alchemists from the latter part of the Middle Ages onwards; they identified it sometimes with the phases of the transmutation process. . . . In Bettini's *Libro de monte santo di Dio* (Florence, 1477), steps are shown superimposed upon a mountain, to emphasize the parallel — and indeed identical — symbolism of the mountain and ladder, the former is portrayed as if it were terraced and the terraces are shown to be the rungs of the ladder. On these rungs are the names of the virtues. . . ."[13]

Now, among the names of the virtues on this ladder/mountain are Temperance, Fortitude (Strength), and Justice, the names traditionally of Keys 14, 11, and 8, in the Major Arcana, and of Keys 14, 8, and 11 in the Waite "switched" deck.

Let us return to the concept of the Stairway of Planets, and we shall see how the Major Arcana are the Stairway of Planets. So far we have established an equivalence of Key 1 to Mercury/Hermes/Thoth; Key 10 to Jupiter; Keys 13, 14, and 15 to Saturn; and Keys 18 and 19 to Moon and Sun. We are left, then, with two of the seven planets unaccounted for, and they are Venus and Mars. Astrologically, it must be remembered that Mars is martial and Venus venereal; and when we look for two such cards in the Major Arcana we find no problem. Key 6 is "The Lovers," and Key 7 is "The Chariot."

The tricky question then is: how can there be a correlation of the Major Arcana with the Stairway of Planets when there are twenty-two Key cards and but seven planets? The answer is simple. One of the Major Arcana is "The Fool," Key Zero, and zero is outside the numerical progression. That is not to say that it lacks importance. Just as the "wild" play of the modern Joker gives that card an exalted role, so too "The Fool" in Tarot has more freedom than any other Key. He is both first (before Key 1) and last (after Key 21) in the sequence, and on the symbolical meaning of this I shall have more to say later. But examining now the twenty-one remaining Keys, and remarking that 21 is 3 times 7, we might ask: What then if these 21 cards should be arranged in seven triads?

Let us see.

The triad of Keys 1, 2, and 3 contains within it a correlation of Mercury with Key 1; the triad of Keys 4, 5, and 6 contains Key 6, signifying Venus; that of 7, 8, and 9 contains Key 7, associated with Mars; triad 10, 11, and 12 contains Key 10, "The Wheel of Fortune," controlled, as above remarked, by Jupiter; while all the Keys of the next triad, 13, 14, and 15, as we have seen, are related to Saturn; the triad of Keys 16, 17, and 18 has within it 18, "The Moon"; and, finally, that of 19, 20, and 21 contains 19, "The Sun." Thus the veil of Isis has been lifted and the Stairway of Planets revealed as the great mystery of the Major Arcana.

Planet	Symbol	Metal	Tarot Keys
Mercury	☿	Quicksilver	1-3
Venus	♀	Copper	4-6
Mars	♂	Iron	7-9
Jupiter	♃	Tin	10-12
Saturn	♄	Lead	13-15
Moon	☽	Silver	16-18
Sun	☉	Gold	19-21

Thus, in the Tarot Major Arcana, the transformational journey of soul or spirit commences with a descent through Mercury to Saturn, that is, from the volatile and mercurial metal to the heavy and gross, and this then is followed by an ascent through the silvery Moon to the gold of the Sun.

CHAPTER III

THE MAGIC NINE ARRANGEMENT

1. *The Three Layers of Meaning*

In 1971, in *Tarot and You,* I hinted at an arrangement of the Major Arcana which would reveal the deepest esoteric meaning of the twenty-two Keys. Rather like deciphering a code, one begins by searching for common elements between the cards. In respect to the Waite/Rider pack one might say that a code had been converted into another code, or a mystery deepened.

Let us begin by looking for the first clue. In Key 15, The Devil, we notice what appears to be The Lovers of Key 6, now chained under the duress of the devil. Symbolic implications aside, the relation of these cards is simply a numerical difference of nine. Nine may very well be called a magical number, because it always returns to itself. Like the elusive Hermes/Mercurius it may take many forms, while yet retaining its essential identity. How so? Any number multiplied by nine reduces again to nine. By reduction numerologists mean the addition of digits. For example, 9 x 2 = 18. Then 1 + 8 = 9. Further 9 x 456,701 = 4,110,309. These digits add to 18, which again reduces to nine. If nine is added to any of the nine primary digits, then reduction restores that number once again, as 1 + 9 = 10. So 1 + 0 = 1. And 2 + 9 = 11. So 1 + 1 = 2. And so forth.

According to Paul Foster Case, "As last of the numeral symbols, 9 represents the following ideas: completion, attainment, fulfillment, the goal of endeavor, the end of a cycle of Activity."[14] Cirlot calls nine the "triangle of the ternary, and the triplication of the triple. It is therefore a complete image of the three worlds."[15] Thus numerological associations with nine cluster about an idea of culmination, substantiating from a source outside Tarot the relation of Keys 6 and 15. Of course, as we have discovered so far, true Hermetic art integrates many apparently diverse disciplines. Although its origins are lost in time, the concept of numbers as archetypes of meaning is Pythagorean.

If the Tarot code is to yield to the magic number nine, then the relation to nine should persist throughout. Furthermore, another dimension of meaning opens before us as we explore the idea of the archetype of each number raised to another level by the addition of nine. Generally speaking, The Lovers gone to The Devil may perhaps represent their damnation for eating of the Tree, Adam and Eve's original sin. But let us proceed from the One, and move through the entire Major Arcana to show how the addition of nine preserves the original archetypal meaning of the number to which it is added, and yet transforms that number as well.

Our layout will then number one to nine on a single line; above or below (as you choose) will be another line of nine cards: hence 1-9 on one line and 10-18 on the next. We shall then have a third line of only four cards, Keys 19, 20, 21, and 0.

Now we are ready to move through the entire Major Arcana. Obviously there is a lateral sequence, but for the moment we shall concentrate on the relations between cards when nine is added to each Key in the vertical sequence. At this point the reader should fold out the reproduction of the Magic Nine arrangement at back of book, enabling him to follow precisely the significance of our explanation as it develops in the subsequent pages.

First comes The Magician. The focus of meaning in Key 1 is the gesture, "As Above, so Below." Numerically, one is unity; yet the question always arises, "Out of what is the One born?" Or, "Which came first, the chicken or the egg?" Our egg is the hatching Zero, which will be discussed later with relevance to The Fool. But we must remember that The Fool and The Magician are aspects of the same being, the spirit Mercurius. Thus the chicken and the egg are finally one and the same. (See Drawing 1.)

60

DRAWING 1.

The uroboric zero out of which the One proceeds from the No-thing, Manifest from Unmanifest, is depicted in Key One by the uroboros encircling the magician's waist. The upraised wand and the encircling serpent recall symbolically the serpent-staff or caduceus of Mercury. The Hermetically benefic aspects of the serpent are suggested in this card; for above the Magician's head is the lemniscate, another, more simplified version of the serpent uroboros. In mathematics this symbol stands for infinity. In metaphysics we speak of eternity, death and life reconciled, underworld and heaven, the *serpens mercurialis* mediating between the two.

Waite's creation is superior, I think, to the exoteric Tarot in which the figure is a juggler. The Magician's wand is not the same wand as that of the suits on the table before him. There are wands and wands! His is transformative. Moreover, in the exoteric Tarot, the juggler's hat is seen to have the form of the lemniscate, or lazy eight. Obviously Waite has put this "out front." Sitting directly above the middle of the pole/spine of The Magician, the lemniscate's two halves, left and right, encompass all pairs of opposites and suggest the two oval faces of King Sun and Queen Moon, the two-headed hemaphrodite of alchemy. Left and right are also the opposed (by function) hemispheres of the brain, as well as being symbolic of conscious (right) and unconscious (left). Further, it embraces the two worlds, above and below, in one, and is even suggestive of the maze, which is symbolic of the soul's path to the underworld.

Since Mercury is a *psychopompos,* guide of souls, represented in Key 1 in the form of The Magician, arm pointing above, he here compels us to recall that our own dull lead is to become as gold of the Sun. Mercury, like our magician, is master of the two worlds and, as Cirlot notes, a "god of roads, that is, potentialities."[16] The compelling quality which this image had for Jung can only be explained by the parallel between Jung's concept of one's life as a "path of individuation" and Hermes/Mercurius as a symbol for "unlimited capacity for transformation."[17]

As we have said earlier, it is impossible to separate the alchemist from his work. Jung has focused on the metaphor of alchemy as true to human psychology. But he has also pointed to the parallel of alchemy and the soul's journey after death, back to the Light or Sun from whence it originated. In individual readings of the Tarot the accent is naturally on the union of conscious and unconscious, and on the personal journey, but not to be overlooked is the larger "Great Myth," of god's descent to man and the ascent of the god/soul within man back to god. Key 1 presents this god in a manifest form, "pointing the way" of ascent and descent, the way above and below; and it is by uniting the powers of the two that eternity is assured.

In a personal sense, The Magician of Key 1 is the reader of Tarot, the one (I) who is to proceed through the entire initiatory experience of the Major Arcana, arriving, finally, back at the place from which he came, Key 0. In a parallel way, The Magician embodies the magic of self-transformation which is the secret essence of alchemy. With this in mind, we shall see how Key 10 is then the opus, and Key 19 the goal of the opus. But in order to simplify our explication of the Major Arcana, we shall do three run-throughs, each treating a different aspect of the message. First will be that which we have commenced already, primarily of the numerical relations. And in this first development, we shall uncover the common elements in each vertical series, such as the judging motif in Keys 2, 11, and 20. Also, in this initial run-through, we shall take cognizance of the symbolic color scheme that Waite has utilized. Every color and shading thereof in the Waite pack has its own specific significance, which is important since the various stages of the alchemical process are designated by colors.

Furthermore, underlying the whole of the Major Arcana, there is a pattern of graphic design that reinforces the numerical symbology. For example, the number four may be depicted geometrically by a square or cross, because of the four points of the figure. A three is rendered as an upward-pointing triangle and stands for "above," whereas the four directions of the square or cross define the field spatially and link it to "below." Present in Tarot are combinations of crosses, squares, triangles, and also interpenetrating triangles, the meanings of the latter being defined by the directions of the apexes. We shall also examine the mandorla, which was a figure present in the religious art of the 14th century, and, therefore, contemporary with Tarot's earliest known pack (1392). Basically, a mandorla is formed when circles or spheres intersect on a plane. The plane may then be thought of as the meeting ground of "above" and "below."

The delight and yet the frustration of the task of elucidating this esoteric Tarot lies in the maze of meanings here confronting the unraveler. If one follows the thread of alchemy, then for a time the link to the Book of the Dead is forsaken. And if too much time is lost in the underworld, then the way back to The Sun (Key 19) may be lost as well. We are going to have to accept these conditions for a time, as we follow our three threads, one by one. However, at the end, at the conclusion of our third run-through, we shall see how all of the threads entwine, and how each supports and enhances the other's significance.

For example, in regard to color: in our first run-through we shall examine a scheme of active and passive, specifically, red and white combinations, with variations thereon. The coloring of the background of Key 1, for instance, heralds the Golden Dawn, the Society that created the deck, the active and passive elements needed to initiate the opus being represented in the magician's garb. In the course of our second excursion through the Keys, after our study of some basics of alchemy, we shall see that active red and passive white signify sulphur and quicksilver, which are presented as glyphs in Key 10, The Wheel, which in turn is symbolic of the whole alchemical process or opus. Further, the Golden Dawn of Key 1 anticipates the *rubedo,* or reddening stage, of alchemical transformation, the moment of sunrise, when the Red King and White Queen celebrate their symbolical "chymical wedding."

Our third and last treatment of the Major Arcana, treating of the astrological thread that runs through the Waite/Rider Tarot, will unite in one great image all the earlier themes, inasmuch as the alchemical gold to be made is "gold of the sun," Key 19; and as we proceed up the Stairway of Planets once more, the Red King and White

Queen come together at only one place in the zodiac, namely the midheaven of the summer solstice as it appeared in 2,000 B.C., on the cusp of Cancer and Leo, which are ruled respectively by the Moon and the Sun. Simultaneously, the individual soul, which itself is "gold of the sun," will be seen to have followed the Great Myth's pathway to immortality. And thus the essence will have been illustrated of the lesson of the *Emerald Tablet's* summary words — "As Above, so Below" — with "Below" understood as the microcosm, the elemental world, "Above" as the macrocosm or universal world, and between, Man, the mediator, the mesocosm.

From the interplay of Above and Below, our subsequent run-throughs appear as follows:

BELOW (Microcosm)	ABOVE (Macrocosm)
Alchemy (Metals)	Astrology (Planets)
Ascent/Descent	Descent/Ascent
Gnosticism	Book of the Dead
Zosimos	The Caduceus Reading

NUMERICAL RELATIONS IN THE MAJOR ARCANA

In the series of numbers 1-9, in the Magic Nine arrangement, five mediates between the first and last four numbers of the series. Five is also known as the number of "man." In the esoteric Tarot of Waite, this figure is not The Pope — as in the Marseilles deck — but The Hierophant, who has at his feet the keys to the two kingdoms, Above and Below, divine and mundane. His gesture indicates Above, while his feet rest firmly on a mundane throne; thus man (five) is the mesocosm between microcosm and macrocosm. The microcosm has as its equivalent the number four, representing the elemental world. In Tarot's Key 4, the emperor's cubical throne stands for the terrestial kingdom "below." The macrocosm, "above," has two associated numerals: nine, since it signifies completion and attainment, and always returns to itself; and ten, the monad of unity combined with the "ellipse of superconsciousness."[18] Key 10 is the wheel of cosmic process, which mirrors the mundane alchemical process below.

Between alchemy and the science of numerals as archetypes of meaning (numerology) there is a profound Hermetic link. Witness a 15th-century text which Jung has interpreted in his chapter on "The Personification of the Opposites." The text reads, "The descent to the four and the ascent to the monad are simultaneous."[19] Jung's interpretation: "The 'four' are the four elements and the monad is the original unity which reappears in the 'denarius' (the number 10), the goal of the opus. . . ."[20] We have above equated "gold of the sun" (Key 19) with the goal of the opus; however, when the digits 1 and 9 are added, reduction yields 10, the denarius, which is the goal as defined in Jung's quotation. The number 4 defines the mundane plane, there being four elements and four directions, which are symbolized in Waite's Key 10, "denarius," by Bull, Lion, Eagle, and Man. In the represented Wheel of Fortune itself, the spiritual Monad takes the form of a golden serpent descending to the elemental world, "Below"; but its ascent is simultaneous in the form of Hermes/Anubis moving *up* the wheel. And so it is that a basic alchemical text has here already served to introduce our numerical reading of the Major Arcana.

Elements of stasis, fixity, and balance are present in all even numbers. These are regarded by numerologists as feminine or passive; and to this we may add the observation that *dualities* are manifest or symbolized in Keys 2, 4, 6, 8, and 10, and that these dualities show a tendency to merge or to "marry" in Keys 12, 14, 16, 18, 20, and "22" or Key 0.

The addition of one, the Monad, to any even number resolves the dichotomy and initiates a numerical evolution. Accordingly, the odd numbers are said to be masculine and dynamic; and, as we shall see in proceeding through the Magic Nine arrangement of our cards, the addition of 1 to any numbered Key initiates a new series, and stasis, therefore, is never permanent. Indeed, the culminating Tarot Key, Zero, is completely regenerative, so that the series does not end but commences again in Key One. Behind this numerical concept is the Hermetic concept of the uroboric cosmos, devouring and reappearing, or in terms of modern physics, contracting and expanding. Therefore, the addition of one is the impetus for a linear progression.

In our Magic Nine arrangement, the addition of the odd number 9 results in relations between the Keys that are truly revelatory, for it is as if the archetype of meaning of a particular Key had been transformed to a higher plane of consciousness, as though with a quantum jump in the archetypal meaning of the number. And this is entirely in keeping with the nature of 9 as signifying "completion, attainment, fulfillment. . . ."[21] All the Keys in our Magic Nine arrangement, when read in vertical series, reveal this transformative relation.

Read in horizontal series, on the other hand, the 1 proceeds from unity to multiplicity, that is, from 1 to 2; and beneath this elementary truth lies the archetype of all creation myths and the whole diversity of form which spirit may manifest. $1 + 9 = 10$. And $10 + 9 = 19$. All of these reduce again to 1, so that 1 is the archetype of the first vertical series: the many are eventually swallowed back by the One.

Here there is a relevance to Jungian psychology, as there is also, as we have just seen, in the relation of Keys 10 and 19, the opus and the goal, paralleling the process of individuation. Read in terms of the psyche: "the painful suspension between opposites gradually changes in the bilateral activity of the point in the centre, the self, or divine Monad. . . . The 'Aurelia occulta' puts this thought in the words of the dragon: 'Many from one and one from many, issue of a famous line, I rise from the lowest to the highest. The nethermost power of the whole earth is united with the highest. I therefore am the One and the Many within me.' In these words, [comments Jung] the dragon makes it clear that he is the chthonic forerunner of the self."[22]

Consequently, the numeral one is the parallel to the archetype of the self in that One is the undivided (into two) archetype of wholeness.

This dragon, then, that rises from the lowest to the highest is the spirit Hermes/Mercurius/Thoth of the *Emerald Tablet,* who "rises from earth to heaven and comes down again." Numerically, the forerunner of the One (Key 1) is Key Zero, the Orphic egg hatched by the dragon/serpent out of which the One emanates. And as the Major Arcana culminate at Key Zero, the many forms of the One are "swallowed" by the uroboric serpent, returning once more to no-thing.

To numerologists the number zero is known as an abysmal number of "the abyss", for it was said to contain the abysmal mystery of God. The mystery's unraveling is the knowledge of the Many in the One and the One in the Many; or the descent of the Monad to the multiple forms of the elemental plane, and ascent again, wherein the human soul attains reunion with its creator. For those who had not caught the connection between the number nine and the Major Arcana, a numerologist analyzing The Fool might have stumbled upon the fact that the meaning of the entire Major Arcana is contained within this card; since Waite's innovation adds an actual abyss to the card, while being careful not to mention the word abyss: ". . . the brink of a precipice among the great heights of the world," and also, "the edge which opens on the depth. . . ."[23] The *spiritus mercurialis,* or Hermes Trismegistos, is according to the *Emerald Tablet,* "He who unites the powers of Above and Below and shows his full power when he returns again to earth." As we gaze at Key 0, we see the fool about to descend once more into "the abyss of the nigredo."[24]

In Gnostic terms this descent is a death of the spirit. Likewise, above Key 0 or 22, The Fool, we see Key 13, namely Death, while at the same time, the vertical sequence of 4 + 9 = 13, which is to say, the elemental, mundane plane leads inevitably to death. But 13 + 9 = 22, and zero does not reduce to thirteen, nor to four, nor to any other number. It is outside numerical law, a cosmic law unto itself. Of all the figures in the Major Arcana only the fool's footwear is golden, hinting that he has walked the golden path of spiritual evolution. Perhaps now he himself has become "the path." Behind him is the color of the golden dawn, linking him to Key 1.

As an active number thirteen resolves the static quality of the elemental world. Death is nature's way of graduating matter to spirit. The pairs of opposites first encountered in the black and white pillars of Key 2, reiterated in the white horse and black rider of Key 13, eventually yield to the golden dawn of rebirth, the impending sunrise in Key 13, which culminates as Key 0's golden dawn.

We have seen the connections between the Keys of the vertical sequences 1, 10 and 19, as well as of 4, 13, and 0. Let us proceed to Keys 2, 11, and 20.

By the simple linear addition of one, the Monad of Key 1 becomes 2, duality, equilibrium, and reflection. In my Jungian Spread,[25] Key 2, the High Priestess, stands for a man's anima, and Key 1, the Magician, for a woman's animus: thus the sexual polarity of these two cards. The Monad, being essentially indivisible, contains within itself the yin/yang polarities, just as Mercurius is duplex, uniting all opposites; but whereas the polarities were only hinted at symbolically in Keys 1 and 10, they are explicit in Key 2 in the columns lettered B and J. In Waite's own words in explanation:

> The two pillars between which she sits are those of Solomon and of Hermes. Opposite in color, but alike in form, they represent affirmation (white pillar, bearing the letter Yod, initial of the word *Jachin*) and negation (black pillar, bearing the letter Beth, initial of the word Boaz). For strength (Boaz) is rooted in resistance or inertia, which is the negation of the activity which is the establishing principle (*Jachin*) of all things. The High Priestess sits between the pillars, because she is the equilibrating power between the "Yes" and "No," the initiative and the resistance, the light and the darkness.[26]

I have a quarrel with the current publishers of the Waite deck; for Waite himself has stated in no uncertain terms that in Key 2 the column representing Jachin is white, and so must be seen as black's opposite. And so it is in my Waite pack; but now, in recent decks grey is its color, and since Jachin stands for light, this is an unforgivable error.

The pillars of light and darkness are symbolic of conscious and unconscious, in the Jungian sense. The problem is to balance these, as in Key 11, Justice. Life itself is born between the pillars of the Great Mother of the mystery of birth and death. Lingam and yoni, male and female symbology, are suggested in the palms and pomegranates on the veil behind Waite's Priestess. Some say her veil has never been lifted, intending by this to mean that the mystery of death has never been disclosed. She is the companion to the solar principle, which acts through Keys 1, 10, and 19, and is his bride at the *hierosgamos,* as the moon is his reflection. That he should not be forgotten in this card, Waite has placed "a large solar cross on her breast."[27] And since he will be the force working through her at the resurrection, our vertical sequence appropriately reads 2, 11, and 20.

The reason for Waite's switch of Keys 8 and 11 will now become manifest. What meets the eye is a continuity of judging figures. In Keys 2 and 11 we are before thrones, TORA in the lap of the High Priestess signifying the Law, and in Key 20 "The Last Judgment" is made upon us. The ultimate Law is not social but cosmic; hence the judgment from "above," in Key 20, which Waite is careful to accent in his symbolization. The figure of Justice performs again the "As Above, so Below" gesture of Key 1; but this time the raised hand holds a sword, suggesting cosmic retribution, while the other holds a scale, while at the same time pointing down to the final judgment of Key 20. The scales suggest the ancient image of the weighing of the soul at death, and we shall have more to say of this in connection with the figures of MAAT, the Egyptian goddess of the soul's last weigh-in, and LE MAT, the name given The Fool in the French Marseilles deck. For in a certain sense, The Fool is the final judge, since he is the last of the Major Arcana. In the Hermetic sense, however, since god is within, he is not "out-there," but a manifestation of the divine within; hence Key 20 bears a strong relationship to one of the pictures in the *Mutus Liber,* an alchemical text of 1677, in which the clarion call of the last trumpet sounded is to awaken those spiritually asleep (dead). Present also in Waite's figure is a ladder, which was the code symbol for the Stairway of Planets.

Whereas active colors (red, orange, and gold) dominate our first vertical series, passive blues and greys predominate in the sequence 2, 11, and 20. The active principle resides *in potentia* in Key 2, as symbolized by the red and gold yoni, the meaning of which is that the goddess actively gives birth to the active masculine. Red dominates, on the other hand, in the robe of the figure in Justice, signifying that 2 + 9 yields a more active judgment than 2, outer-directed rather than inward-turning, since it is an uneven, active, masculine number. Note the almost meditative posture of the High Priestess, Key 2, whereas the figure in 11, Justice, holds a sword on high as though to mete out justice in the social sphere. And finally, a red and white solar banner, pairing with the red banner of the sun-child of Key 19, dominates the scene of Key 20, the *cosmic* judgment.

Horizontally, three is a product or active offspring of the action of one on two (1 + 2 = 3). Waite describes his Key 3, The Empress, as "universal fecundity and the outer sense of the Word,"[28] that is, the Logos clothed materially. "In another order of ideas," he continues, "the card of The Empress signifies the door or gate by which an entrance is obtained into this life . . . the way that leads out therefrom, into that which is beyond, is the secret known to the High Priestess."[29].

Our next vertical series, then, is 3, 12, and 21, and there is a clue in Waite that links 3 and 21, where he writes of the Empress that "There are also certain aspects in which she has been correctly described . . . as the woman clothed with the sun [2 + 1] as *Gloria Mundi* . . ."[30] He does not apply the words *Gloria Mundi* to Key 21, The World; yet his description of this card is of the mundane world transformed and raised to the celestial—or, once more an ascent of spirit. This card, in his words, refers "to that day when all was declared to be good, when the morning stars sang together and all the Sons of God shouted for joy."[31]

To comprehend what Waite means by "the woman clothed with the sun," we must have the cards in the special arrangement that I have outlined, since only the addition of nine to Key 3 gives us Key 12, which is one of the great enigmas of the esoteric Tarot. Here we note that the active solar principle is present in the red tights covering The Hanged Man's lower body, whereas the blue tunic refers to the feminine lunar element. Waite has surrounded the head with a golden nimbus or sun disc, implying some sort of breakthrough in consciousness. But even before Waite's illumination, this card had ties to the sun; for in *A History of Playing Cards,* Catherine Hargrave tells us that "Le Pendu, The Hanged Man, symbolizes the universal sun myth, which has been called the basis of religion wherever a dying god is worshipped. Its meaning, of course, is emblematic of the winter solstice and the coming of spring. La Roux de Fortune can be plainly traced from the earliest sun glyphs, which were wheels."[30] We shall have more to say about this in our astrological, third run-through. Basically, however, "the woman clothed with the sun" in Key 3, and the inverted figure in Key 12 bear the same essential meaning, *as do all of the cards by the process of reduction to the numerical essence.* Our further run-throughs will demonstrate this in precise detail, but what can be said here is that as Keys 1, 10, and 19 are basically 1 in essence (that is, $1 + 0 = 1$, and $1 + 9 = 10$, which in turn reduces to one), a similar play around 2 applies to the 2, 11, and 20 series. Key 12 reduces to three, as does also 21. 13 reduces to 4; 14 to 5; 15 to 6; 16 to 7; 17 to 8; and 18 to 9. The relationships of all these cards will presently be made clear, but that of 12 to 3 is particularly rich in meaning, since at the winter solstice the sun has descended to the abyss from the heaven of the summer solstice, and thus spirit has interpenetrated matter. The same idea is conveyed in the Gnostic myth of the descent of Nous, to become locked in the embrace of Physis, and it is in this way that the woman is "clothed with the sun." The addition of nine elevates this same principle to a new plane, akin, as we have said earlier, to the mystic liberation of the soul of the world, *anima mundi.*

In the way of personal discovery, the reader may now find it stimulating to analyze the cards for their integral relationships. These could fill an entire book, but a few examples may here be cited as follows. 4 is composed of 2 and 2, as well as of 3 and 1; thus each number has an archetype which functions in essence, and the new totality preserves those essences up to and including number nine, beyond which all numbers reduce to their archetypal essences, e.g., $9 + 1 = 10$ and $1 + 0 = 1$.

So five is 4 + 1 and 3 + 2
Six is 5 + 1, 4 + 2, and 3 + 3
Seven is 6 + 1, 4 + 3, and 5 + 2
Eight is 7 + 1, 6 + 2, 5 + 3, and 4 + 4
Nine is 8 + 1, 7 + 2, 6 + 3, and 5 + 4

If the inner meaning of the card is understood, then these relations are clear indeed.

Now let us proceed to the vertical series 5 + 9 = 14, since we have already dealt with 4, 13, and 0. Ostensibly, concepts of mediation, as evident in Key 5, and Temperance, Key 14, are related in that one element tempers the other. The winged angel of 14 suggests "above" and the divine plane; yet its feet are grounded in the mundane. So too the ancient interpreter of sacred mysteries, The Hierophant, while sitting on his mundane throne, points "above." Since water frequently signifies spirit, the two domains, "above" and "below," may be what is represented by the positions of the angel's feet, one on land and one on the water. The wings are fiery red, and the robe white, reiterating the colors of Key 5. In some of the later decks the wings are purple, which may be either an inaccuracy or a "tempering" of red with blue. My deck has a rainbow above the halo on the angel's head. Iris, who personified the rainbow for the Greeks, was Zeus' messenger, which links her with Hermes/Mercury/Thoth, and suggests that this card may be playing once more on the theme of the reconciliation of opposites, more particularly those of "above" and "below."

Above and below appear symbolically in the sign upon the angel's breast, "the square and triangle of the septenary."[33] The square = matter, or the four points and elements of bound nature; the triangle, as the Egyptians knew, channels the spiritual forces of the universe into the mundane. Their interpenetration is also the meaning of the flow between the golden chalices. A cross, because of its four points, has the same significance as a square, and Key 12 (4 x 3 = 12) has both the cross and triangle represented in the positions of the legs and arms of The Hanged Man. Waite's Tarot plays upon the theme of the Great Myth, with all its variations and profound implications; and once the code is cracked, the esoteric meanings become crystal-clear.

Let us move on to the series 6 + 9 = 15. Six = 4 (the elemental world) + 2, duality; hence, Adam and Eve in the world, or Garden. Waite was willing to reveal more of this card's meaning than of any other, and so we read in his own words: "The suggestion in respect of the woman is that she signifies that attraction towards the sensitive life which carries within it the idea of the Fall of Man [Key 15, The Devil], but she is rather the working of a Secret Law of Providence [3 + 3 = 6] than a willing and conscious temptress."[34] The above brackets are mine, not Waite's, lest the reader think he had forsworn secrecy. He continues: "It is through her imputed lapse that man shall arise ultimately, and only by her can he complete himself."[35] Five, the number for man + one = six, The Lovers.

Key 15, The Devil, presents an image of the underworld, or winter solstice, with the sovereign lord of the abyss, Saturn/Capricorn. The serpent is of course a form of this so-called Devil, and appears in Keys 10 and 6, in the latter entwined about the Tree of the Knowledge of Good and Evil, that is, of the pairs of opposites. In this card, the lovers of Key 6 are given tails and horns to indicate their dominance by the chthonic realm. Adam's tail is fiery, indicating the active masculine principle, whereas Eve's is formed from a natural cornucopia of fruit. They are chained to a cube of matter, which is similar to the foursquare throne of Key 4, The Emperor, which yields ultimately Death (4 + 9 = 13).

Crowning the Devil's head is a five-pointed star, which is significantly inverted. Five is the number of man. The numerological significance of this is the submission of man to the diabolical, dark element. Astrologically, this would be the point in the sun's annual journey when it submits to the Saturnian dominance, the winter solstice of 4,000-2,000 B.C., in Aquarius and Capricorn, both of which are ruled by Saturn, the dark sun or *sol niger* of alchemy. Key 6 anticipates the descent (and subsequent ascent), as is shown by the sun above the angel, and the distant mountain, symbol of the Great Work.

The background color for Keys 6, 7, and 8 is golden, whereas for Keys 13, 14, 15, and 16 it is either grey, black, or some combination of these, the colors of Saturn. We cannot mistake the fact that we are at the nadir. "Above" is the solar, spiritual element, which descends "below" for the salvation of both man and matter. In Gnosticism we shall see how this is regarded as a tragic "fall" from light, and our next vertical sequence depicts this most vividly in The Tower, Key 16.

Exoterically this card is called "The House of God." Because of the destruction shown it is one of the less welcome cards in a reading. The lightning-struck tower is another form of the stone to which the lovers of Key 15 are chained; hence liberation rather than ruin is the esoteric meaning of this Key. From the nadir only one direction is possible and that is up. Significantly, the golden bolt comes from aloft and reunites above and below, seemingly kindling in matter the fiery essence that is to be unlocked. This in alchemy is known as the "active sulphur," the red lion of Key 8.

Our linear sequence, meanwhile, can be read as follows: The Lovers, or pairs of opposites, appear in Key 7, in transformation, as the yin/yang sphinxes, charioteered by the wand-carrying magus of Key 1 in a new form, surmounted "above" by a starry canopy. Thus 6 + 1, The Lovers plus The Magician, have become 7, The Charioteer. Suggested also is man (5), plus the pairs of opposites (5 + 2 = 7), as well as the foursquare elemental throne of Key 4, The Emperor, plus 3, The Empress, a spiritual principle pregnant with the Word, interpenetrating with these; hence 4 + 3 = 7.

Alchemically, the solid must be dissolved and rendered volatile so that the essence may be liberated, and in order to accomplish this the opposites must be separated. In Key 16, The Tower, they are shown as the falling King Sun and Queen Moon, masculine and feminine, active and passive, sulphur (note the King's red cape) and salt (or quicksilver). Unlike Humpty-Dumpty, they will be put back together again at Keys 18 and 19, Moon and Sun.

Mastery of the pairs of opposites, which is the esoteric meaning of Key 7, The Chariot, leads to "Strength," Key 8, which is not brute force, but rather that spiritual (alchemical) strength which results when the power of Key 1, The Magician, is added to the mastery of the Charioteer, Key 7; thus 7 + 1 = 8.

In the following vertical sequence, 8 + 9 = 17, the eight-pointed star crowning the Charioteer has become the great star that is Key 17, "The Star." And in our next linear series this same eight-pointed star reappears as the light within the lantern of The Hermit, Key 9. Note, too, the starry diadem of The Empress, Key 3, and again, the Charioteer's starred crown. The connections are as follows:

Three is the number of the celestial or heavenly realm. In the words of Cirlot: "Hence, seven is the number expressing the sum of heaven and earth" [3 + 4 = 7]. . . . Seven, with its characteristic quality of synthesis, is regarded as a symbol of the transformation and integration of all hierarchical orders as a whole, hence there are seven notes in the diatonic scale, seven colours in the rainbow, and seven planetary spheres together with their seven planets. . . . Seven is represented graphically by the joining of the triangle and the square, the triangle being either superimposed upon or inscribed within the square."[36] This combination of the three and four is depicted graphically in Key 7 by the triangular form of the Charioteer's body within the square of the starry canopy and the solid, square base of the chariot proper, the meaning of which is the interpenetration of the heavenly and the mundane, or spirit infusing matter. Pointing upward, such a triangle represents aspiration towards the spiritual, and alchemically symbolizes fire, or the aspiring, fiery spirit of man desirous of reunion with its source. Key 14, Temperance (two 7's), presents a variation of this theme of the angelic (heavenly) and mundane realms in dynamic interplay. On the angel's breast is a triangle within a square, and the rainbow's seven colors are symbolized by the iris. (See Drawing 2.)

Proceeding with the linear sequence, King Sun and Queen Moon become, next, the red lion and white woman of "Strength," Key 8. But since both this card and The Star,

DRAWING 2.

VII

Key 17, its vertical companion, receive an extensive analysis in our alchemical run-through, we shall pass over them, for the time being, and move on to the final linear card, Key 9, The Hermit. Nine is the final archetypal number as well, for all subsequent numbers beyond it are of two or more digits, hence reducible. The Hermit appears to be looking back along the long line of the preceding Arcana, and by the same token he appears to halt the linear movement, almost like a bookend at the edge of a shelf. So, too, The Fool concludes the entire Major Arcana, and both Hermit and Fool appear in a common topography of icy heights, connoting a theme of spiritual elevation. The Hermit's wand is also The Fool's, a long staff suitable for the spirit's eternal journey; and, like The Fool, The Hermit, too, is a transformation of the Magician/Alchemist of Key 1.

Waite translated a number of books on alchemy, one of which is *The Hermetic Museum* (1892), the original of which was published in Frankfurt in 1678. Waite used one of the pictures from this text as a model for his hermit, without revealing it in his explanations of the Major Arcana. At right we present The Hermit and his prototype.

As to the star in The Hermit's lantern, it is composed of two interpenetrating triangles, which have a specific alchemical meaning that we shall treat in our second run-through. The alchemists are following the light carried by *anima mundi,* or spirit in nature, who appears in Keys 17 and 21 as The Star, respectively, and The World. By placing her light within The Hermit's own lantern, Waite makes The Hermit a light unto himself. Such a star of light, so placed, signifies the aspiration of the material plane for the spiritual, and the descent of the spiritual to the material. And this completes the numerical cycle that was initiated by the Magician's "above/below" gesture, with the two planes now conjoined within the one lantern.

In Waite's description of this profoundly significant card, there should be a clue to the feasibility of our Magic Nine arrangement and, indeed, there is. Waite writes: "I have said this is a card of attainment."[37] The words match what we have said of the attributes of 9 as representing attainment, realization, and completion. Symbolically as well,

DRAWING 3.

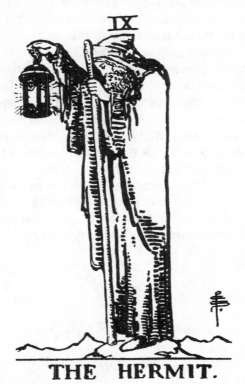

THE HERMIT.

The Hermit concludes the series of the various pairs of opposites that we have noted in the first linear sequence, 1-9. He is a solitary figure, but we have the two triangles of the starlight in his lamp to convey this truth.

Generally speaking, in our decimal system, the number ten concludes numerical series; but since ten reduces to one, the Tarot series would then run from one to one, with 2-9 intervening. More properly, it is the archetypal, or mystical, meaning of numbers that applies here, and not that of their mathematical utility. Waite's color schemes and underlying graphic designs are amplifications of the numbers' archetypal meanings. And when, following our second and third run-throughs, we shall have integrated alchemy, astrology, and Gnosticism into our reading of the Major Arcana, it will be seen that Tarot is a compendium of Hermetic wisdom unmatched by any other document extant today.

3. Numbers as Archetypes

Now that we know something of the basic meaning of the figures in the Keys, let us review their underlying numerological meanings. For this we shall need some such authority as J. E. Cirlot's *A Dictionary of Symbols*. He writes as follows:

"ONE: The number one is equivalent to the 'Centre,' to the non-manifest point, to the creative power of the 'unmoved mover,' "[38] In Key 1, The Magician, encircled by the uroboric serpent, pointing both upward and downward, is a visual representation of this idea. Reduced to its underlying pattern, the figure would be rendered thusly: ⟀ And in Key 0, The Fool, as well, we recognize the irony in the name of The Fool, for he is in reality "the sage . . . who has attained the central point of the Wheel. . . ."[39] The bond between Fool and Magician, Omega and Alpha, survives through incarnation upon incarnation. Furthermore, if the first vertical series is examined solely from the view of number and

80

underlying design, it will be realized that all of its numbers reduce to the One, and that both the Wheel and the Sun are circles moving about axes. Hence, they are essentially the same figure as Key 1.

"TWO: Duality is a basic quality of all natural processes insofar as they comprise two opposite phases or aspects. When integrated within a higher context, this duality generates a binary system based on the counterbalanced forces of two opposite poles. . . . The right hand and left hand, corresponding to the two pillars Jachin and Boaz in Hebrew tradition . . . can be taken to symbolize a binary system. This is also the case with the King and Queen in alchemy."[40]

Here Cirlot is discoursing on number symbolism, not Tarot, so it is rather startling to come upon direct references of this kind, which apply as well to Tarot features. As we have seen, with Key 2 once the natural process had commenced, various binaries of opposites continued through the whole of the Major Arcana. "True reality," according to Marcus Schneider, "resides only in the synthesis" of opposites. This is what the Tarot "message" is all about, and it certainly is the capsule meaning not only of alchemy and astrology but also of Jungian psychology, which we shall bring to bear on Tarot.

With a solar cross on her breast, the lunar crescent at her feet, and her crown marrying the two, the High Priestess of Key 2 anticipates the *hierosgamos* of Moon and Sun in Keys 18 and 19. If The Magician of Key 1 is to be likened to spirit, she is soul, spirit's bride. She is passive, whereas he is active. Case notes that she sits on a cubic stone, which he identifies as a symbol of salt and describes as one aspect of the feminine side of Mercurius. The other side is of quicksilver, which is penetrating; and so she sits between these two, as the "equilibrating power."[41]

Evil is thought to have come into the world with duality, the two, and the female, Eve; or, according to another image, with all that is separate from the undifferentiated One, namely the Many. But what was brought into the world by the two was *tension,* the pull of polar opposites. And in our second vertical series this tension is a matter of life or death, appearing in the polarities of Key 11, the sword or mercy, and Key 20, death or resurrection. For salvation the soul must learn to know and follow the Law (Torah) which the High Priestess of Key 2 bears in her lap.

"THREE: As Lao-Tse declared: 'One engenders two, two engenders three, three engenders all things.' Hence three has the power to resolve the conflict posed by dualism; it represents also the harmonic impact of unity upon dualism, symbolizing the creation of spirit out of matter, the active out of the passive."[42] All of which is rendered in the formula $1 + 2 = 3$. In alchemical terms: 1 is active sulphur, and 2 is passive, material salt, then 3 is like quicksilver, the catalyst that makes everything work. The opposed worlds of the polar opposites come into dynamic interplay when the third factor is introduced. Three, therefore, as Cirlot tells us, is "the number pertaining to heaven."[43] Union, or synthesis, proceeds linearly 3-9, or vertically 3-12-21, but in either case is *attained*.

The interplay and exchange of the opposites is represented graphically by a figure known as the mandorla. Behind the High Priestess it appears in the pomegranate symbol, which is significant, since this seed was associated with Persephone's descent to the other world. In appearance it resembles an almond seed, and is formed by two intersecting circles, the spheres of heaven and earth generally, but often the mandorla encompasses all polar opposites posed by dualism. "Hence it is a symbol also of the perpetual sacrifice that regenerates creative force through the dual streams of ascent and descent, appearance and disappearance, life and death, evolution and involution."[44]

The vertical series 3, 12, and 21 explores the possibilities of the mandorla. Geometrically, this symbol is the *third* born of the interpenetration of the two. It may also be thought of as the product of the longing of the one for the other, its bride; thus a heart suits it, and this is the figure that Waite introduces in Key 3. In medieval religious art, Christ appears within the mandorla, often surrounded by the four evangelists, as The World appears in Key 21. However, here we have the dancing *anima mundi,* which in alchemy is equated with Christ as the spiritual essence in

DRAWING 4.

the world. The symbol for Venus, goddess of love, appears within the heart of Key 3; thus the Eros principle, the heart-felt desire of spirit for matter and matter for spirit, *animates* the universe. (See Drawing 4.)

The desire of spirit for matter and matter for spirit is the highest esoteric meaning of The Lovers, and it is the aspiration of man for the divine creator that is the impulse of the Sufi "love" poetry. Graphically a triangle with the apex pointing down symbolizes spirit's involution to matter (Key 12), whereas a triangle with apex pointing up symbolizes man's (and matter's) aspiration towards spirit, the desire for union. Esoterically, then, these two kinds of triangles convey the same meaning as the mandorla; and if we examine imaginatively the graphics of Key 6, The Lovers, we may identify, above and below, two trines with apexes *nearly* touching. Within this figure we may also discover "the St. Andrew's cross, with its two intersecting and opposing lines standing for fall and ascent respectively, symbolic of the intermingling of the 'two worlds.' . . ."[45] The fall is indicated in the tree and serpent of Adam and Eve in Key 6, and the descent (6 + 9) is to Key 15 (6 + 9 = 15). But as we have already remarked, ascent commences at the nadir, and it here is symbolized by the lower trine in Key 6, the mountain of the work to be done to attain gold of the sun (ascended matter). In Key 10 the St. Andrew's cross again appears, in the center of the ROTA; and in Key 9 the two symbolic triangles are conjoined in the eight-pointed star in the lantern. This recurrent motif is played out numerically as 3-6-9, or 3, 6, (3 + 3), 9 (6 + 3). (See Drawing 5.)

The mandorla resembles the vagina, and Case, in assigning the Hebrew letter Daleth to The Empress, notes that "Daleth represents the womb, as the door of life. . . . East, the direction assigned to Daleth, is the doorway through which the sun enters the world at the beginning of a day."[46] This suggests the incarnation of the Holy Ghost, and in his design for this card, Case places a dove on her shield.

Waite tells us, "the card of The Empress signifies the door or gate by which an entrance is obtained into this life."[47] She bears the sceptre of mundane authority and yet

DRAWING 5.

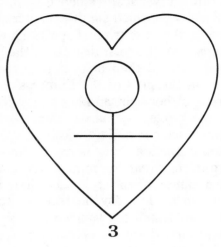

3

6

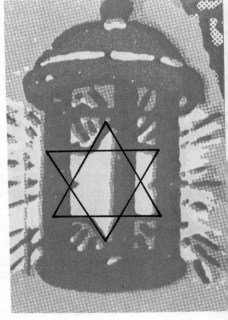

9

wears a crown of the starry zodiac. In her the two worlds interpenetrate. In the vertical sequence of 3, 12, and 21, numerically 12 is 4 x 3, which signifies the cross of matter multiplied (fertilized) by the trine of spirit. Thus Key 3 is a tableau of fertility, and the solar disc about the head of The Hanged Man of Key 12 then links him to the fertilizing spirit suggested in the gold of the Empress' background, the golden corona of her hair, and her starry diadem.

By Key 21, the circle is squared; that is, the material realm is revealed as containing within it "infinity, the universe, the all."[48] Such a shape is not common in nature, but best known to the dreaming mind as a mandala, which appears to the dreamer when integration, individuation, or wholeness is attained. The psyche receives the message from the Center (self), and the two worlds (conscious and unconscious) are married (*coniunctio, hierogasmos*) in mutual fertilization. Thus the accent on womb, fecund nature, and dancing goddess throughout this series of 3, 12, and 21. Moreover, the esoteric meaning of the symbols of the four evangelists of Key 21 associates them, as well, with the four elements. Raised to the heavenly world (note clouds surrounding them), the elemental or natural world has attained divinity, which is the meaning of the circle squared, the mandorla with the four apostles, and also the meaning of the St. Andrew's cross, which appears if lines are drawn connecting the polar opposites, earth and water, fire and air. The St. Andrew's cross intersects at the *navel* of *anima mundi,* resurrected nature! Thus *anima mundi* as World Tree/Axis, the Stairway of Planets in another form.

Then at Key 0, a most interesting thing happens. The mandorla shape becomes zero: the early form of the organ of birth returns to the infinity of the All on that archetypal plane from which all form evolves; for, as we read, again in Cirlot: "the actual digits are, as it were, only the outer garments . . . idea-forces, each with a particular character of its own."[49] Simultaneously, The Fool of this Key prepares to return to chaos, "below," the abyss of the alchemical *nigredo:* so that even the archetypal numbers that gave form to The World and all the Keys from 1 to 21, return to the nothingness (Zero) out of which they themselves evolved.

DRAWING 6.

Naturally, there cannot be any further Keys beyond Key 0, and our interpretation resolves the question of where this enigmatic card is to be placed in the sequence of our Tarot. Nothingness follows Death (4 + 9 = 13 + 9 = 22, or Key 0 in our numeration). Waite set a blind alley for his readers by placing the Zero "after No. 20, but I have taken care not to number The World or Universe otherwise than as 21. Wherever it ought to be put, the Zero is an unnumbered card."[50] Such tactics were designed to preserve the secrets of the Golden Dawn's esoteric Tarot. But one comes away wondering at the level of unconsciousness that would withhold from man the marvelous truth of Tarot.

By the time the journey recommences in Key 1, The Magician will be seen to be bearing above him the sign (∞) of his infinitely foolish heritage. One final note on Waite's deception. In Key 13 (Death), one meaning he gives to the card is "ascent in the Spirit" therefore, 13 + 9 = 22 or The Fool, the ascended spirit. Furthermore, Waite tells us, "The mysterious horseman moves slowly, bearing a black banner emblazoned with the Mystic Rose, which signifies life." We shall have more to say on the white rose during our alchemical run-through, but the whitening was one of the stages in alchemical process, calcination representing the death of the profane. It is no coincidence that the Fool carries a white rose, signifying, as Waite states, "the extinction of all interest in life and in the manifest world. . . ." Thus the propriety of our sequence 13 + 9 = The Fool.

"FOUR . . . is equated with the square and the cube, and the cross representing the four seasons and the four points of the compass."[51] The "manifest world" is what this number represents. There are four directions and four elements to the terrestial world, and in Key 4 of the sequence of Waite's Tarot, The Emperor's throne symbolizes all the meanings constellating about the archetype of four. All material forms die, that is to say, are transformed. 13 is the number of Death, to be followed by 22, Resurrection. Hence, when Key 13 appears in my readings, I associate it with a death of the old consciousness of the person for whom I am reading, and a rebirth of consciousness. And in this sense Key 13 is similar in divinatory meaning to Key

16, the stricken Tower. Add 1, the enlivening spiritual center (the One) to matter (4 + 1), therefore, and we have 5 Man (4 + 1 = 5).

"FIVE: Symbolic of Man . . . and of the quintessence acting upon matter. It comprises the four limbs of the body plus the head which controls them, and likewise the four fingers plus the thumb and the four cardinal points together with the centre. The *hierosgamos* is signified by the number five, since it represents the union of the principle of heaven (three) with that of the *Magna Mater* (two). Geometrically, it is the pentagram, or the five-pointed star."[52] In Tarot, therefore, Key 5 is the combination of "heaven (three)," or The Empress, with "the *Magna Mater* (two)," The High Priestess, as well as of 4 (matter) and 1 (spirit). In The Hierophant, the pillars of the High Priestess are presented again, emblematic of the dichotomy of spirit and matter, the two worlds of which The Hierophant is the initiate and mediator. By the same token, 5 mediates between 1 and 9, standing at the midpoint of our numerical series.

"Traditionally," states Cirlot, "the number five symbolizes man after the fall."[53] Since spirit has now descended, the inverted triangle no longer appears, and its place is taken by the aspiring triangle (apex *up*), symbolizing man's desire to ascend to spirit, as a kind of spiritual fire. Our indicated geometrical graphics for Key 5 are accordingly of a triangle within the pillars, similar to the emblem on the angel's breast in Key 14, since 5 + 9 = 14. (See Drawing 7.)

The fall of spirit to the condition of man is a mutual tempering of both spirit and matter; hence Key 14 is called Temperance. The angel (heaven) whose feet rest on the earth represents this interrelation, as do the color scheme and the act of the angel, pouring water from one vessel to another. In the Marseilles deck, the red and blue in the robes symbolize the active and passive, or spiritual and mundane; and the chalices are said to be gold and silver, which portends the *coniunctio* of Moon and Sun in Keys 17 and 18. Waite opted for the alchemical symbology of color, which, as we have seen, is of red and white as active and passive, sulphur and salt, spirit and man as the salt of the earth. These are the two colors seen in the Hierophant's

DRAWING 7

THE HIEROPHANT

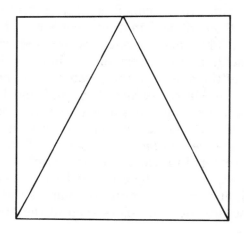

garb and on the Angel's robe and wings. But in both cards gold is the color for the head, the head being the highest point in the pentagram for man, and thus the anatomical "seat" of the spirit.

The angel, as agent of the heavenly realm, is pouring from one chalice to another, symbolizing in this act the etheric flow of spirit into the world. But, at the same time, the exchange is not to be in one direction only; for through ascent the spiritual essence will also return above, bearing with it the *anima mundi* as risen matter. In a sense, therefore, Keys 5 and 14 both divide and mediate between spirit and matter, just as they each mediate, appearing in the centers, respectively, of the series 1-9 and 10-18.

5 + 1 = 6, or Man after the Fall (The Lovers, Adam and Eve), and 14 + 1 = 15, The Devil, the bright angel of Heaven, Lucifer, after his Fall, whereupon the angelic, golden wings of Keys 6 and 14 became leaden-colored bat wings.

"SIX: Symbolic of ambivalence and equilibrium, six comprises the union of the two triangles (of fire and water) and hence signifies the human soul."[54] The number also combines four and two, that is, the polar opposites of the binary and the elemental, mundane plane. We have said that these are masculine and feminine, active and passive as well, and they appear as the archetypal lovers Adam and Eve. Paradise, the Garden, is the world, or number four, before the Fall. The other combination possible for six is three and three, which appears as the two triangles of the graphic pattern. The number three, we recall, combined the heavenly and earthly planes as a number of incarnation. Here in Key 6, therefore, the Angel, the Tree of Life, and the Earthly Paradise evoke the archetype of three.

The equilibrium of Key 6 becomes the stasis of Key 15. The serpent appears, coiled about the World Axis/Tree in Key 6, having descended — along with the angel — from the heavenly realm. In the round of time it will be the golden serpent of Key 10 that will shatter the stasis of Key 15, appearing in Key 16 as the bolt of the lightninglike Logos; whereupon the Devil, who is shown rising in Key 10, will be in ascent again. Thus 15 (The Devil) + 1 (The Magician), the One of Spirit = 16 (The Tower).

"SEVEN: Symbolic of perfect order, a complete period or cycle. It comprises the union of the ternary and the quaternary."[55] Here we may take issue with Cirlot; for the Great Work is only commencing, and ascent only beginning. Paul Foster Case comes closer to the truth. "To the ancients 7 represented temporary cessation, not final perfection, as some have thought."[56] Final perfection, a truly "complete cycle," will occur only when spirit has attained "Above" once more, and the human soul is united with the One. Numerically such a fulfillment is indicated by the addition of 3, the ternary of spirit, to 7: $7 + 3 = 10$, which then reduces to the archetype of the One. In graphics such a design appears as the kabbalistic Tree of Life. (See Drawing 8.)

This design incorporates the watery and fiery trines of man's aspirations towards spirit, and spirit's longing to be clothed materially. The mediating square implies that earth is the plane of this dynamic process and ultimately is elevated by the process, which is the alchemical purpose. Such a design does not underlie any of the Major Arcana, but the archetype of meaning behind it is present in Key 10. That is to say, "above," the watery trine, and "below," the fiery trine, appear within the wheel of Key 10, and become "One" in the cyclical unity of the wheel, which has no static points but is ever becoming something else, above descending, below ascending. The square of our design becomes the elevated, or ascended, elemental world, winged earth, air, fire, water; and thus the circle is squared.

Numbers 8, 9, and the addition of the final 1, which closes the cycle, are the final stations in the path to perfection.

"EIGHT: The octonary, related to two squares or the octagon, is the intermediate form between the square (or the terrestrial order) and the circle (the eternal order) and is, in consequence, a symbol for regeneration. By virtue of its shape, the numeral is associated with the two interlacing serpents of the caduceus, signifying the balancing out of opposing forces, or the equivalence of the spiritual power to the natural. It also symbolizes — again because of its shape — the eternally spiralling movement of the heavens (shown

DRAWING 8.

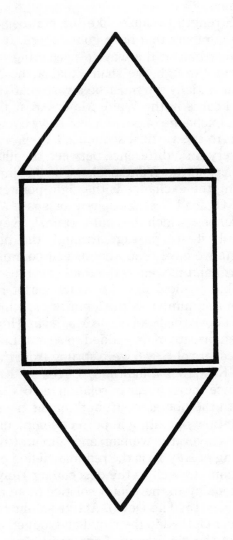

THE TREE OF LIFE

by the double sigmoid line — the sign of the infinite). Because of its implications of regeneration, eight was in the Middle Ages an emblem of baptism. Furthermore, it corresponds in medieval mystic cosmology to the fixed stars of the firmament, denoting that the planetary influences have been overcome."[57]

Key 8 is Strength because, like the number 8, it harmonizes all the numbers that have gone before. It is the circle not yet perfect but on the way to perfecting itself. In our alchemical run-through, we shall exhaust the meanings of this Key, but initially we must be aware that this is one of the switched cards in the Waite Major Arcana. I am going to justify the exchange of positions of Keys 8 and 11 by calling attention to the vertical sequence 8 + 9 = 17.

There is very little difference between the illustrations in the Marseilles and the Waite packs. The one important feature justifying the exchange is the eight-pointed star, symbolizing the Ogdoad, or that sphere or space "above" the planetary archons, which the soul "attains" (Key 9) through its successful rite of passage through the planets upon ascending. As we have seen, that ascent commences at the abyss (Saturn) and moves to the midheaven (Sun).

The "double sigmoid line" to which Cirlot refers in his discussion of the number is the lemniscate, which in Key 1 is to be seen above the head of the Magician. Hence, eight is 7 + 1, the lemniscate of one added to seven. Likewise, 6 + 2 = 8. The Lovers of Key 6 were sprung from their material bondage in Key 15 by lightning Logos of Key 16, The Tower; whence they appear in relation (as 6 + 2) to Key 8, endowed with the liberated strength of the polar opposites of Key 2, but now operating in perfect complementary harmony as quicksilver (the woman) and sulphur (the lion). The red-caped king of Key 16 is the red-maned lion of Key 8. He was once Adam, as well as the descending Holy Spirit and the sun descending to the winter solstice (note the inverted firebrand in Key 15, The Devil). Active sulphur is the solar, spiritual power clothed in the metal and lodged in the earth. Quicksilver is the yin aspect of the same power, although now not passive but active in a complementary way. This is the esoteric meaning of eight as 4 + 4, or the natural world

94

harmonized with the spiritual.

What we see here in our first run-through is a materialization of spirit and then a return to spirit; for the archetypal essence of each number resides in a nonformal, universal, collective unconscious, which is unconscious only from the point of view of consciousness. It is the reductive view that regards matter as inert and "dead." From the atomic point of view, a divine dance is taking place within all particles, similar to the allegory of risen *anima mundi* in Key 21, the spirit of the world. Thus out of the Zero, the No-thing, comes the One, followed in multiplicity by its many forms. For purposes of our Tarot analysis, the nonformal essence manifests as a number, which, although having some form, is more abstract than specific. The number then actualizes in the geometry that suits it, such as a trine and square for the seven. And these in turn specify further, becoming the illustrations (or enigmas) of the Major Arcana. And so it is with all things in the world. Behind one's name, number, and horoscope lies the archetypal essence (or god, if you will), that uses these to specify one's divinity. But like the eight's "eternally spiralling movement," one's life is recycled too, and the matter of one's life is regenerated by return to the No-thing.

This is the feeling The Star evokes. The pool, into which dips Ator, *anima mundi,* or Mercurius in his feminine guise, is the "cosmic mind-stuff" which will take many forms on the mundane plane, symbolized by the dry land surrounding the pool. To the medieval mind, the abode of the divine was in the starry firmament, the sphere above the seven planets. This star symbolizes not only that "place" but the way forms flow into the world from it, since the figure dips into this pool to renew the world. Literally, it is an irrigation process that the card illustrates. Behind this lies the esoteric meaning of spiritual irrigation, the descending water-trine of spirit materialized as a pool. It may be thought, as well, that the waters return to this pool, just as Tarot returns to the No-thing, Key Zero. This is the abyss, the great depth of nothingness, out of which the One evolves. But it is *not* the same abyss to which the Fool descends, which is the abyss of the *nigredo,* or the *prima materia,* bottoming out as Key

15. The Fool's descent is a materializing, clothing, involutive fall, not into a pool of spirit, but all the way down into the cold, hard reality of lead (Saturn).

Keys 17 and 18 present two illustrations of the abyss, but these are the evolutive depths out of which forms are born, as in Key 18, The Moon, where an emerging crayfish is to be seen. Such forms may have been low at first, but through centuries of evolution they have yielded man. In Key 10, for comparison, a half-animal, half-human form moves up the evolving side of the wheel.

The vertical sequence of Key 3 culminated, in Key 21, in the mandorla in which *anima mundi* appeared as spirit's manifestation. Obviously Keys 21 and 17 are similar, specifically in their depictions of the naked *anima mundi,* who in Key 21, The World, has draped herself in the blue (heavenly) stream of cosmic essence, which in Key 17 she pours out.

Since Key 17 is an expression (by reduction) of the archetype of 8, we see in it two halved mandorlas which correspond to the two halves of the lemniscate and the number eight. (See Drawing 9.)

Nature, the figure of *anima mundi,* mediates at their convergence. The mandorla above is filled with the symbol of the celestial dwelling-place of the divine, whereas the lower mandorla has only Mother Nature's foot in the door, so to speak, which she will fill by Key 21. The esoteric meaning of this seems to be the spiritualizing of nature and the eventual elevation of nature to the Eighth Sphere, at least, that of the Ogdoad. The clay pitchers of Key 17, held in both hands, become the transformative wands, held in both hands, of *anima mundi* in Key 21. From this we may surmise that clay (matter) has been regenerated, or the alchemical transmutation effected.

Anima mundi is the natural bride of the One, sun, or spirit. For her completion at the end of the cycle (Keys 10-17), she requires the marriage with the One (17 + 1 = 18), which is illustrated by the alchemical *hierosgamos* of sun and moon. Most persons, in examining this card, completely miss the fact that it depicts a *coniunctio,* joining, as in marriage, sun and moon. The phallic rays of the sun, ap-

DRAWING 9.

pearing from behind the moon, make this evident, which is not Waite's alchemical interpretation of Tarot but present as well in the exoteric Marseilles deck.

But before we go on with The Moon, let us analyze Key 9, which is the root source of Key 18, which reduces to 9. At first glance the cards 18 and 9 are vastly dissimilar, with no apparent elements in common. On the face of it The Hermit is a totally masculine card, while The Moon has traditionally feminine associations. However, Key 9 also contains a *coniunctio,* as it should, since its number is that of attainment, completion, and fulfillment. The water and fire trines are present in the star of the lantern, where they symbolize soul and spirit, Moon and Sun, the Moon ruling the watery sign Cancer and the Sun the fiery Leo. In a very esoteric way, which we shall pursue in our alchemical run-through, the pairs of opposites and the mediating Mercurius are symbolized by Key 18's dog, wolf, and crustacean, the last representing the "volatile" Mercurius, and the dog and wolf, moon and sun.

Evolving from the abysmal waters, the crustacean, "like the Egyptian scarab, has as its function that of devouring what is transitory — the volatile element in alchemy — and of contributing to moral and physical regeneration."[58] This is the same role that the crocodile fulfilled in Egypt, and why he appears in the abyss of Oswald Wirth's Fool card. Scarab medallions comprised a *coniunctio;* for the scarab ruled Cancer, and this royal beetle rolled the sun ball before him. Since sun ruled Leo in Egypt as well as in our modern zodiac, the symbol united Leo and Cancer.

But besides the *coniunctio,* there are other common features recognizable in Keys 9 and 18. The hermit's face and that of the woman in the moon show identical profiles, both with eyes downcast towards the abyss. The moon looks down on the golden path or spiritual way, which evolves from the abyss, while the hermit looks down his straight and narrow golden staff, the *way* having become his personal support. He looks down, moreover, into another kind of abyss, the same as that of The Fool; for they both occupy the great heights which symbolize spiritual ascendance. The golden spiral of the serpent of Key 10 might well coil about his staff as it involutes to the abyss. As we have said before, this golden spiral is the sun's course to the abyss. It is all but lost by Key 13, Death, between the distant pillars, which are the same as those of The High Priestess. And now, in Key 18, they appear almost in the foreground, between the reunited sun and his nocturnal (underworld, unconscious) bride. Death is thus one kind of abyss out of which new forms are born. The newer Waite decks present a golden wolf, rather than a grey one, improving the symbology, as we shall see.

And now, finally, our Magic Nine arrangement culminates laterally with 9, 18, and 0, on the top, middle, and bottom lines respectively. All three of these cards share a couple of symbolic features which confirm me in my confidence that the Magic Nine is the correct arrangement in order to read the true meaning of the cards *and how they work together!*

First of all, all three of the figures in these cards face right to left, in the direction of the preceding cards. This is appropriate for cards that culminate series. And secondly, the abyss-feature occurs in each, with the Hermit and Fool at the heights of attainment, gazing downward, so that "Above" may be reunited with "Below," and the work of the sun thus perfected in its return to earth (the *Emerald Tablet*).

The return to earth, or descent, has been our chief concern in this prelude to our second — or alchemical — runthrough. Whereas Jung was correct in stating that the usual pattern of descent/ascent is reversed in alchemy, what we must realize is that before ascent commences in alchemy a descent is understood to *have already occurred.* That is to say, the mundane metals are thought to be the planets in earth; hence, in this way Above has already descended to Below, and here exists as spirit-infused matter. The alchemical process is the means of freeing that spirit from material bonds, the released spirit then perfecting "the work" (*opus*) by returning to earth as the saviour of matter.

Relegated to the status of naive chemistry by reductive science, alchemy's relevance for modern man may be found in Jungian psychology and also in what has lately become known as the human-potential movement; for the body is thought of, more and more, as the reflection of an individual spiritual essence which possesses its own healing potential. The connection between body-chemistry and personal psychic factors is very much in the foreground of medicine today, and this idea is commensurate with the alchemical approach. In the same sense, Tarot presents a series of transformative images which — although in code — may be instructive for the psyche. And that code is rooted in alchemy.

Earlier, we called attention to Key 8, Strength (Key 11 previous to Waite), as having remained relatively unchanged, as a tableau of Mercurius, since the period of the prototypical fourteenth century Tarot. Waite's alchemical accent in his deck brings elements to the fore that may have been lost or submerged over the years. We are now going to examine the roots of alchemy in Gnosticism, particularly its descent motifs, and when we come to Zosimos (c. 300 A.D.), all the strands of alchemy and Gnosticism will come together in an Ariadne thread which we may follow down Tarot's fifteen steps to the abyss, and thence up again.

CHAPTER IV

ALCHEMICAL DESCENT

The basic premise of alchemy is that a spiritual essence interpenetrates matter. In our numerical run-through we have connected this essence with the One, the undivided unity before duality, and, therefore, the number one. The One makes a vertical descent to earth, and in this way the spiritual and mundane, above and below, are joined as in the symbol of the uroboros. Salt is often taken to mean the passive material element, or the *prima materia* in its pure, receptive state prior to impregnation by spirit. Here a parallel is apparent to the Christian figure of the Virgin. Indeed, an incarnating dove signifies both Holy Ghost and Mercurius. Salt has obvious associations with earth, and with Queen Luna as the feminine side of the *coniunctio*. The enfolding, nourishing, matriarchal quality of earth is suggested, and not the Gnostic connotations of an *evil* Fall and the concept of spirit *imprisoned* in matter. In Drawing 10, we see represented the way in which the One descends to earth.

Symbols and glyphs are of the same esoteric shorthand as numbers; thus, the symbol for earth and the mundane plane $\oplus$ is compounded of the glyph for salt and the descended One. *To understand alchemy, we have only to think of it as a process whereby the One may be liberated from world/matter in order to ascend once more to its original state of undivided unity.* Further, the One (1) may be likened to the divided circle of original unity, the Zero, now split into the pairs of opposites. This bisected or descended Zero is esoterically symbolized by the axis/spine of The Magician which divides the encircling serpent at his waist. The making of gold

DRAWING 10

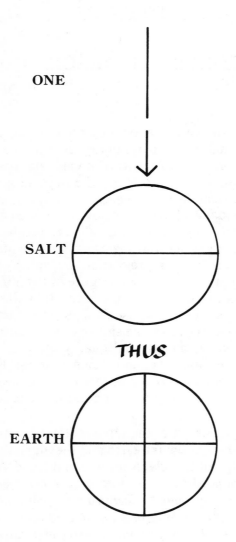

ONE

SALT

THUS

EARTH

recalls the correspondence which the metal has with the sun. In turn, sun is spirit/light/Logos.

When spirit is turned inside out, a cosmic mandala appears in which the "impossible" squaring of the circle is attained. Liberated soul/spirit, the goal of alchemical process, is presented in the four cards of our third plane in the Magic Nine arrangement. Key 21, the dancing *anima mundi,* is the redeemed One represented as soul of the world. The four fixed signs in the corners of the card square the circle (or mandorla) of the world. Thereby the symbol for the world becomes the symbol for the *lapis,* or philosopher's stone, ⊕ yielding ▣ , with the womblike, circular earth no longer restricting the imprisoned cross, the 4, which, as a square, is now outside, enfolding the circle of earth.

In Key 19, The Sun, the liberated One, appears in two forms symbolizing the end of the process, "gold of the sun," and the homunculus born of the alchemical retort. Key 20, Judgment, depicts the liberation of the One in the form of the individual soul, since if spirit interpenetrates inert matter, it infuses the body and soul of man as well. And finally, on our third plane, the ascended One appears in the guise of The Fool, who, as we have seen, has many ties with Mercurius, the animating spirit of the world. But now, the earliest Tarot presents the same sequence (19, 20, 21, 0), and our esoteric reading of these four mysteries seems, therefore, both to justify the Magic Nine arrangement and to lend added support to the argument that Waite may have been restoring Tarot's original meaning.

Once the subtleties of alchemy have been understood, we shall be able to do much more numerically with this third plane. Zero is the circle of the world, now empty. This emptiness connotes maximum freedom in that the One is no longer bound; it is now *not there,* the "no-thing." The same implications come to mind in the Easter story of Christ's empty tomb.

The number zero suggests the circular Wheel of Fortune of Key 10, which contains the Roman number X in the form of a St. Andrew's cross of fire/water, spirit/matter, as well as another cross composed of the line of "Salt" crossed by the digital "One." As already said, this card symbolizes the alchemical process, and as ten, 1 + 0, it contains both the descended One (Key 1) and the ascended One (Key 0). Key X contains within the wheel four glyphs (☿ ⊖ ♒♄). Reading counterclockwise, from twelve to three o'clock, these symbolize mercury, salt, dissolution, and sulphur. This arrangement bears a strong resemblance to a schema which appears in Jung's *Mysterium Coniunctionis*;[59] however, Jung places sulphur at the left-hand pole and salt at the right, which is not precisely proper since salt is passive and belongs at the left or involuting direction. Active sulphur best suits the right side. Waite's wheel shows the involuting golden serpent at the left, being a form of the descending One. The psyche of man contains the Jungian Self, or the divine Monad, at the center. Earlier we mentioned the dragon ("I therefore am the One and the Many . . ."), which as fabulous beast symbolizes the spirit, and because of his wings and chthonic form (reptile) unites in one above and below.

The bottom glyph is ♒, the abyss, into which the serpent involutes. Here Jung places "Mercurius Serpent," while at the top is "Mercurius lapis," that is, philosopher's stone, another name for the One at the end of the process. Waite's wheel has at the right a *red* Hermes-Anubis evolving from the abyss, rising to the position of sulphur, which as we have noted is symbolized by the color red. In alchemy, according to Jung, sulphur "is the active substance of Sol."[60] Thus, it is thought of as possessing the spiritual qualities of the creative Monad (One), although retaining many of the diabolical attributes of its opposite. "Sulphur dioxide and sulphuretted hydrogen give one a good idea of the stink of hell."[61]

Nearly all alchemical symbols embrace pairs of opposites, since any imbalance in the work prevents the successful conclusion of the process. Spiritual salt, sulphur, and Mercurius, therefore, have their earthly, abysmal, chthonic, even devilish aspects. "Mercurius is not only split into a masculine and feminine half, but is the poisonous dragon and at the same time the heavenly lapis. This makes it clear that the dragon is analogous to the devil and the lapis to Christ, in accordance with the ecclesiastical view of the devil as an autonomous counterpart of Christ. Furthermore, not only the dragon but the negative aspect of sulphur, namely *sulphur comburens,* is identical with the devil, as Glauber says: 'Verily, sulphur is the true black devil of hell who can be conquered by no element save by salt alone.' Salt by contrast is a 'light' substance similar to the lapis. . . ."[62] To the alchemists, then, the Trinity corresponded to sulphur, Mercurius, and Salt. A quaternity is formed by the addition of ⊕,earth, or the mundane plane (*prima materia*), required for the completion of the work. This bears a relation to another pattern of Jung's in which Mary corresponds to earth, while above is the Holy Ghost (Dove).

In Waite's Ace of Cups, the descending dove bears a Host-marked wafer, a cross within a circle, the same symbol as that of earth, or the mundane plane. The dove descends to Mary on earth, just as the One descends to salt and is fixed in earth as the Many. The Assumption of the Virgin into heaven corresponds to the liberation of the *anima mundi,* adding One to the Trinity, and squaring the circle, as in Key 21, The World.

Jung has made quite a case for the affinity between lapis/Mercurius and Christ. In the comparison of the two diagrams, we note that Christ and salt are at the same pole. Since Christ = lapis, then if a case can be made for salt = lapis, our parallel of Jung's schema and Waite's Key 10 is even more exact. Jung devotes an entire chapter to this relation in *Mysterium Coniunctionis.* For our purposes a few lines suffice. "In philosophical alchemy, salt is a cosmic principle. According to its position in the quaternity, it is correlated with the feminine, lunar side and with the upper, light half. It is therefore not surprising that Sal is one of the many designations for the arcane substance. This connotation seems to have developed in the early Middle Ages under Arabic influence. The oldest traces of it can be found in the *Turba,* in which text salt-water and sea-water are synonyms for the *aqua permanens,* and in Senior, who says Mercurius is made from salt."[63]

Aqua permanens is merely another of the many forms of the One, extracted or liberated by the alchemical process. If the reader can hold mentally to the idea of liberation of the

One, and recognize that it is a simultaneous process in man, then he will not bog down as we wind through the labyrinthian maze of symbols and ciphers that is alchemy. At the same time, the relevance becomes clearer of Jungian psychology to Hermeticism (Tarot, astrology, alchemy, etc.), for realization of the Self (Creative Monad) from the abyss of the unconscious is the goal of both alchemy and Jungian psychology.

Light and spirit are basically synonymous in Gnosticism, a subject as difficult as alchemy to treat succinctly; however, in the descent (or Fall) of Light (or spirit) to earth, we have the essence of Gnosticism. This descent results in spirit's entrapment in matter, whereas in alchemy spirit *animates* matter. Uniting the powers of the two worlds, alchemy's descent is a conscious willing, seemingly, on the part of spirit; yet Gnosticism's concept of the Fall is seen as an evil because any separation from Light is viewed as painful.

The primary names for the spirit in matter are *anima mundi* and Mercurius, while in Gnosticism they are Nous, Anthropos, and Sophia, the latter bearing a relation to *anima mundi* since she is feminine, although often androgynous like Mercurius. Too, Mercurius is sometimes regarded as virgin, especially since the planet Mercury rules Virgo, the first sign of descent on the Stairway of Planets. In some depictions, Mercurius is the *anima mercurii,* with the upper body of a woman and the tail of a fish or serpent, sometimes known as the *melusina.* We see the relation between *"anima mundi,* imprisoned in the dark depths of the sea" and melusina in the following Plate from the *Mutus liber,* an alchemical text of 1702.

At the top of the picture, God the Father presides over the pageant within the circles. His position is rather like that of the Sphinx in Waite's card, The Wheel of Fortune. Instead of the four fixed signs of the zodiac, the pairs of opposites are represented by Sun and Moon. The upper and lower dichotomies of Mercurius are symbolized within the first circle by the figures of Hermes/Mercurius at the top and the melusina at the bottom, the latter being the abysmal, unredeemed aspect of him/herself as *anima mundi.* Now this pic-

106

ture is instructive for us because of its relation to Keys 10 and 15, Wheel and Devil. Mercurius points down towards the abyss, and the birds (doves?) descend in a lefthand direction that parallels the serpent's descent in The Wheel. The net which shall ensnare the birds is an important motif, rather Gnostic in tone because the heavenly principle is then fixed or locked materially.

The apex of the wheel, or midheaven astrologically, is the place of the sun at the summer solstice. As we saw in the Stairway of Planets, the sun's "house" or sign is Leo, and the descent commences with the left hand sign, Virgo, of which Mercury is the ruler. The abyss to which Mercury descends may be thought of as watery, chaotic, or dark, but it may be fiery as well, since Mercurius is also "the universal and scintillating fire of the light of nature, which carries the heavenly spirit within it."[64]

In descending, spirit gradually becomes clothed materially as it takes on the qualities of the metals associated with the planets of each sign. From gold and quicksilver to lead, the progress is increasingly dense and gross. Waite's Key 15 depicts the abyss as hell. In Gnostic terms the devil is adversary, whereas in alchemy he is the lower component which must be redeemed, the fires of hell being the chthonic aspect of the light/fire of the spirit Mercurius. Again, the same resolution of opposites is implied here as in the symbol of the uroboros. According to Jung:

> Mercurius, the revelatory light of nature, is also hell-fire which in some miraculous way is none other than a rearrangement of the heavenly, spiritual powers in the lower chthonic world of matter, thought already in St. Paul's time to be ruled by the devil. Hell-fire, the true energic principle of evil, appears here as the manifest counterpart of the spiritual and the good, and as essentially identical with it in substance. After that, it can surely cause no offense when another treatise says that the mercurial fire is the 'fire in which God himself burns in divine love.'[65]

In Tarot's Devil, we have noted that Adam bears a fiery tail. Tails suggest lower forms of life, and in our preceding picture the melusina's tail is hooked as a means of drawing her from the waters, in the same way that spirit is liberated from the abyss of nigredo by the alchemical process. Not by coincidence, it is the alchemist and his wife (or personal *anima*) who fish for the melusina. One of them points above to indicate the beginning of the ascent; within the second circle are ram and bull, for Aries and Taurus, the signs at the spring equinox when the work (opus) was said to commence.

Ascent, therefore, is a return to Light, sun, or spirit, the end of alchemical process symbolized by Mercurius as *lapis,* liberated *anima mundi,* or — in the picture at hand — peacock, whose tail symbolizes Mercurius' exotic quality by reiterating all the colors connected with the steps in the alchemical process.

In Tarot we have called attention to the descent sequence of Keys 1-15 and the relation to the Stairway of Planets. Some form of descent is symbolized or depicted in all cards from Keys 10-15, and even though ascent commences with Key 16 and the sequence 16, 17, and 18 signifies The Moon, there are still some hidden esoteric elements of descent in these cards as well. Therefore, we can say that all cards of the second plane (Keys 10-18) have some descent motifs. All the Keys of the third plane, Keys 19-0, have an ascended motif, which The Fool culminates by his imminent descent and return to the abyss. Examples of descent are so diverse that we shall do well to elaborate on many of these in order to comprehend what meanings lie beneath the Tarot mysteries. We shall reserve for later those descents that involve the macrocosmic world above, such as the sun's annual journey through the zodiac.

We have already seen the greater implications of numerical descent. "Evil and matter together form the Dyad, the duality. This is feminine in nature, an *anima mundi,* the feminine Physis who longs for the embrace of the One, the Monad, the good and perfect."[65a] Too, we have discussed the elemental world's fall to death (4 + 9 = 13) and Adam and Eve's Fall (6 + 9 = 15). Precisely what is entailed in the archetype of the Fall, and what are its origins? Pagan man attributed the soul's source to the sphere of the sun, which was manifestly "Above"; hence the soul was thought to descend to earth. Subsequent Gnostic sources also saw the soul as originating in the Ogdoad, a starry realm beyond the seventh planet. Once a transcendent value had been placed on soul or spirit, it followed that it could not originate within man or on earth; therefore it *fell* to earth, and one day would return to its spiritual Creator by the process of ascent. This spiritual redemption by the Creator is analogous to the creation of the alchemist, as we read in an excerpt from "The Creation," the eighth chapter of an alchemical text of 1732:

> Take of common rainwater a good quantity, at least ten quarts, preserve it well sealed in glass vessels for at least ten days, then it will deposit matter and faeces on the bottom. Pour off the clear liquid and place in a wooden vessel that is fashioned round like a ball, cut it through the middle and fill the vessel a third full, and set it in the sun about midday in a secret or secluded spot.

> When this has been done, take a drop of the consecrated red wine and let it fall into the water, and you will instantly perceive a fog and thick darkness on top of the water, such as also was at the first creation. Then put in two drops, and you will see the light coming forth from the darkness; whereupon little by little put in every half of each quarter hour first three, then four, then five, then six drops, and then no more, and you will see with your own eyes one thing after another appearing by and by on top of the water, how God created all things in six days. . . .

> By this you will see clearly the secrets of God, that are at present hidden from you as from a child. You will understand what Moses has written concerning the creation; you will see what manner of body Adam and Eve had before and after the Fall, what the serpent was, what the tree, and what manner of fruits they ate: where and what Paradise is, and in

110

what bodies the righteous shall be resurrected; not in this body that we have received from Adam, but in that which we attain through the Holy Ghost, namely in such a body as our Saviour brought from heaven.[66]

The result of the *opus* is a liberated or spiritual body, both *within* the soul (psyche) of the alchemist and *without,* manifest in the elemental world, just as God's own creation put on an earthly body. As we know, each day of the week is named after a *planet;* hence the mundane week of creation has a cosmic equivalent in the soul's manifestation of a material body as it descends the seven degrees of the Stairway of Planets. Once again the parallel is unmistakable to the creation that takes place in the alchemist's crucible, as we read in the ninth chapter, "The Heavens," of the preceding text:

You shall take seven pieces of metal, of each and every metal as they are named after the planets, and shall stamp on each the character of the planet in the house of the same planet, and every piece shall be as large and thick as a rose noble. But of Mercury only the fourth part of an ounce of weight and nothing stamped upon it.

Then put them after the order in which they stand in the heavens into a crucible, and make all windows fast in the chamber that it may be quite dark within, then melt them all together in the midst of the chamber and drop in seven drops of the blessed Stone, and forthwith a flame of fire will come out of the crucible and spread itself over the whole chamber (fear no harm), and will light up the whole chamber more brightly than sun and moon, and over your heads you shall behold the whole firmament as it is in the starry heavens above, and the planets shall hold to their appointed courses as in the sky. Let it cease of itself, in a quarter of an hour everything will be in its own place.[67]

Descent has been through the planets, but the way back to Light is fraught with peril, because of "the antagonisms or combined influences of the signs of the zodiac, the stars, the planets. The starry firmament is peopled with oppressors and despots; the planetary spheres are customs stations or jails . . . where demonical guards do their utmost to hold back the souls which strive to escape from the perpetually reforming chains of becoming."[68] These words present the essence of the Gnostic attitude towards descent and the near-futile attempt of the individual soul to ascend. What a contrast to the carefree manner of the fool in Key Zero as he is about to descend into the abyss! The sense of terror which the Gnostics felt in the face of an alien universe is echoed today in the writings of the existentialists.

The relevance of Jung to these myth-pictures is that he recognized in them the human psyche turned inside out. Indeed, one's personal myth is the wishing ring that brings to pass the life's events. Here we may see the parallel to alchemy in that salvation is not external, as in Gnosticism and Christianity, since the redeemer is the alchemist himself. Furthermore, we have seen that in all Hermetic arts God is within. With the reins of salvation firmly in hand, one cannot rail against fate. The ultimate wholeness, or spiritual completion, which the alchemists sought to perfect in themselves and in matter (the psyche turned inside out), bears a profound relation to Jung's process of individuation, and he has written several volumes on this. In order to keep the idea of *personal transformation* in the reader's mind, I wish to investigate these myths with relation to the archetypes of the collective unconscious, which are psychic components undergoing transformation in the direction of consciousness, although never fully integrated into consciousness. The psychic balance thus attained is symbolized by the *coniunctio* of Sun and Moon, conscious and unconscious, above united with below.

One word of caution. By saying that these myth-pictures are the psyche outpictured, I am not implying that the universe is a "nothing but," possessing no transcendental value. On the contrary, the psyche has conferred value on the universe through its own evolution of consciousness, in

112

the same way that the alchemist redeems the spirit in matter. With this in mind, the reader may reflect on the numinous effect of the Tarot images within the crucible of his own soul. In such a way, traces of the archetypes may surface like the skin of metals emerging from the *prima materia.*

ARCHETYPES OUTPICTURED

If the projections of the unconscious confront us in outer life, as Jung has demonstrated in cases of animus/anima attraction, then the planets of the inner psyche may take equivalent forms. For example, the archtyrant/despot of the cosmos in Gnosticism, creator of the material world after being engendered by Sophia, is equivalent to the planet Saturn, whose effects in the personal horoscope are harsh, restrictive, and unremitting. In Christianity we have noted the correspondence of this figure to Death and The Devil. Astrological associations for the planet Saturn parallel these restrictive qualities, the metallic equivalent being lead, the heaviest, grossest, blackest of the seven metals, that is, the least conscious. So, too, the inner planets of the synchronous moment of birth actualize personality characteristics.

Dividing our world-pictures into two categories only, for the sake of initial simplification, they polarize on the shadow-Self axis, evil versus good, light/darkness, devil/god, antagonist and protagonist. Alchemically these polarities are symbolized by sun and *sol niger,* the dark sun, that is, Saturn. Astrologically the configuration "above" is Sol in the sign of Leo, opposed by Saturn across the zodiac in Aquarius and Capricorn. To know which archetype a myth manifests, we have only to judge the effect. A "starry firmament people with oppressors and despots" obviously projects Saturn/shadow's heavy hand. Conversely a process that seeks to make man's dull lead "gold of the sun" leads upward on the Stairway of Planets toward light and liberation from all restriction. Ultimate freedom may be one definition of Jung's concept of selfhood. This is manifest in The Fool, enabling him to descend freely to the abyss, where he *appears* as his opposite, the union of the above and below being the reason for his descent. In this sense, the features in Waite's The Fool unite the polar opposites of Mercurius and abyss, or ☿ and ♒ as they appear at top and bottom of the wheel in Key 10. Also implied is the resolution of polar opposites Sun in Leo and Saturn (*sol niger*) in Aquarius as they line up across the zodiac at winter and summer solstice. Symbols for the Self, then, may be said to have devoured (or integrated) their shadowy opposite, "poison and yet healing draught,"[69] and in that way, like the uroboros, they stand as symbols for wholeness or psychic totality; the numerical One returns to itself from duality and diversity.

Practically every myth includes an Antagonist, the shadow principle which at first may vanquish/swallow the Protagonist before wholeness is achieved; yet in this way the dark powers are added to the light, and below unites with above.

From the point of view of the ego, the descent to the underworld of the unconscious is extremely threatening. According to Jung, "the dread and resistance which every natural human being experiences when it comes to delving too deeply into himself is, at bottom, the fear of the journey to Hades."[70] For the most part, the ego does not acknowledge the existence of the archetypes in the unconscious, or if it does, it treats them condescendingly, like stepchildren. This is what psychologists mean by the "one-sided" attitude of consciousness. In one's personal psychology, spirit swallowed by matter has its parallel to consciousness overwhelmed by the dark world. The theme of being devoured is one of the most common elements in fairytales, and my thesis is that this is another example of an outpicturing of the psyche's dynamics. Further, I believe that most fairytales are disguised alchemical texts. For example, the theme of rebirth or regeneration appears frequently, which is the end of the alchemical process; but, more than that, stomach/womb is analogous to the athanor/retort in which the homunuclus appears.

Without developing this thesis in detail, we can say that

one other element occurs in fairytales which has an alchemical parallel, and which may be the source of the Grail legend. This is the sick, dying, dismembered or put-to-death king, for whom a hero embarks upon a journey in order to effect the king's salvation, the king having associations with sun and the metal gold. Great riches are bestowed upon his saviors, but we may take these to be metaphors for spiritual gifts. Often his daughter is the reward, she being the hero's anima or the rescued *anima mundi* imprisoned in matter. By reviving the king, his savior makes him whole once more, particularly if his body has been cut up and the parts scattered. This again parallels the One, who assumes the forms of multiplicity. A hierarchy of value may be present which constellates about the planet/metal progression of baseness versus preciousness, that is, from Saturn/lead to King Sol/gold. Dead or ailing King Sol also has a relation to the sun at the winter solstice in the sign of Saturn's rulership. Like the phoenix, his rebirth commences when he is weakest (the winter solstice), and his ascendency is in the fire of the summer solstice in his own sign, Leo. In Tarot the theme of the death of the king is inherent in the sequence $4 + 9 = 13$, the emperor descending to death. We recall that the next vertical card beneath Death is Key 0, The Fool, which places the fool below the emperor, a symbolic reminder of their relation in life, since the fool/jester is usually at the king's feet. Deflating the king's pompous authority with his wit, the fool functions as his polar opposite, foolish misrule being the shadow side of court protocol.

Base matter, *prima materia*, Saturn, or Physis in Gnosticism, feeds on spirit, Nous, an emanation from the godhead, when spirit descends to the mundane plane, or to the abyss of Saturn's realm. The correspondence of king and sun implies that the physical world draws strength from the interpenetrating solar principle. In one version which Jung recounts, "Mars feeds the body of the King to the famished wolf . . . the son of Saturn (lead). The wolf symbolizes the *prima materia*'s appetite for the King. . . ."[71]

By alchemical process, the *prima materia* is made volatile, or sublimated, sublimation equated with ascent; for the soul in matter went up through the metals corresponding to the planets on the Stairway of Planets, like the alchemical fire rendering the metal volatile and enabling the soul to obtain liberation. This parallels precisely the *solificatio* initiation, which Apuleius described, in which the initiand was *crowned* as Helios (sun). Again we see the relation of sun and king. Let us look now at two pictures, one of which is solely alchemical, and the other Key 20, an Italian Minchiate deck, very probably of the 15th century. (Drawing 11.)

A comparison of these pictures reveals a common element, the wolf in the fire, which indicates alchemical symbology in even very early Tarot; therefore, Waite's deck may not be as far afield as it first appears to the uninitiated eye. In the foreground of the first picture, *prima materia,* Physis, or the elemental world, devours the king. In the background, the base *prima materia* is consumed, or transformed, and the king makes his exit from the fire. The flames are purgatorial in that they purge the gross and permit the resurrection of the king, who parallels anima mundi as the soul of matter. Recalling that Key 20 in the Waite Tarot is Judgment, in which we see the resurrected bodies emerging from graves, the connection is clear that the reborn king is a metaphor of the individual soul as well. When we do our astrological reading of the Major Arcana, the reborn sun serves as a metaphor of the personally resurrected soul to those who look above (the stars) rather than below (the elements and metals).

In a sense, the king need not appear, and he does not in the Italian Tarot card, since the ascending flames connote the upward, fiery triangle of ascent. In Waite's Key 20, and in the Marseilles, the trumpet has the same symbolical meaning as the interpenetrating triangles of fire and water, matter and spirit, and wolf and king. In the making of a trumpet, because it is a metallic instrument, both water and fire combine to temper the metal. Earlier we called attention to the combination of heavenly (above) and mundane (below) in the angel/grave symbology. The function of Gabriel's horn specifically matches our esoteric symbology, since it is the call of spirit to the mundane world to awaken and ascend. As a final note on the symbol of fire, frequently

116

DRAWING 11.

a salamander or phoenix is present in the fire, the former usually a symbol of Mercurius, the latter Mercurius and/or the sun, both being metaphors of the spirit in the process of liberation from matter.

Mercurius' power to penetrate matter is likened to the *lapis,* the stone, blue flower, or extract produced at the end of the process. Be not confused; these are all names for the One. The *lapis* transforms metals from base to noble by a projection of spiritual power. According to Jung, "This 'spirit-substance' is like quicksilver, which lurks unseen in the ore and must first be expelled if it is to be recovered *in substantia.* The possessor of this penetrating Mercurius can 'project' it into other substances and transform them from the imperfect to the perfect state. The imperfect state is like the sleeping state; substances lie in it like the 'sleepers chained in Hades' and are awakened as from death to a new and more beautiful life by the divine tincture extracted from the inspired stone. It is quite clear that we have here a tendency not only to locate the mystery of psychic transformation in matter, but at the same time to use it as a *theoria* for effecting chemical changes." Jung adds in a footnote, "It is indeed remarkable that the alchemists should have picked on the term *proiectio* in order to express the application of the philosophical Mercurius to base metals."[72]

When we consider myth-pictures as the psyche inside out, the archetypes of anima and animus deserve attention. The former is the unconscious component in the male. Since these archetypes are unconscious, they are never observed directly by the conscious mind. Rather, their effects may be seen in dreams and in the relations one has with the opposite sex, that is, what sort of persons attract the individual. When the projection of the archetype is spiritualized, then one is led out of the personal sexual sphere of relations and a transformation to higher consciousness occurs. This is possible because the last portal to the Self (god within) is guarded by the contrasexual archetype. It is as if one must marry conscious and unconscious, sun and moon (the *hierosgamos*), before the Self can be born, since it is the offspring of that marriage. The *homunculus* or little man in the glass retort may be read as the new birth in the psyche. At the same time, this figure is a symbol for wholeness, the One. Thus, animus and anima lead through sexual duality (two) back to the last portal, which opens on the One once more.

The spiritualized anima and animus are present in Tarot as Keys 2 and 5, The High Priestess and Hierophant. In earlier decks of predominantly Catholic countries, such as France and Italy, they are called The Pope and "Papess," or "Pope Joan." The last portal on the path to psychic wholeness may be symbolized by the pillars behind these figures. Beyond the pillars is the mystery dimension of the psyche. Read in this manner, the psyche turned inside out, Tarot may be used not as mere fortune-telling, but as a demonstration of the principle that life events are actualized from the individual, archetypal level of the psyche. To illustrate this as simply as possible, the cards representing the persons with whom one is involved reflect the level of the archetype. Wherever the projection lights, the impetus of a relation begins.

Keys 1 through 7 "proceed from the One" to illustrate variations on the pairs of opposites which by Key 7 come under the domination of the will and consciousness. Subsequently, Keys 8 and 9, and their vertical progressions Keys 17 and 18, symbolize the harmony that is the result of the unity of opposites. These *four* cards are associated with the significance of the number four in Jungian psychology as a totality; thus four functions, four quarters, four elements, four evangelists, etc.

As to mythic equivalents of the spiritualized animus/anima, we may begin with Thoth himself, who is said to have created the world from his Breath, that is, spirit as Pneuma. In other parallel variations, spirit is Logos, or Word of God.

Perhaps the best exposition of the characteristics of animus/anima was written by Emma Jung, Jung's wife. In *Animus and Anima,* she states as follows:

> The ability to assume different forms seems to be a characteristic quality of spirit; like mobility, the power to traverse great distances in a short time, it

is expressive of a quality which thought shares with light. This is connected with the wish-form of thinking already mentioned. Therefore, the animus often appears as an aviator, chauffeur, skier, or dancer, when lightness and swiftness are to be emphasized. Both of these characteristics, transmutability and speed, are found in many myths and fairy tales as attributes of gods or magicians. Wotan, the wingéd god and leader of the army of spirits, has already been mentioned; Loki, the flaming one, and Mercury with winged heels, also represents this aspect of the logos, its living, moving, immaterial quality which, without fixed qualities, is to a certain extent only a dynamism expressing the possibility of form, the spirit, as it were, that 'bloweth where it listeth.'[73]

Our study of the spirit Mercurius shows the relation to the evolving animus, and our correlation of Tarot's Key 1, The Magician, to Hermes/Mercurius/Thoth demonstrates the propriety of the association of this figure with the personal animus. There is yet another link between Key 1 and Hermes as the personal animus; for in his role as psychopompos he mediated between Above and Below. In terms of the psyche this signifies the harmonizing of conscious and unconscious, preparatory to the magical transformation that occurs with the emergence of the Self, the divine within.

PROJECTIONS

The descent of spirit into matter has its parallel in the projection of the archetypes and in projection into the metals. The projected anima has been discussed with great insight by von Franz in her commentary on *Aurora Consurgens, 1625,* "a document attributed to Thomas Aquinas on the problem of opposites in alchemy," germane to our Tarot discussion in that the numerous queens and goddesses that appear in both the Major and Minor Arcana of Tarot are clearly anima figures which the reader must understand if he wishes to divine their meaning for himself. Again, he will be reading his own inner life outpictured.

120

The projection of the anima-image into Physis . . .
left its mark on practically all the Gnostic systems,
where it can be found in the motif of the 'fallen
Sophia.' The latter is a feminine hypostasis of the
deity, sunk in matter. . . . Thus the followers of
Simon Magus revered Helen, his companion, as the
'Ennoia' of the Primordial Father, as the 'virgin
Pneuma' and the 'All-Mother' (Prunikos, Holy
Spirit, etc.), and taught that she had descended into
the lower world and there produced the angels and
archons by whom she was afterwards devoured.
After many incarnations and much suffering she
even sank so low as to become a whore in a brothel
in Tyre, from which she was rescued by Simon. In
Barbelo-Gnosis a similar goddess sunk in the world
and in matter was worshipped as the 'Mother of All
Living,' and was also named the 'Holy Spirit.' The
Sophia of the Ophites was not only a 'virgin
Pneuma' but had even sunk down into the intermediate realm between God and the world. She
signified 'Life,' or, in Leisegang's interpretation, the
'soul embodied in earthly things.' She was also con-
sidered to be the mother of the seven planets, and
hence of Heimarmene ('compulsion of the stars')
and the earthly world.⁷⁴

Another manifestation of divine descent in feminine form
is found in the Babylonian myth of Inanna, circa 1750 B.C.
Here the descent is not only to earth but also to the "great
below" beneath earth. In this respect, associations are with
the anima in the nether world of the unconscious, or to the
abyss of the nigredo in the outer world of metals. As in
other mythologies of the Fall, there are indications that the
"goddess of Light" was once part of consciousness in the
godhead.

From the 'great above' she set her mind toward the
'great below,'
The goddess, from the 'great above' she set her mind
towards the 'great below,'
Inanna from the 'great above,' she set her mind towards the 'great below,'

My lady abandoned heaven, abandoned earth, to the
    nether world she descended,
Abandoned lordship, abandoned ladyship, to the
    nether world she descended.
In Erech she abandoned Eanna, to the nether world
    she descended . . .
She arrayed herself in the seven ordinances,
She gathered the ordinances, placed them in her
    hand,
All the ordinances she set up at her waiting foot,
The *Sugurra,* the crown of the plain, she put upon
    her head,
The wig of her forehead she took,
The measuring rod and line of lapis lazuli she gripped
    in her hand,
Small lapis lazuli stones she tied about her neck,
Sparkling . . . stones she fastened to her breast,
A gold ring she put about her hand,
A breastplate which . . . she tightened about her
    breast,
With *pala*-garment, the garment of ladyship, she
    covered her body . . .'[75]

Further, this early example of descent in literary form
presents an illustration of spiritual divestiture; for the
"seven ordinances" which she puts on to descend must be
given up at the seven gates of the nether world, which are
analogous to the seven gates of the Stairway of Planets.
Rather than a putting on of material clothes in descent, in
this version Inanna is forced to do a kind of spiritual
striptease. Submission of the higher world (consciousness)
to the nether world (unconsciousness) is what is demanded.

Upon her entering the first gate,
The sugurra, the crown of the plain of her head was
    removed.
'What, pray, is this?'
'Be silent, Inanna, the ordinances of the nether world
    are perfect,
O Inanna do not question the rites of the nether
    world.' . . .

[To pass through each gate Inanna removed one of
   the ordinances and at the last gate—]
Upon her entering the seventh gate,
The *pala*-garment, the garment of ladyship of her
   body, was removed.[76]

We have stated that images of descent appear in Keys 10
through 16. The Lord of the nether world, antagonist of
Light (consciousness) reigns in Key 15, The Devil. He
corresponds to what Jung calls the shadow. Seemingly this
archetype is in opposition to the birth of new Light; yet
ironically this birth cannot occur unless the journey is made
"below" to unite the powers of the two kingdoms. In terms
of the revelations made about consciousness by Tarot divination, one finds a distinct phase or phases in the life pattern in which the shadow realm is confronted, things "looking black" for a time while the resistances of the conscious
mind are overcome. Where sometimes too entrenched, they
then are overwhelmed by the unconscious. The lesson is
hard, but once learned Light recognizes *sol niger* as its own
dark brother, or in Jungian terms, consciousness accepts its
shadowy component. This journey through the underworld
restores the "sick" King Sol, born anew in Key 19, The
Sun. The Wheel of Key 10 marked his progress as a golden
spiral down to the abyss, where he confronts his antagonists
and receives the powers of the underworld, and then moves
up the Wheel in the form of Hermes-Anubis. A transformation has occurred. Jung tells us that what is transformed is
the planetary demon Saturn;[77] thus a transformation occurs
within the psyche and without in matter, above and below.
   The chthonic, infernal, or polar opposite of the divine
becomes the guide aloft, as in Key 10. In *The Gnostics and
Their Remains,* C. W. King cites the frequent depiction of:

   . . . the Jackal-headed *Anubis* . . . bearing the
   caduceus of Hermes to denote his office of conduct-
   ing souls, not as of yore through the shades of the
   lower world, but along the planetary path to their
   final rest in the Pleroma. . . . This Anubis-Hermes
   appears sometimes waving a palm-branch [this may
   be a feather since the role supplanted is Maat's] to

123

proclaim his victory over the Powers of Evil; or presiding at the *psychostasia* 'weighing of the soul,' the scene commonly pictured in the Egyptian Ritual of the Dead. In the latter character he stands here for Christ, the Judge of the quick and the dead; but his successor in medieval art is the Archangel Michael, who holds the scales. In the old Greek gems Hermes is often represented as bending forward, caduceus in hand, and by its mystic virtue assisting a soul to emerge from the depths of the earth—a strange coincidence in form, probably too in origin, with the medieval picture of the Saviour lifting souls out of Purgatory. The Zoroastrian Hell, a burning lake of molten metal, into which, on the Judgment-Day, Ahriman with his followers where to be cast, had for object the ultimate *purification* and restoration to their pristine state of the condemned—a merciful doctrine, held by Origen, and partly allowed by Jerome.[78]

In the foregoing paragraph we note several elements common to Tarot's Major Arcana, not only Hermes-Anubis of Key 10, but also Christ's "successor in medieval art" as judge of the quick and dead, the figure in Key 11 who may be Michael, since he holds the scales and the sword, which — enflamed — guarded Paradise. Too, this card anticipates the Judgment of Key 20 in the vertical sequence, depicting souls emerging "from the depths of the earth." However, what I find most compelling here is the possible source of alchemy in Zoroastrianism, a Persian religion of which the Zendavesta is the principle text (1200-1000 B.C.). The lake of molten metal in which Ahriman is purified suggests the heating of metals to extract the divine essence, and Ahriman's devilish role parallels Saturn's as planetary demon and metal-to-be-transformed.

A thumbnail sketch of Zoroastrianism shows Gnosticism's derivations. According to C. W. King, "The first emanation of the Eternal One was Light, whence issued Ormuzd (Ahuramazda), the King of Light . . . By means of his 'word,' Ormuzd created the pure world of which he is the preserver and the judge. . . . Ahriman, the

Second-born of the Eternal One — like Ormuzd, an emanation from the Primal Light, and equally pure, but ambitious and full of pride — had become jealous of the Firstborn. On this account the Supreme Being condemned him to inhabit . . . the black Empire of Darkness . . . Ahriman, in order to oppose his rival, created . . . the *Arch-Devs,* chained each one to his respective planet, and of whom the chief is Astomogt, 'the two-footed serpent of lies.' These Devs are the authors of all evil, both physical and moral, throughout the universe."[79] Thus we see the origin of the Gnostic planetary demons who seek to impede the soul in its journey back to Light.

ZOSIMOS

Let us examine now the writings of a man who unites both Gnosticism and alchemy. Zosimos lived circa A.D. 300. In "The Visions of Zosimos,"[80] the rite of redemption is contained in Tarot in symbolical form, since it parallels exactly the Major Arcana's sequence of 15 cards of descent and seven of ascent. The introduction by Zosimos commences with a general commentary which hints at the alchemical orientation of the treatise. However, the rite is experienced firsthand and is of such a bloody and horrendous nature that the words have great numinous effect:

And as I spoke thus I fell asleep, and I saw a sacrificer standing before me . . . saying to me: 'I have performed the act of descending the fifteen steps into the darkness, and of ascending the steps into the light. And he who renews me is the sacrificer, by casting away the grossness of the body . . . and by the transformation of the body that I had become spirit. And that is my unendurable torment.' And even as he spoke thus, and I held him by force to converse with me, his eyes became as blood. And he spewed forth all his own flesh. And I saw how he changed into the opposite of himself, into a mutilated anthroparion, and he tore his flesh with his own teeth, and sank into himself.[81]

Earlier we called attention to the relation of Keys 0 and 1 in the self-devouring dragon (uroboros), which is also self-generating. We said that Keys 0 and 1 were aspects of the same figure, Mercurius. In the same way, all numbers are "swallowed" by zero and disappear into nothingness, out of which the One is born again. Zosimos continues:

> I saw the same bowl-shaped altar and, on the upper part, boiling water, and a numberless multitude of people in it. . . . And I perceived an anthroparion, a barber grown grey. . . . 'The sight that you see is the entrance, the exit, and the transformation.'[82]

Presently Zosimos sees a "brazen man" who writes on a tablet of lead, and commands those in the "bath" to do likewise. Jung tells us that the barber is grey because "he represents the lead."[83] Bronze is an alloy of copper and tin, the metals of Venus and Jupiter; so Zosimos' vision is an allegory of the transformation of metals and the parallel transformation of man.

> At last I was overcome with the desire to mount the seven steps . . . so I went back in order to complete the ascent.[84]

On the Stairway of Planets, the descent is from Mercury, Venus, Mars, Jupiter, and Saturn, equivalent to Keys 1-15, as we noted. The corresponding metals being quicksilver, copper, iron, tin, and lead, ascent is back the same way, with an additional *seven* steps, or seven cards, which are Keys 16, 17, 18, 19, 20, 21, and Zero, which we assigned to Moon (silver) and Sun (gold). The parallel with Zosimos' vision is precise. He descends fifteen steps and mounts "the seven steps . . . in order to complete the ascent." The Tree of Metals and the Stairway of Planets are one and the same, the former being the microcosmic view and the latter the macrocosmic outlook. Man is the mesocosm who stands between the two, mindful (as alchemist) of the tortures the psyche must undergo to ascend to the higher consciousness of "gold of the sun." Zosimos continues:

> The priest, that brazen man, whom you see seated in the spring and composing the substance, look on

him not as the brazen man, for he has changed the colour of his nature and has become the silver man; and if you will, you will soon have him as the golden man.

But as I was about to ascend, I lost my way again; greatly discouraged, and not seeing in which direction I should go, I fell asleep. And while I was sleeping, I saw an anthroparion, a barber clad in a robe of royal purple, who stood outside the place of punishments. He said to me: 'Man, what are you doing?' and I replied: 'I have stopped here because having turned aside from the road, I have lost my way.' And he said: 'Follow me.' And I turned and followed him. When we came near to the place of punishments, I saw my guide, this little barber, enter that place, and his whole body was consumed by the fire.

On seeing this, I stepped aside, trembling with fear; then I awoke, and said within myself: 'What means this vision?' And again I clarified my understanding, and knew that this barber was the brazen man, clad in a purple garment. And I said to myself; "I have well understood, this is the brazen man. It is needful that first he must enter the place of punishments.'[85]

The brazen man has a curious relation to Moses' brazen serpent on a cross, and here we come upon Christ's parallel to *prima materia* in that *the cross is a refining ritual of torture which culminates in the ascent of the soul.* We should not overlook the link of Christ and serpent. "Christ as Logos is synonymous with the Naas, the serpent of the Nous among the Ophites. The Agathodaimon (good spirit) had the form of a snake. . . ."[86] This brings us full circle to Zosimos' next guide, who is named Agathodaimon, and is specifically associated with lead; therefore, the divine and daimonic, celestial and chthonic, are again but dual aspects of the One, who descends and ascends, and descends once more. This duality, which the serpent uroboros symbolizes, has a connection to the mesocosm (man) in that it stands "for the two aspects of the unconscious: its cold and ruthless instinctuality, and its Sophia quality of natural wisdom, which is embodied in the archetypes. The Logos nature of Christ represented by the chthonic serpent is the maternal wisdom of the divine mother, which is prefigured by Sapientia in the Old Testament. The snake-symbol thus characterizes Christ as a personification of the unconscious in all its aspects, and as such he is hung on the tree in sacrifice (wounded by the spear like Odin)."[87]

> And again I followed the road alone, and when I was near the place of punishments, I again went astray, not knowing my way, and I stopped in despair. And again, as it seemed, I saw an old man whitened by years, who had become wholly white, with a blinding whiteness. His name was Agathodaimon. Turning himself about, the old man with white hair gazed upon me for a full hour. And I urged him: 'Show me the right way.' He did not come towards me, but hastened on his way. But I, running hither and thither, at length came to the altar. And when I stood at the top of the altar, I saw the white-haired old man enter the place of punishments. O ye demiurges of celestial nature. Immediately he was transformed by the flame into a pillar of fire. What a terrible story, my brethren. For, on account of the violence of the punishment, his eyes filled with blood. I spoke to him, and asked: 'Why are you stretched out there?' But he could barely open his mouth, and groaned: 'I am the leaden man, and I submit myself to an unendurable torment.' Thereupon, seized with great fear, I awoke and sought within myself the reason for what I had seen. And again I considered and said to myself: 'I have well understood, for it means that the lead is to be rejected, and in truth the vision refers to the composition of the liquids.'[88]

The whiteness of the nigredo recalls the "Book of Ostanes" in which the philosopher's tears transform the stone from black to white, again suggesting that certain qualities of the planet/metals are projections of the psyche, or inside turned out. Certain of the alchemists evidence this in their writing, particularly Gerhard Dorn. According to Jung, in Dorn's *Physica Trismegisti*, "he even declares that the time-honored blackness (*melanosis, nigredo*) is a projection: 'For Hermes said, "From thee shall all obscurity flee away," he said not "from the metals." By obscurity naught else is to be understood save the darkness of disease, and sickness of body and mind.' . . . The 'Consilium coniugii' equates the *nigredo* with melancholia. Vignenere says of the Saturnine lead: 'Lead signifies the vexations and aggravations with which God afflicts us and troubles our senses.' This adept was aware that lead . . . was identical with the subjective state of depression. Similarly, the personified prima materia in the 'Aurelia occulta' says of her brother Saturn that his spirit was 'overcome by the passion of melancholy.' "[89]

In the Waite Minor Arcana, there are many "black" cards which stand for the restricted and depressed states which beset human life. In divination these should be placed in the proper perspective and seen as situations which are the psyche outpictured, with the cause within, rather than events which have randomly "happened" to the person; hence the importance of "getting the lead out." Key 15 depicts the gross, restricted condition of Devil/Saturn, the antithesis of Keys 19, 20, 21, and Zero, which are the free, liberated, unrestricted cards of higher consciousness (sun). The correlation of the dichotomy to psychology is manifest; lead versus gold means that restricted consciousness is higher consciousness *in potentia*. In the same way, consciousness is associated with the sun, Light, and day, and darkness associated with the unconscious, lead being prima materia, the primal matter out of which the Self (sun) evolves. The macrocosmic outlook presents the polar opposites in terms of summer and winter solstice, ruled by Sun and Saturn in the signs of Leo and Aquarius. The synchronous relation to man the mesocosm may be seen in the affects associated with the holidays and sacred calendar events honoring these days. At Christmas the Light is near extinction until the new Light (Nous, Christ) is born. The pagan celebrations of the summer solstice were significantly joyous, since they made a more direct correlation between the sun and salvation. Recalling the *solificatio* in Apuleius, our next revelation from Zosimos parallels that revelation:

> Again I beheld the divine and holy bowl-shaped altar, and I saw a priest clothed in a white robe reaching to his feet, who was celebrating these terrible mysteries, and I said: 'Who is this?' And the answer came: 'This is the priest of the inner sanctuaries. It is he who changes the bodies into blood, makes the eyes clairvoyant, and raises the dead.' Then, falling again to earth, I again fell asleep. And as I was ascending the fourth step, I saw, to the east, one approaching, holding a sword in his hand. And another came behind him bringing one adorned round about with signs, clad in white and comely to see, who was named the Meridian of the Sun.[90]

Commenting on this in a completely different context, Jung says "the apotheosis means no more than maximum consciousness, which amounts to maximal freedom of the will. This goal cannot be better represented then by . . . the (position of the sun at noon) in Zosimos."[91] In *The Golden Ass,* or one might say *The Transformed Nigredo,* Apuleius tells us that he was garbed in "a white palm-tree chaplet with its leaves sticking out all round like rays of light," and when revealed to the people he is "dressed like the sun," which he had seen at midnight, the daily equivalent of the yearly abyss of the solstice, "shining as if it were noon."[92]

Now let us look at the Major Arcana once more in order to see the progressive transformation from Key 15 to Key 16. Adam and Eve are chained, depicting the restrictions in man and mesocosm. As a very general rule, these restrictions are on the side of an imbalance between conscious and unconscious minds; so that the wedding of the two is a sought-for alchemical goal. Silver and gold, locked in lead (Saturn, Key 15) are symbolized by Queen Moon and King Sun, manifest in Key 16 when the liberating flash of lightning appears. The torment of Adam and Eve in hell is thus an apt metaphor for the tortures of the metals. In Sir George Ripley's *Theatrum chemicum britannicum,* he writes, "the unnatural fire must torment the bodies, for it is the dragon violently burning, like the fire of hell."[93] The chthonic dragon is the hellish aspect of the *spiritus mercurialis*, just as devil is his dark side, and as Adam and Eve are the primal King and Queen in restricted, unevolved form. Too, Mercurius contains not only dark and light aspects, but dichotomies of sex, which King and Queen portray. Light, fire, or revelation, whether macrocosmic, microcosmic, or mesocosmic, are the means of driving out the darkness and loosing the primal pair who commence (in Key 16) the ascent to their union on high at the summer solstice, equivalent in man to the marriage of conscious and unconscious, and the actualization of the philosopher's stone, the Self.

CHAPTER V

THE ALCHEMICAL ASCENT

1. *Waite's Alchemical Texts*

It has been my thesis that Waite's Tarot is specifically alchemical in theme, restoring what may have been the original orientation of Tarot. In order to substantiate this further, I should like to present some excerpts from three texts on alchemy in which Waite had a hand. By correlating these with specific cards, it should be apparent to the reader that Waite's deck is a highly conscious creation with the disguised (esoteric) intent to present the tenets of alchemy. The three texts are titled *The Secret Tradition in Alchemy*, *The Hermetic Museum Restored*, and *The Brotherhood of the Rosy Cross*, the latter referring to the Rosicrucian Society, whose founders undoubtedly knew the alchemical secrets.

These Waite books were known to Jung, who corrects Waite in his opinion that "the first author to identify the stone with Christ was the Paracelsist Heinrich Khunrath... Waite's assumption is undoubtedly erroneous, for we have much earlier testimonies to the connection between Christ and the *lapis*, the oldest that I have so far been able to discover being contained in the Codicillus (Ch. IX) of Raymond Lully (1235-1315)."[94]

Further on in *Psychology and Alchemy*, Jung tells us, "Additional evidence, which ought to have been known to Waite is furnished by his countryman Sir George Ripley (1415-90), canon of Bridlington, whose main work, 'Liber duodecim portarum,' is prefaced by a table of philosophical correspondences ... between the seven metals and chemical substances and what are called 'types,' by which are meant the alchemical symbols . . . signs of the zodiac, and so forth. These correspondences include seven mysteries, the *Mysterium Altaris* (i.e., the Mass) being attributed to gold, whereas the alchemical equivalent is the *transmutatio* [transmutation]."[95]

By a nice synchronicity, this table of correspondences may have been the organizing principle for Waite's correlation of his Major Arcana with metals, planets, and signs of the zodiac, that is, the signs ruled by the planets on the Stairway of Planets. Too, Ripley's dates (1415-90) place him in the initial mainstream of Tarot's appearance in Europe.

Jung cites many references to Waite's translation of *Musaeum hermeticum,* originally published in 1678 and "restored" by Waite in 1893. As far as precise correlations to the Major Arcana, we may note the following: The title page contains a picture of an ancient alchemist, with staff, lantern, and exactly the same peaked cap and length of beard as in Waite's Key 9, The Hermit. In *The Hermetic Museum Restored, anima mundi* leads the alchemist, with the *lumen naturae* (light of nature) rendered as two interpenetrating triangles. Waite places these within the alchemist's own lantern, which contains a feeble candle in the original, as we saw in Drawing 3.

Literary relations are manifest in *The Hermetic Museum Restored,* but since Tarot is visual symbology, let us move on to Waite's *The Secret Tradition in Alchemy,* particularly noteworthy for his analysis of the *Mutus Liber* (Dumb Book), sometimes called *The Book of the Silence of Hermes.* The *Dumb Book* takes its name from the gesture made by the alchemist and his wife in a depiction at the end of the opus. One hand is either raised in caution or perhaps makes some secret gesture, while the other touches the lips in admonishing silence. Waite certainly took this to heart!

The entire sequence of plates from the *Mutus Liber* is reproduced in Mangetus' *Bibliotheca Chemica Curiosa,* available for viewing in the Rare Book Room of the University of California's Medical Library. The first plate contains two elements common to Waite's Tarot, only one of which appears in prior decks. The artist has made a mandorla of branches of roses. Waite forsakes the mandorla symbol in Key 1 as perhaps too far removed from the design of the exoteric Juggler, but he does surround his Magician with roses, symbolical of the opus. For the rest of Plate 1 of the *Mutus Liber*, let us learn from Waite's description.

"The first design represents the symbolical ladder of Jacob with angels descending thereon. They are in the act of sounding trumpets to awaken one who is asleep on the ground beneath; thus symbolizing the quickening of an artist who is called to the Great Work."[96]

We are safe in assuming that Waite knew of the Stairway of Planets. His Magician of Key 1 is the descended form of the *spiritus mercurialis*, Key 0. Hence this gesture, "As above, so below," has the same meaning as the ladder with angels descending. Furthermore, this Magician has the same meaning as the sleeping alchemist in Plate 1 of the *Mutus Liber,* unawakened in consciousness. Waite's Key 1 thus incorporates and identifies as one the descended spirit and awakened adept.

The primary symbol in Plate 1 of the *Bibliotheca Chemica* is that of the angels sounding trumpets, and this is primary also in Key 20, Judgment. But since Waite did not seriously alter Key 20 in borrowing from the earlier exoteric deck, this connection gives evidence of alchemical influence already in that version of the Major Arcana. Or rather, it might even be more correct to say that *Mutus Liber* (1702) may reflect the alchemical elements in Tarot (c. 1400). At all events, the angels announce a higher reality to man, which may become his own through a transformation of consciousness. And we may note in addition that the prototype Tarot deck of 1391 has *two* angels sounding trumpets in Key 20.

Plate 2 of *Mutus Liber* presents two angels holding a retort which contains a boy-sun and girl-moon, the microcosmic equivalent of the conjunction of sun and moon at the solstice on the cusp of Cancer and Leo. Between these angels there is the figure of Mercurius holding a trident, a variation of the caduceus. In Waite's words: "The second plate shows that he [the sleeping alchemist] has responded forthwith and has entered into consultation with a female collaborator, who may be regarded as his wife. The symbolic sun of philosophy is shining in the midheaven and beneath are two angels, having one foot on the earth and another on the water, presumably to indicate that dryness and moisture both enter into the work. . . ."[97]

The *Mutus Liber* always presents the alchemist *and* his "wife," as Waite calls her; however, she is the *soror mystica,* that is, not necessarily a flesh-and-blood companion in the work, but the feminine, unconscious component (anima) of the adept. He corresponds to Sol and she to Luna, growing in the retort which the angels hold. The point is that the one-sided attitude of consciousness can never complete the work of psychic wholeness, which is the goal of the opus.

Now as to the correlations with the Waite deck, what Waite has utilized from this plate is the arrangement of the angel's feet. In the Marseilles Tarot, The Star shows a figure with one foot in water and the other foot on land, whereas the angel's feet in the Waite Temperance Key are covered by a long gown. Waite has turned stylist, shortening the hemline to permit us to see "one foot on the earth and another on the water."[98] Dryness and moisture are polar opposites, indicative of Sol and Luna, since the sun's rays dry the earth, while at night the moon's "vapors" were thought to be the source of nocturnal dew. At the same time, active sulphur and passive mercury are connoted, since Mercurius in his feminine aspect is linked to Luna, while the dry (earthly), fiery sulphur is the active component of Sol.

Waite continues, in comment on the *Mutus Liber,* Plate 3: "The last design signifies completion, and therein Jacob's ladder, symbolizing the path of ascent from the earth of ordinary life to the heaven of philosophy, is seen laid upon the ground, because the work is done. The Alchemical King of the third plate has been brought from heaven to earth; and his flight is restrained by a rope which the adepts hold between them."[99]

As we know, the end of the process is represented by Key 21, The World, in both exoteric and esoteric Tarot. Another mandorla of branches appears in the *Mutus Liber* design,

136

paralleling that of The World in this Tarot Key. Jung reproduces the picture in *Psychology and Alchemy,* interpreting it as "Hermes as Anthropos, united with the artifex and *soror.*"[100] The union implies the conjunction of above and below, since the artifex and soror are earthbound and require the ladder to ascend: i.e., Hermes/Mercurius/Anthropos is to be liberated from the bounds of matter through the opus of this artifex and soror. What strikes me as most interesting in regard to the design is that Waite's depiction of The Sun is an almost exact reproduction of the sun in *Mutus Liber,* as seen below. If he had not been influenced by this work, he would surely have followed the tradition of the Marseilles design; yet such was not the case. Furthermore, at the top of his mandorla in Key 21, The World, there is a red knot. The color red, in alchemy, as we have said, symbolizes active sulphur or the sun, whereas here it takes the place of the sun in the *Mutus liber* mandorla and occupies the point symbolic of the midheaven. All in all, the case is convincing for significant influences in Waite's Tarot from *Mutus Liber.* (See Drawing 12, next page.)

Next, let us have a look at Waite's *The Brotherhood of the Rosy Cross.* Rosicrucianism, of which this work is a major document, is a latter-day version of alchemy, having originated about the time of alchemy's decline in Europe in the seventeenth century. Jung comments that "This was the age that saw the rise of the secret societies, above all the Rosicrucians — the best proof that the secret of alchemy had worn itself out. For the whole *raison d'etre* of a secret society is to guard a secret that has lost its vitality and can only be kept alive as an outward form."[101]

"Now we know," he states again, "that the regression to the Helios [sun] of antiquity vainly attempted by Julian the Apostate was succeeded in the Middle Ages by another movement that was expressed in the formula 'per crucem ad rosam' (through the cross to the rose), which was later condensed into the 'Rosie Crosse' of the Rosicrucians. Here the essence of the heavenly Sol descends into the flower — earth's answer to the sun's countenance. . . . Seven-petalled rose as allegory of the seven planets, the seven stages of transformation, etc."[102]

DRAWING 12.

The heavenly sun in the earthly rose has the same symbolical meaning as all of the descents we have examined, namely spirit interpenetrating matter. There is one more descent, however, which we should consider at this point because it throws new light on Key 12, The Hanged Man, and paves the way for our approach to Waite's study of Rosicrucianism. Manly P. Hall is the author of an encyclopedic work entitled *The Secret Teachings of All Ages*, subtitled "Masonic, Hermetic, Cabbalistic and Rosicrucian Symbolical Philosophy." It is an attempt to touch all the occult bases, and very nearly succeeds. In one chapter he reprints "fifteen diagrams which appear in *The Magical, Cabbalistical, and Theosophical Writings of Georgius von Welling, on the Subject of Salt, Sulphur, and Mercury*. This extremely rare volume was published at Frankfort and Leipzig in 1735 and 1760, and its fifteen charts constitute a remarkable and invaluable addition to the few other known admittedly authentic Cabbalistic and Rosicrucian diagrams.

"Lucifer," we read in Hall's words, "is the greatest mystery of symbolism. The secret knowledge of the Rosicrucians concerning Lucifer is nowhere so plainly set forth as in these plates, which virtually reveal his true identity, a carefully guarded secret about which little has been written. Lucifer is represented by the number 741."[103]

Now if we recall the significance assigned to numbers, 741 adds to 12, the number of The Hanged Man. Upside down as he is, parallels are suggested to Lucifer pitched headlong from heaven, and Hall's reproductions seem to support this contention. One plate is said to have designated "the symbolic tomb of Christian Rosencreutz, founder of Rosicrucianism." "The upper circle," states Hall, "is the first world — the Divine Sphere of God. The triangle in the center is the throne of God. The small circles at the points of the star symbolize the seven great Spirits before the throne, mentioned in the Book of Revelation, in the midst of which walks the Alpha and Omega, the Son of God. The central triangle contains three flames — the Divine Trinity. From the lowest of these flames proceeds the first divine outflow, shown by two parallel lines descending through the throne of Saturn (The Spirit *Orifelis*, through whom God manifested Himself). Passing through the boundary of the celestial universe and the 22 spheres of the lower system, the lines end at . . . the throne of Lucifer, in whom the divine outpouring is concentrated and reflected."[104]

Thus Lucifer descends into matter, and the concern of the text is in part with "the liberation of Lucifer and return to his original state."[105] Waite seems to have employed the symbolism of this mystery of Lucifer, at least in his addition of the light/flame nimbus to the Hanged Man's head, where it is intended to indicate a reflection of "the first divine outflow" in the form of a flame, Lucifer's name, as we know, signifying "light."

By far the most interesting of the early Rosicrucian documents which Waite discusses, however, is *The Chemical Marriage—or Nuptials—of Christian Rosencreutz* (1459). The form of this work is an allegorical romance, with the seven planet/metals appearing as kings and queens and with the marriage chamber described as a "laboratorium, to intimate that the whole pageant of the nuptials conceals — *ex hypothesi* — an experiment in secret chemistry." Waite describes this symbolical pageant as follows:

"The Virgin President of the Mystery bound the eyes of the six royalties with black taffeta scarves, after which six coffins were brought in and set down, with a low black seat in their midst. A giant negro entered with naked axe and proceeded in a solemn and reverent ceremony to decapitate the kings and queens — male and female indifferently. This terrific pageant began with the ancient monarch. . . . The business had been done expeditiously but there was to be yet another episode, for when the headsman prepared to retire he was added also to the shambles. The blood of the kings was received in golden goblets, which were placed with them in their coffins." [106]

Associating the royal couples with planets, Waite assigns Saturn to one of the black kings, but this correlation really does not work, since there are two black kings. Iron and tin being dark metals, Mars and Jupiter, their planets, are more likely attributions, especially since the negro with the axe is certainly Saturn as *nigredo*. Too, Saturn is the executioner of the zodiac in his role as Father Time bearing the scythe, and as Chronos he devours his children, the other planets.

When the executioner's head was deposited with his axe in a chest, there were then seven coffins. About midnight C.R.C. (Christian Rosy Cross), from his room looking out on a lake, "beheld from afar 'seven ships making forward, all full of light.' Over each of them hovered a flame, which he judged to be 'the spirits of the beheaded.' When the vessals had come to land he saw the Queen-President going towards them, bearing a torch and followed by the six coffins, and also the chest. Each of these was laid secretly in a ship; the lights were extinguished, save one for a watch on each vessel; and the spiritual flames 'passed back together over the lake.'"

The next day, Waite continues, a "voyage began with the ships in due order, as shown in the following diagram."

In Waite's diagram, I have connected the dots to reveal the interprenetrating triangles of spirit and matter: the same that shine in the lantern of Key 9, The Hermit. The planetary lights are arranged in this order into three pairs of polar opposites, with Mercury the equilibrating light at the center.

Later C.R.C. and the voyagers are led into "a subterranean laboratory, where they extracted the essences from plants and precious stones. . . . C.R.C. went out to contemplate the stars, and from one of the walls he beheld not only a memorable conjunction of planets, but the seven spiritual Flames passing over the sea to rest on the summit of the Tower."

"Of that which followed . . . it is scarcely possible to

speak in a summary manner, as it is exceedingly involved. Above the subterranean laboratory the Tower of Olympus was raised in eight stages or storeys and . . . access from storey to storey was through a trap opened in the ceiling."

Let us pause here for a moment to analyze this structure. There are *seven* levels before the top is attained, the trapdoor of which opens out on the starry sky, equivalent to the Ogdoad or Starry Firmament of the Gnostics, the eighth sphere. This corresponds also to the eight-pointed star in Key 17, The Star. We have noted that the tower is a symbol of ascent, with its name denoting the *heavenly* gods and its specific form of the Stairway of Planets, each level of which is also one of the seven stages in the alchemical process. To go into detail on the names and procedures takes us too far afield; so let me make the point that Waite undoubtedly knew the Stairway of Planets, and despite his secrecy, the triadic arrangement reveals this in his Major Arcana.

The concluding events which C.R.C. relates are as strange as those of Zosimos' document. The Moor's head, draped in green taffeta, is placed in a kettle and "the liquid essences prepared on the previous day from plants and precious stones were poured therein." A great snow-white egg, distilled from the bodies of the royal couples, is cooked in a square kettle until "a bird with black plumes broke through the shell and was fed with the blood of the beheaded kings and queens." Because of its coloring, the bird is another form of the nigredo, as the crow is the peacock (end of opus) without his feathers. At the next level, the bird does lose his feathers when a milky-white bath is heated until they fall off, tinting the bath blue, which condenses into a blue stone used to paint the bird, "the head only excepted, 'which remained white.' The Virgin departed with her Bird, and the Guests were thereafter called up to the sixth storey. In this place the Bird was fed with the blood of a white serpent and then decapitated, the body being burnt to ashes, which were deposited in a box of cypresswood."

Here we have motifs associated with the phoenix, alchemical symbol of resurrection, and as such related to Christ and the *lapis*. On the eighth floor, the Bird's ashes are moistened to a thin dough, "which was then heated over the fire and cast 'into two little forms or moulds,' where it was left to cool. Subsequently the moulds were opened, discovering 'two bright and almost transparent little images, a male and female, the like to which man's eye never saw.'" These homunculi, miniature Sol and Luna, anticipate the *hierosgamos,* or marriage of opposites. Blood of the phoenix-like bird then effects the resurrection of the couple fed on it. C.R.C. witnesses "the entrance of the souls into their bodies through tubes placed in their mouthes. . . . He testifies that the souls descended through an open space in the vaulted roof, after the manner of streams of fire poured through the tubes, and thence into the two bodies." This presents an image similar to the Gnostic concept of descent of the Breath/Pneuma through the spheres of the Stairway of Planets. Sol and Luna are then placed in a " 'travelling bed' and the curtains drawn about them. They were left to sleep in this manner for a considerable time, but were ultimately awakened by the Virgin in white garments. . . . It is said that the young King and Queen 'imagined that they slept from the hour in which they were beheaded.' "

The subsequent two quartos of the text are missing, but undoubtedly the hierosgamos, conjunction of Sol and Luna, or the "chymical wedding" does take place, just as it does at the end of Tarot's opus.

2. Keys 16-21, The Alchemical Ascent

Let us look now at the Major Arcana with regard to alchemical influence. As we recall, alchemy commences with an ascent, the subsequent descent uniting above and below. Since Tarot begins with a descent, Keys 1-15, we shall begin our discussion from the place of the abyss, Keys 13-15. The archetypal, unmanifest One descended to duality down the Stairway of Planets, where at the abyss, in Saturn's realm, the help of the alchemist had to be sought to liberate (volatilize) the now-concretized One. The ascent will then occur through the stages of the metals, Saturn's equivalent metal being lead, the blackest, heaviest, and grossest.

Coloring is important to symbology, as we saw in our first reading. Lead, being black, is the *nigredo,* and generally speaking there are two other colors associated with stages of the alchemical process. These are white, of the *albedo,* whitening, and red, of the *rubedo,* or reddening, sometimes known as "the tincture." These three color stages bear precise relationships to Keys 13-15, 16-18, and 18-21 of the Tarot, which, it will be recalled, we have already related to Saturn, the Moon, and the Sun. Let me commence our study of their symbologies with the words of another authority, Charles Poncé.

"The nigredo was the most frequently discussed stage of the alchemic process. It symbolized the death stage, the time when the matter being worked was 'killed' [Key 13, Death], its basic form broken down so that the spirit believed to be contained within it could be set free. This initial stage of the work was the most feared, and the alchemist likened it to a descent into hell [Key 15, The Devil]."[107] The bracketed notations are, of course, my own, as will be those in the texts quoted below.

Now, before the *albedo* could be achieved two operations were necessary; and if we examine the Arcana Keys following that of The Devil, the sense of these stages in the alchemical opus will be apparent. The *athanor,* or alchemical oven, was used for heating, in order to free the volatile quicksilver (Mercury) and so to release spirit (Mercurius) from matter. Sometimes the heat was gentle, but often *calcination* was required, i.e., a burning that reduced the prima materia to a white ash. (Compare Key 16, The Tower.) Such incineration was the initial step in a separation of opposites, active and passive, masculine and feminine, King and Queen, Sol and Luna, sulphur and salt.

Dissolution, the next step, was a watery process that leached out impurities in the white ash; and in this way fire and water (heat and cold) were combined in the alchemical process, just as are above and below, symbolically in the fiery and watery triangles. Let us hear again from Charles Poncé:

144

"Because the albedo represents the transition from base lead to silver we often find it symbolized by a feminine figure [Key 17], a personification of either the moon [Key 18] or nature. If nothing else the transition points to the emergence of a new awareness of consciousness and for this reason is often associated with symbols of rebirth. Intimately connected with this stage are the ideas of washing, cleansing, and purification [Key 17]. Whereas the first stage stood for the moment of spiritual death, the albedo was thought of as a moment of baptism or return from the depths of the ocean [Key 18]. Its association with the dawn lead to the idea that the new awareness was as yet a dim perception, that the sun had not yet made an appearance."[108]

In Key 18, The Moon, the crustacean, symbol of Cancer, ruled by the moon, emerges from the watery depths at the beginning of the golden path of ascent. This golden path is a frequent symbol in esoterica of the spiritual Way of evolving consciousness. Its appearance here, in the figure of Key 18, The Moon, suggests that an alchemical transformation of consciousness of the alchemist himself is about to take place, "gold" appearing in the outer world when the inner "gold" is being realized. Or in Jungian terms, as selfhood is attained, the path of individuation leads to increasing heights of consciousness. We note that in the Tarot Keys the golden path leads ever higher, into distant mountains, until in Key 19 "the initiand is crowned as Helios." The ascending path of Key 18 thus reminds us that the seven cards, from 16 to 22 (= 0), represent the seven "steps" of the ascent in the Major Arcana.

In Keys 17 and 18 the Moon and Sun are conjoined by their proximity; yet there are other, more esoteric ways in which the sacred marriage (*hierosgamos*) is represented in these cards. One of the most interesting is that suggested by the eclipse shown in Key 18, where the sun has been "swallowed" by the moon. The suggestion is of the alchemical myth of Gabricus swallowed by Beya. Something similar is suggested in the Marseilles Tarot, since the Moon, there also, is shown eclipsing the sun.

There are two different versions of this myth. In one, the active masculine principle is represented as an old king, dead or ailing, who is restored to youth by descending into the body of his feminine opposite. "Gabricus . . . is dissolved into atoms in the body of Beya," states Jung, "this being equivalent to a form of *mortificatio.*"[109] In another version, Gabricus and Beya are the old king's two children whom he has hatched in his brain. Other variations are of the King (Sol) drowning in the mercurial bath, or of a green lion devouring the sun. "In the *Rosarium* version," as Jung describes it, "the death of the son is the result of his complete disappearance into the body of Beya during coitus."[110] Behind the nocturnal purple color of its moon shine forth the bright red rays of a rising sun. Waite alters this image significantly by changing one of the two dogs of the Marseilles version into a wolf, which is an animal symbolic of the soul (or sometimes of the body), whereas the dog connotes the spirit. Sol and Luna, likewise, stand for spirit and soul respectively, so that Waite is fully justified in his choice of these animals. Indeed, he is in effect only reinforcing the basic symbolism.

In our numerical analysis earlier, we pointed out that active numbers and colors were indicative in alchemy of active sulphur, the spiritual essence of the sun, while passive numbers and colors (white, blue) indicate the moon, quicksilver, and salt. Therefore, it is significant that an Arabic word for sulphur is the source of the name Gabricus of the King or King's son of the alchemical myth. The etymology is described by Jung as follows: ". . . Gabricus, Cabricus, Cabritis, Kybric: Arabic *Kibrit* = sulphur. Beja, Beya, Beua: Arabic *al-baida* = the white one."[111]

The union of sun and moon as depicted by Waite is often interpreted in divination, by readers of Tarot, as an evil sign, but this is because they do not realize that a *hierosgamos* is what is represented in Key 18, The Moon, and their reaction to the scene is one of uneasiness and foreboding. This is proper, since Luna's kingdom is on the edge of hell, so to speak, even though the ascent has commenced. Also, *albedo* is adjacent to *nigredo* in alchemical process, and *nigredo* contains the *mortificatio,* or death. In discussing the Sol-Luna allegory, Jung catches the feeling of Key 18. The moon, "standing on the borders of the sublunary world ruled by evil, has a share not only in our world of light but also in the daemonic world of darkness. . . . That is why her changefulness is so significant symbolically: she is duplex and mutable like Mercurius, and is like him a mediator; hence their identification in alchemy."[112]

What then of the *rubedo* and our attribution of Keys 19-21 to that stage of alchemical transformation? As we view Key 19, The Sun, we may recall my earlier remarks about the midheaven of the horoscope between the Ninth and Tenth Houses in the chart. Our sun in Key 19 straddles this midheaven line, the red banner of active sulphur proclaiming the "reddening."

3. Descent To The Monad

By whatever name Mercurius is known, the *Emerald Tablet* tells us, "its power is made perfect" when it returns to earth, thereby uniting above and below. Recalling our numerical attributions to the Major Arcana, Key Zero represents the archetypal power of the Unmanifest, Uncreated World, while Key 1 is that aspect of the same principle with manifest form and creative actuality. The lemniscate (horizontal eight) is a symbol of these dual aspects of the divine One, one half tending towards form, the other towards annihilation of form, as in the serpent shape which devours itself. At the same time, all polar opposites arise from this dynamic tension and are embodied in the two ovals of the lemniscate, which suggest the circular sun and moon at the *coniunctio.* Jung tells us that the royal marriage of King Sol and Queen Luna "is simply a variant of the Uroboros, which, because it is by nature hermaphroditic, completes the circle in itself."[113]

Completion of the circle recalls the cyclical nature of the alchemical process, and the wheel of ascent/descent in Key 10, wherein "above" is represented by the glyph for Mercurius, and below by the symbol of dissolution. Fool and Magician are twin aspects of the involuting/evoluting cosmic uroboros. The Fool's waist is encompassed by twelve lights, corresponding to the celestial zodiac. Below is his chthonic aspect, the Magician's waist engirdled by a *serpent* uroboros. The Magician points above and below, reminding us that the descent will continue down the 15 steps to the depths of the nigredo in the abyss known as Hell. The symbols on the table before him are the symbols of the four Tarot suits, also of the four elements; thus the Unmanifest Zero appears as the manifest One in the elemental world. Along with the descent, the One now faces *multiplicity* of form.

Now let us consider the dog with The Fool, since the Marseilles deck shows a dog biting him. We know that the European period of history out of which Tarot evolved had a strongly alchemical undercurrent. Since we have established the parallel between Mercurius and the Fool/Juggler/Magician, when we learn that "the dog is also the symbol for Mercury,"[114] it is evident that man's best friend does not appear accidentally as companion to the fool. Furthermore, since the Hermes of Greek mythology and dog-headed Thoth of Egypt are ancient prototypes of the Mercurius of alchemy, Manly Hall's words are relevant to an interpretation of the companionship of fool and dog. "Cynocephalus, the dog-headed ape," he writes, "was the Egyptian hieroglyphic symbol of writing, and was closely associated with Thoth. Mercury rules the astrological Third House of writing and communication. Cynocephalus is symbolic of the moon and Thoth of the planet Mercury. Because of the ancient belief that the moon followed Mercury about the heavens, the dog-ape was described as the faithful companion of Thoth."[115]

Like Hermes/Mercurius/Thoth, the dog has a guiding role. Also, since our dog is white, he is linked symbolically with the lunar, quicksilver aspects of Mercurius. The spirit Mercurius has its equivalent in the Gnostic Logos, and since dog = Mercurius, we may also say dog = Logos. This is substantiated by Hippolytus; in the *Elenchos* we read: "*For the Logos is a dog* who guards and protects the sheep against the wiles of the wolves, and chases the wild beasts from Creation and slays them, and begets all Things. For Cyon, they say, means the Begetter."[116]

Hippolytus continues: "But with the rising of the Dog-star, the living are distinguished by the Dog from the dead, for in truth everything withers that has not taken root. *This Dog, they say, being a certain divine Logos,* has been established judge of the quick and the dead, and as the Dog is seen to be the star of the planets, so in the Logos, they say, in respect of the heavenly planets, which are men. For this reason the Second Creation Cynosura stands in heaven as an image of the rational creature."[117] In this passage we have perhaps the precursor of the *Emerald Tablet*'s "As above, so below."

A second look at The Moon with regard to dog and wolf definitely establishes the alchemical symbology of this card. We must remember that Western alchemy has its origins in Egyptian sources. Jung tells us that symbolic interpretations of the dog "entered western alchemy in Kalid's 'Liber secretorum,' originally, perhaps, an Arabic treatise. All similar passages . . . go back directly or indirectly, to Kalid [c. 700]. The original passage runs:

> Hermes said, My son, take a Corascene dog and an Armenian bitch, join them together, and they will beget a dog of celestial hue, and if ever he is thirsty, give him sea water to drink: for he will guard your friend, and he will guard you from your enemy, and he will help you wherever you may be, always being with you, in this world and in the next. And by dog and bitch, Hermes meant things which preserve bodies from burning and from the heat of the fire.

Some of the quotations are taken from the original text, others from the variant in the *Rosarium,* which runs:

> Hali, philosopher and king of Arabia, says in his Secret: Take a Coetanean dog and an Armenian bitch, join them together, and they two will beget for you a puppy [filius canis] of celestial hue: and that puppy will guard you in your house from the beginning, in this world and in the next.

As explanatory parallels, the *Rosarium* mentions the

union of the white and red, and cites Senior: 'The red slave has wedded the white woman.' It is clear that the mating must refer to the royal marriage of Sol and Luna."[118]

In an analysis of a patient's dream, Jung subsequently mentions Gabricus and Beya, usually depicted as two dogs, one devouring the other; in the same way the moon swallows the sun. Key 18 says the same thing twice through the two dogs and also through the *coniunctio*. To my mind, this leaves no doubt about Tarot's alchemical persuasion, although previous texts on Tarot have not delineated the alchemical symbols. For example, in regard to The Moon, authors speak of the animals as symbolic of lower instincts. At the same time, they miss the crucial fact that sun and moon are in conjunction. The most unenlightened view of all is simply that dogs bay at the moon; hence their presence in Key 18.

Waite, however, says absolutely nothing in his explanation which possibly would reveal the card's esoteric meaning. Given his vast knowledge of alchemy, we may then ask, why the change of the two dogs (Gabricus and Beya) in the Marseilles Tarot into dog and wolf? By the leaden-colored wolf, Waite reminds us esoterically of the devouring aspect of the conjunction. Moon swallows sun at the eclipse just as wolf as Saturn/*prima materia* "has an appetite for the king." Rex is also Leo (lion), the sign which the sun rules. "Luna is the 'shadow of the sun, and with corruptible bodies she is consumed, and through her corruption . . . is the Lion eclipsed.'"[119] Corruption has its analogy in alchemical *putrefactio;* so the wolf is an apt symbol for *prima materia* as chaos, grinding, mutilating, indeed, torturing the spiritual gold. In the same way Christ as Logos is tortured on the cross, that is, the elemental world. The Marseilles version of Death is particularly gruesome, the skeletal reaper surrounded by a field of amputated heads, hands, and feet. But we must remember that the process of sun/spirit's descent to earth refines the gold, and the bodies sown in the earth will have their resurrection (Key 20), just as the sun/spirit will be reborn from the earth as ascended gold, and Mer-

150

curius born of the *hierosgamos* of sun and moon. "In alchemy . . . a dog devoured by a wolf represents the purification of gold by means of antimony."[120] Since antimony has the same symbol as that for earth, $\oplus$, the parallel is manifest of the action of earth on sun to produce gold, the planet in the earth, and the action of earthly life on spirit (One) to promote ascended consciousness. Sun, in becoming gold in the earth, retains its same symbol, $\odot$ standing for both. Similarly, the descending spiritual One, 1, interpenetrating salt of the earth, $\ominus$, becomes antimony, $\oplus$, as well as world, $\oplus$, in our earlier formula.

Returning to the Marseilles version of The Fool, since dog and fool are aspects of the Logos, what is the meaning of the dog's biting the buttocks (tail) of the fool? It appears that this is a variant uroborus, the serpent biting its tail. At all events, here the dog is the chthonic, dangerous aspect of the Logos principle. And Jung concludes, "Because of its rich symbolic context the dog is an apt synonym for the transforming substance."[121]

There are two rather remarkable variations on The Fool which we shall treat because they have additional symbols which corroborate our interpretation, and there is some evidence as well that the two men who created these decks had access to the same Hermetic material utilized by the Golden Dawn and A. E. Waite. Paul Christian's pseudo-Egyptian deck is 19th century, and Oswald Wirth's appears about the same time as Waite's deck. Both Fool cards contain a crocodile.

In the Egyptian judgment of the dead, to the crocodile-god known as "The Devourer"[122] were thrown the hearts of those found guilty; and indeed, Paul Christian's Fool card is entitled "The Crocodile: Expiation." The Wirth Arcanum 0 also contains a crocodile, and a white lynx biting the fool. Associated concepts accent the destructive power of jaws, like wolf and dog. In this sense, the connection to abyss is clear. Abyss also signifies chaos, that is, one is rendered into many parts, or phrased numerically, One is divided (duality) and then scattered in many parts (multiplicity). Abyss = Logos, or the solar spiritual principle. Wirth's Key 0 also contains an obelisk, which Cirlot tells us is a solar symbol; thus, "the Logos . . . must be returned to chaos."[123] Instead of an obelisk, Waite depicts the sun, which other decks do not.

Let us examine in detail a small area of Waite's Key 13, as shown below.

DRAWING 13.

Obviously there is an affinity between the two towers and the sun. They appear again in The Moon, when the sun is devoured by Beya (Moon). The fool descends to death, Key 13, and an equation for the Logos runs as follows: Logos = Fool/dog/sun/obelisk. We may then look in Waite for the crocodile of Paul Christian's and Oswald Wirth's earlier decks, and this figure is to be found disguised in the form of the cleric's miter in Death (see above). Now if the crocodile represents chaos, *prima materia*, as does the wolf, the Logos "returned to chaos" is represented by the proximity to the sun of the crocodile shape. One is given the impression that the sun is sinking into its jaws and about to be devoured. Again this seems to substantiate the Magic Nine arrangement, since these symbols properly belong in The Fool, which says the same thing in another way, by utilizing the abyss. Waite's Key 13 anticipates the descent (return) of Logos to chaos.

In the creation myths of the world's origin, the World-Egg (0) is said to have been engendered by Chaos and Wind, the latter being nothing less than the Logos, or God's creative Word. In other languages, equivalent words are Latin *spiritus*, as in *spiritus mercurialis*, *prana* (Sanskrit), and *Pneuma* (Greek). In a Gnostic creation myth, the creator is known as Saklas, The Fool, which is perhaps one reason for associating the creative principle with the name "Fool." Our own belief is that the medieval tradition of fool as scapegoat is linked to the early rituals of sacrifice of the solar gods. Sir James Frazer has written on this in *The Golden Bough,* and we shall explore this relevant to our astrological run-through of the Major Arcana.

As to taking the title "Fool" literally, the reader of Tarot who does this is himself the fool. In *Maps of Consciousness* Ralph Metzner cannot be further off the path in saying of Waite's The Fool, "But in the Tarot path he has no place, no number, and is not on the path. He is usually depicted as a carefree young man, wearing a richly embroidered tunic; with his face up in the air, he is about to step off the edge of a precipice. He is caught in dreams and images, self-created fantasies preventing him from seeing the world as it actually is, which *may* plunge him to his death. Note that he has not yet fallen off the precipice; but he may very well unless he wakes up."[124] Perhaps Metzner should wake up. Talk about taking symbols at face value! He continues, "in some decks he is called *le mat*, the materialist, and indeed his sumptuous clothes indicate great interest in externals."[125]

Who ever heard of a materialist in motley? The fool's garb is not exactly the social prescription for materialistic success. We have called attention to the belt and the reproduction of the eight-spoked Wheel of Fortune. It may be added that this design appears in ten places on the fool's tunic, and that is the number of the Wheel of Fortune. Ten also reduces (descends) to one (the One), which is what the fool is about to do in manifesting as One, The Magician. The eight-spoked wheel is analogous to alchemical process, as Drawing 14 demonstrates.

Furthermore, the fool is the *spiritus mercurialis* born of the celestial *hierosgamos* who appears as the child in The Sun. The descending spiritual trine composed of the three points of his nipples and navel is reproduced on the chest of the fool by three of the ten wheel glyphs. The eight-spoked wheel motif is also the Stairway of Planets (7) plus the Ogdoad, the eighth star in The Star, which is the Highest of the high, akin to the Gnostic Pleroma wherein dwells the formative creative power before manifestation. In conclusion, as to whether the fool ranks high or low spiritually, if one were to forget all that we have delineated heretofore, one symbol of perfection remains. "The single rose [which the fool carries] is, in essence, a symbol of completion, consummate achievement and perfection. . . . The mystic Centre [hence Zero]."[126] And, finally, the Masonic All-Seeing Eye on the fool's wallet is akin to the Egyptian Eye of Horus, enlightened vision transcending the material plane and opening onto the light of eternity.

The Fool is not to be thought of as an actual man; rather the card stands for the abstractions we have discussed. Even in physical manifestations such as the sun, dual concepts are involved, the body and spirit which created the material Sun. For example, Helios was a name given to *the* sun, and also to the *divinity* of the sun. We noted Saturn as the *sol niger* that swallows the sun at the abyss of the winter

DRAWING 14

solstice. The crocodile who may devour the fool parallels the abyss in Waite and has relations to Hell, Saturn, and the Christian Devil. According to the "Magic Papyri," in the second hour Helios takes the form of a dog; thus solar/Logos = dog, an equation we have seen in Gnosticism. But then we learn, "In the twelfth hour he appears as a crocodile."[127] This must be midnight, not noon, when the dark, chthonic aspect of the One swallows the sun.

To the Christian mind, a reorientation of thinking is required because the antagonist principle is deemed evil and rejected (damned). But in Hermeticism and Jungian psychology, the seeming destruction which the antagonist wreaks (death, swallowing, dismemberment, etc.) works to the will of the One in accomplishing the higher purpose of integration and rebirth. Relevant to Tarot interpretation, the reader may say that personal adversity has a long-range regenerative effect.

Now let us push the fool over the brink, assigning a temporal quality to the descent, so that—like the Gnostics—the descent to matter is seen as a death of spirit. Reversing the vertical line of ascent in Keys 4, 13, and 0, the fool descends to Death, Key 13, and from there to Key 4. Or if the uroboros follows its winding, serpent shape, Zero manifests as One. The Monad and Key 4 are similar. Key 1 contains the symbols of the elemental world, the *four* suits being equivalent as follows: earth = pentacles, cups = water, swords = fire, and wands = air. In Key 4, the cubic form of the emperor's throne symbolizes the basic shape of matter, as well as the *four* elements and directions which constitute our mundane plane.

Since human thought is linear and sequential, it is at this point that gnashing of teeth may begin for "fallen" spirit; yet if we recall again Dorn in his *"Philosophia speculativa,"* "The descent to the four and the ascent to the monad are simultaneous."[128] Viewing the Magic Nine arrangement, the fool *simultaneously* descends and ascends. Up and down are all at once! The reborn homunculus of The Sun may descend to the denarius (Key 10) as the golden serpent, and thence to the Monad (Key 1), or the Monad may ascend to the denarius. So, too, for all our vertical series. The insight we may draw from this is that spirit interpenetrates matter always, there being no such thing as empty or dead matter. In psychological terms, when we feel particularly leaden we must remember that the spiritual self resides *in potentia* within the unconscious, awaiting the transmutation of consciousness that will effect its liberation.

Since we commenced our examination of alchemical elements in the Major Arcana with the cards of ascent, let us now analyze Keys 1-15.

In Key 1, Mercurius (the Monad) is as yet undivided. His form integrates fiery, active sulphur and moist, passive quicksilver; or, in the other scheme we have seen, spiritual sulphur and mundane salt. Too, being androgyne he is a *coniunctio* already.

By Key 2 he becomes his feminine opposite, first emanation from the original One. Yet, again, in all the forms of multiplicity and polar opposition, we are to cling to the underlying harmony which our senses all too easily refute. Between the polar opposites (pillars) we see either a veil of embroidered pomegranates or an actual garden of pomegranates. In the Bible, this fruit is "a symbol of the oneness of the universe."[129]

Psychologically, The High Priestess represents the dark antagonist to light (consciousness). As moon she will swallow the sun in the *coniunctio*. The pillars in the card present the pairs of opposites as light and dark, and this is apt symbology since spirit = Light, and the descent to matter is regarded as a darkness (*nigredo*). But darkness is the womb or matrix for light (spirit), which is conceived when darkness reaches its maximum. Key 2 reminds us of underlying unity through the active, solar colors in the pomegranates, the solar cross on the priestess' breast, and the solar globe resting in the crescent moon of her crown. But primarily this is a lunar card because of the white and blue robe, colors for moonlight and water, which element the moon rules in the sign of Cancer. Alchemically those qualities of matter associated with the moon are moistness and coolness, opposed to the sun's heat and dryness.

A great paradox is contained in Key 2. In connection with this card, antagonist is also redemptrix. Waite speaks of "the Sanctuary of Isis."[130] According to Jung, she "unites the hostile elements into one. This synthesis is described in the myth of Isis, 'who collected the scattered limbs of his body [Osiris'] and bathed them with her tears and laid them in a secret grave beneath the bank of the Nile.' The cognomen of Isis was . . . the Black One. . . . She signifies earth . . . and was equated with Sophia. . . . She is named . . . the redemptrix.

"All these statements apply just as well to the prima materia in its feminine aspect: it is the moon, the mother of all things, the vessel, it consists of opposites, has a thousand names . . . it contains the elixir of life in potentia and is the mother of the Saviour and the *filius Macrocosmi,* it is the earth and the serpent hidden in the earth, the blackness and the dew and the miraculous water which brings together all that is divided. The water is therefore called 'mother,' 'my mother who is my enemy,' but who also 'gathers together all my divided and scattered limbs.' "[131]

Isis has so many universal associations that her presence is justified perhaps in the European Tarot pack. She even has a relation to the Stairway of Planets and the seven metals. "At the top of the tree is the lapis. Its father is 'Gabritius,' who in turn was born of Isis and Osiris. After the death of Osiris Isis married their son Gabritius; she is identified with Beya—'the widow marries her son.' "[132] Since Horus is the traditional son of Isis and Osiris, Gabritius corresponds to the son of god; yet his marriage (*coniunctio*) with the mother suggests that—like the uroboros—the god is capable of self-renewal. Alchemically this is correct in that the King's son is apparently the King in renewed form. In the same way the child in Key 19, born of the *hierosgamos* of sun and moon in Key 18, will later mate with mother moon in a subsequent conjunction. Implicit in these symbols is the cyclical nature of regeneration: "'The form of the birth is a turning wheel, which Mercurius causes in the sulphur.' The 'birth' is the 'golden child' (*filius philosophorum* = archetype of the divine child) [= Self] whose 'master-workman' is Mercurius. Mercurius himself is the 'fiery wheel of the essence' in the form of a serpent."[133] Mercurius, then, is his own father, as in Keys 19 and 1.

In reading Tarot, The High Priestess may stand for an anima encounter in a man's life, in which case consciousness is possessed (swallowed) by the unconscious arche-type. The next vertical card, Key 11, depicts the scales, in-dicating that in the psychological realm an equilibration must be sought. In alchemy, the high priestess of the work is the *soror* to whom the alchemist is wedded. That is to say, the anima has been brought into partial consciousness so that she can be a partner in the Great Work, which can never succeed without commencing from some measure of psychic wholeness.

In an abstract sense, Key 2 is Ator, Nature, world, and *prima materia* personified. In this way she is thought of as antagonist to formless spirit, if one forgets that the two are always married (in union) through spirit's immanence in matter.

As we have said, a trinity resolves a dichotomy, and is born of the world (3 + 9 = 12 + 9 = 21 The World). Sol/sulphur/spirit appears in the red covering of the Empress' throne, balanced by the Luna/quicksilver/soul attributes of her white gown.

The union of above and below is evident in Key 3, since the Empress wears a starry diadem of twelve stars for the zodiac, while she wields the sceptre of earthly autonomy. Below, at her feet, is the grayness of the nigredo. Sprinkling her gown are blossoms in the shape of Venus glyphs to sug-gest the erotic element that entices spirit to wed matter. We noted spirit's connection to the inverted water trine which descends to earth. Here in Key 3 the water *falls* to earth, uniting above and below. As does the Empress, earth be-comes fertile from spirit's action, resulting in the flourish-ing wheat surrounding her. Golden grain sprouting from the earth conveys the same meaning as the metal gold "grow-ing" in the earth as a result of the descent of the sun; thus woman = earth, both "clothed in the sun."

The vertical series 3, 12, 21, resolves the life-and-death tension created by the polar opposites of series 2, 11, 20. The "new birth" is the salvation, and the elemental world exalted to the macrocosm with *anima mundi* in Key 21.

Key 4, The Emperor, stands for the leaden grip of Physis, just as does The Devil in Key 15. One rules on the meso-cosm plane of man, the other is the supreme ruler of the underworld. The dead are the property of The Devil until resurrection. In the vertical sequence 4 + 9 = 13, Death, the underworld commences with 13 and moves linearly to Key 15. But above Death rules The Fool, or pure spirit; hence we have planes heavenly, hellish, and mundane. The Fool requires no throne or form at all, since he is a personified abstraction. The emperor and devil sit on cubic thrones. As to the symbolical import of the cube, "Among solid forms, it is the equivalent of the square [Key 4]. Hence, it stands for earth, or the material world of the four elements . . . cubic objects are not capable of rotation as are spheres, and therefore they represent stability."[134] This stability, or the all-too-solid grip of Physis upon Nous, must be shattered, as in The Tower, which itself has a *cubic* form. Esoterically we may say that the emperor is not the father of the child to be born of the empress. Her fertilization is celestial in origin.

Lest the dichotomy between matter and spirit seem too great, let us recall that in alchemy all opposites contain an element of the other. The cube is the glyph for salt, which we saw as both *lapis* and *prima materia.* Jane Leade, an English mystic of the 17th century, presents the psychic implications of the cube's meaning. (Jung, of course, equates this stone with the self.) "Hereupon I was moved (because I well knew and was certain that this heavenly stone already had its birth and growth in me) [Rebirth = the cubical stone's change from potentiality to actuality]."[135]

If Key 4 is primarily the elemental world, and lapis only *in potentia,* Key 5 restores the balance by adding the One. Keys 1 and 5 have many common elements, obstensibly the red and white robes.

There are also the gestures, the hierophant giving "the well-known ecclesiastical sign which is called that of esotericism, distinguishing between the manifest and concealed part of doctrine." Waite also calls him "the ruling power of external religion."[136] Whereas the hierophant may pass on external religious tradition, the magician functions as shaman, inviting the initiate to "go it alone." A close scrutiny of the garments of the hierophant's attendant monks reveals the red roses and while lilies of Key One's rose garden. This garden is alone sufficient to convey the esoteric meaning of Key 1, and to set the tone for the entire

Major Arcana. " 'Rose garden' . . . was a name applied apparently to alchemistic lodges. The philosophical work itself is compared to the rose, the white rose is the white tincture [albedo], the red rose is the red tincture [rubedo] . . ."[137]

By changing the white roses to lilies, Waite avoids the charge of giving away lodge secrets, and his explanation of the garden again scatters dust in the eyes of the uninitiated. "Beneath are roses and lilies, the *flos campi* and *lillium convallium*, changed into garden flowers, to shew the culture of aspiration."[138] But we have seen that the fool in descending brings to the magician a single white rose. Since fool and magician are dual aspects of Mercurius, it is as if two sides of one picture are put back together to supply the garden of red and white roses. Furthermore, Key One may be associated with Mercurius' active nature because it presents *red* roses and commences the numerical cycle which will be swallowed into nothingness by Zero. According to Herbert Silberer's *Hidden Symbolism of Alchemy and the Occult Arts*, "As the circle symbolized the all and the eternal or the celestial unity of all, and the divinity, so the number one, the single line, the staff or the scepter, represented the terrestrial copy of the power, the ruling, guiding, sustaining and protecting force of the personality that had attained freedom on earth."[139] Again we see the connection between The Fool and The Magician.

Now the connection between Keys 1 and 5 is based upon some very deep esotericism indeed. Even more interesting is the line between Key 5 and the vertical series 4, 13, and 0, because Keys 13 and 0 each contain a white rose; yet in Key 1 Waite substitutes lilies for white roses to disguise the alchemistic rosegarden.

What can we say about the number 5? It may be rendered as a pentagram, which we noted earlier, but when four is depicted as a square, rectangle, or cube, the addition of the one to make five may be symbolized by a dot within the cube. This is the Mystic Centre and also the glyph for sun and gold, when placed within a circle. The One then has a circular rather than linear form. In the glyph for the lapis, the circle enfolds the elemental square, being another variation of 5 (4 + 1 = 5). The lapis is also known as the *quinta essentia,* similar to a *fifth* element that merges and resolves the polar oppositions, and in this way is linked to Mercurius, who contains and reconciles all antitheses.

In terms of Masonic rite, in which the metaphor of building stands for personal transformation, a rectangular glyph represents the lodge. The addition of the One in the form of a center (spirit) may symbolize "in antithesis to the terrestrial house of God, the temple built with hands, . . . the holy number five denoted the celestial abodes of the souls that had attained perfection, and therefore represented both the House of Eternity or the City of God and the Heavenly Jerusalem. The holy pentagram in the form of the rose, not only in the ancient but in the early Christian world, decorated the graves of the dead, that in their turn symbolized the gardens of the blessed."[140]

What this means in terms of Key 5 is that God (as One) has been placed in the House of God. At the feet of the hierophant we see four symbols, each containing a cross enfolded by the circle of the infinite One. We saw this before as the One (1) descending to salt $\ominus$ to make the glyph for earth and the Host $\oplus$; thus the four of the elemental world, encompassed by the infinite, yields five. Another interpretation of this equates the hierophant himself with Spirit, since his throne contains the four $\oplus$ symbols, and he makes up the *quinta essentia*. His red robe is the color of sulphur, sun, spirit; yet like Key 1 this card and the vertical series of both Keys 1 and 5 comprise a union of opposites.

If we examine the black banner of death, we note that the white rose has five petals, as it should symbolically. Also, the square banner (4) contains the rose's mystic center, making it a symbol for five. Accoding to Silberer, "the number five is symbolized by five-leaved plants (rose, lily, vine)."[141] The reason for the appearance of the white rose in Death, and white lilies in The Hierophant, is to clearly present an idea of spiritual resurrection. In other words, the eternal One is reborn from the elemental four. This suggests a new numerical cycle, which is exactly what commences with number five, and we shall touch on that very soon.

Waite's intent of resurrection in Death is substantiated by two more symbols, which also corroborate the Magic Nine arrangement. Death wears a red, feathery plume atop his

162

helm. Beneath this card is The Fool, and he wears a red feather. The significance of the feather was discussed previously as the ideogram for Maat, who presided at the weighing of souls, that is, the judgment of the dead. Before the figure of Death stands a cleric in golden robes, gold being the color we have equated with the eternal, spiritual principle, the reborn sun, and gold reborn from the "death" of the nigredo condition. Over the cleric's head, this reborn sun appears between two grey towers, the same two that frame the *hierosgamos* in The Moon. Now in the next series the cleric appears as The Hierophant in Key 5, and he sits between two grey pillars. Are we not to assume that he is in a reborn or spiritual condition?

Recalling our association of colors with the three primary alchemical conditions, *nigredo*, *albedo*, *rubedo*, we may say that the rebirth of *albedo* from *nigredo* is prefigured by the white rose on the black banner. Indeed, Key 13 is the first card in the series 13-15 (*nigredo*), while Key 18 is the last card in the *albedo* series (16-18). The two grey towers appear in cards that commence and terminate these conditions.

What of the grey pillars? Analyzing this color, we may say that it blends black and white, the yin/yang opposition of Key 2. Additionally, the semicircular crowns atop the phallic pillars present a lingam-and-yoni symbology, the union of masculine and feminine. Key 5, therefore, presents the symbology of a *hierosgamos*. We have seen how five is 4 + 1. The blue color of the High Priestess' gown also appears beneath the red and white garment of the hierophant. Red and white were the empress' colors for throne and gown.

As we have said, color symbology is an aspect of the numerical meaning of a card, The Hierophant containing a triangle and two pillars as a graphic expression of the archetype of five. The numerical meaning of five enforces this. According to Cirlot, "the *hierosgamos* is signified by the number five, since it represents the union of the principle of heaven (three) with that of the *Magna Mater* (two)."[142]

Other pairs of opposites resolved by Key 5 are those of above and below, his ecclesiastic role being one of mediation between the heavenly and mundane realms. The last union of opposites occurs in the crossed keys at the feet of the hierophant. Case, himself one of the Golden Dawn in America, explains them: "The crossed keys at the Hierophant's feet are the familiar symbols of the power of The Papacy. Yet they have a deeper meaning. . . .

"The golden key is the key of heaven, wherein the sun is ruler. The silver key is associated with hell because of the correspondence between the Moon and Hecate, whom the Greeks worshipped as a deity of the underworld. Thus the silver key relates to the powers of subconsciousness, and the golden key represents the powers of superconsciousness."[143]

To this we may add, the two keys are the *hierosgamos* of sun and moon, presented with marvelous symbolic economy before its actual appearance in Key 18. But sun and moon have two associative qualities, fire and water, or heat and coldness, which are depicted by two trines, and marry in the lantern of The Hermit, Key 9. From what we have said of yin/yang, lingam/yoni, sulphur/quicksilver, gold/silver, hot/cold, fire/water, above/below, sun/moon, a pattern emerges in regard to the three vertical series (1, 10, 19), (5, 14), (9, 18). Clearly they are all cards of union!

Immediately one begins to look for other patterns in the vertical series which follow a sequential order. If there is a pattern, then the vertical series commencing with Key 2 has its essential meaning repeated after the next union series, which is 4 and 14. Also, we may expect similarities between the series 3, 12, 21, and that of 7 and 16. The following diagram will clarify these vertical patterns in the Magic Nine.

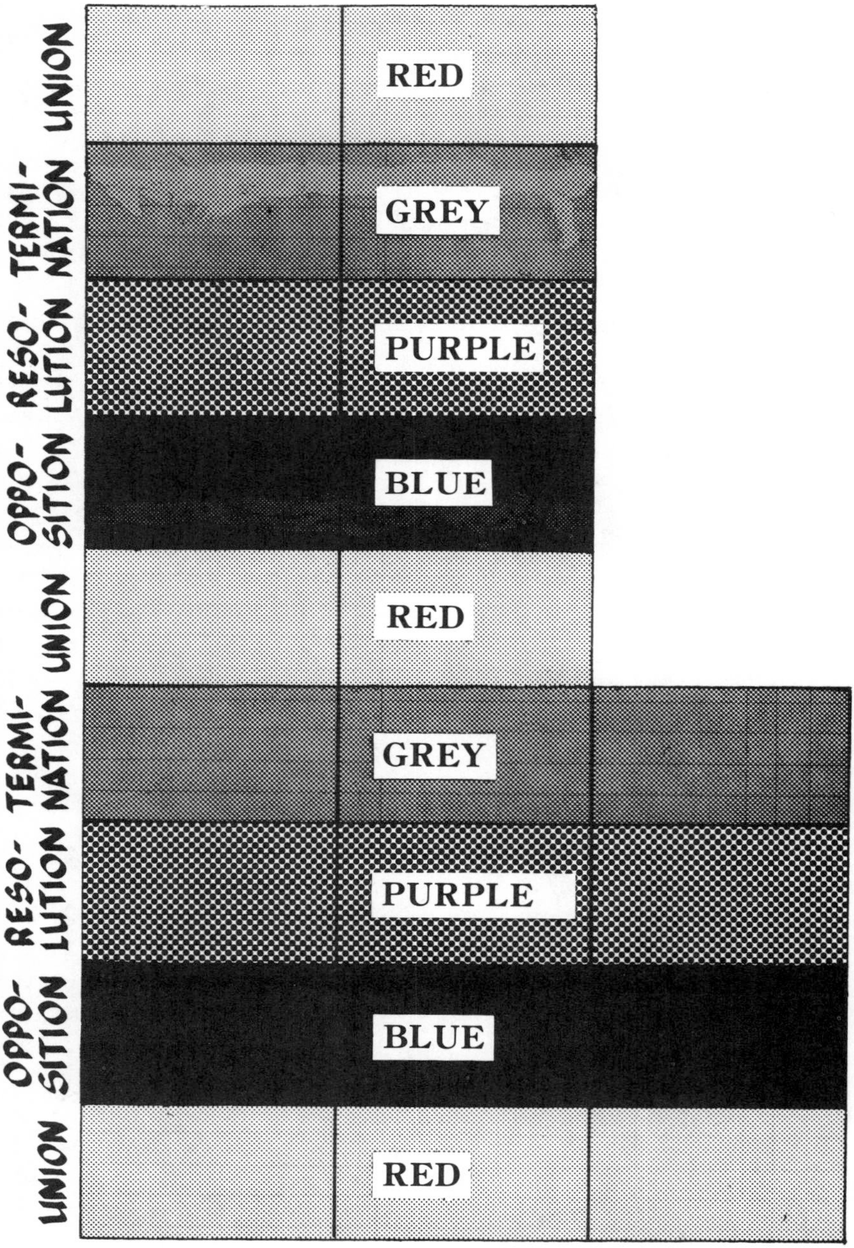
UNION
RED
TERMI-
NATION
GREY
RESO-
LUTION
PURPLE
OPPO-
SITION
BLUE
UNION
RED
TERMI-
NATION
GREY
RESO-
LUTION
PURPLE
OPPO-
SITION
BLUE
UNION
RED

CHAPTER VI

PATTERNS IN THE MAGIC NINE

The patterns are most easily defined by the use of colors in our diagram, although we do not intend to imply that each vertical series is dominated by a single color. Rather, the color delineation separates each series so that the eye may discern the pattern more clearly. Unity and union are in red, opposition in blue, resolution in purple, and termination or fulfillment in grey.

Out of this pattern, we see a sort of miniseries, for numbers one through four constitute a cycle similar to 1-10. The same cycle recommences with Keys 5-8, returning to essential unity in Key 9. After the first cycle (1-4), the spiritual One must initiate a new cycle; thus the hierophant reminds us of another order of reality, which numbers 5-8, and those numbers below them, depict on a transcendent plane. The final vertical sequence is a *coniunctio* of Above and Below in both Keys 9 and 18.

In view of what we have said before, if the reader looks in retrospect at all of the "Union" Keys (1, 10, 19, 5, 14, 9, and 18), the symbology of this unity should be apparent. Now in regard to the Keys of "Opposition," let us have a closer look. Key 2 presents the symbolic pairs of opposites in the pillars, as well as in the feminine principle, antagonist of masculine consciousness. Key 2 contains ideas of antagonism in sword and scales, death or mercy, condemnation or pardon. The vertical series ends with "Judgment," and the underworld yields up its dead to the celestial realm. The next "Opposition" series, Keys 6 and 15, utilize the sexual opposites in addition to the antagonism of the underworld.

In a numerical sense, the "Resolution" sequence adds the One to the antagonism of duality to produce the solution.

We have discussed this relevant to vertical series 3, 12, and 21, and the same ideas prevail in Keys 7 and 16, king and queen, black and white sphinxes standing for the opposites, and charioteer and lightning (as Logos) for the One.

In a sense, four is a numerical cycle that terminates in death (4 + 9 = 13, "Death"), which is to say four is the limit of the *material* order, there being four elements, directions, seasons, etc. Keys 5-8 and their vertical equivalents are *transcendent* in that each card contains symbology of Above and Below. For example, a double four is an eight, completed by its other half; hence, the lemniscate in Key 8. Termination of the series has occurred on a higher plane than in the previous series of four numbers. As in Keys 4 and 13, Keys 8 and 17 do not symbolize an elemental stasis but an equilibrium that has been accomplished by the integration of the antagonist. The resolution is attained in Key 7, sometimes called "Victory," the distant mountain in Key 8 symbolizing successful completion of the opus. Key 17 symbolizes the victory over the planetary archons, since there are seven stars plus the transcendent eighth, the Ogdoad. Eight also has a geometric form which conveys this same meaning, the octagon being "the intermediary form between the square (or the terrestrial order) and the circle (the eternal order)."[144] Again, we must remember that the double sigmoid line of the lemniscate, over the woman's head in Key 8, symbolizes the eternally spiraling movement of the heavens. Finally, nine constitutes "a complete image of the three worlds":[145] macrocosm, microcosm, and meocosm.

Let us return to the center of our Magic Nine arrangement and continue with Temperance, Key 14, the vertical companion of The Hierophant. The tempering referred to in this card is one opposite with another. These were discussed in detail earlier, but in summary they are above (angel) and below (earth), spirit and matter, sun and moon, sulphur and salt. As usual, Waite is his old enigmatic self in describing this card, particularly with sentences such as, "Hereof is some part of the Secret of Eternal Life, as it is possible to man in his incarnation. All the conventional emblems are renounced herein."[146]

To understand better the meaning of this card, it is necessary that we examine what Waite has left *out* of his deck; for the esoteric Tarot of Oswald Wirth colors the chalices silver and gold, to which colors Waite makes no mention, and the current versions of his deck depict both chalices as golden. The significance of this: "The act of pouring denotes the transformation of water as it passes from the lunar order (of silver) to the solar order (of gold), that is, from the world of transient forms and feeling to the world of fixed forms and of reason. . . ."[147]

In the series of Keys 13-15, forms are truly fixed, since this is Saturn's realm, where the metallic order is lowest, heaviest, and most gross. Spirit touches bottom here, so to speak, when "devoured" by Physis. Yet obviously Key 14 does not inspire the same negative connotations as "Death" and "The Devil," between which it mediates. There are also four cards to the left of this card, and four cards to the right, so in the word "temperance" we may read the same sort of equilibrium of opposites which The Hierophant symbolizes. There is also a rather interesting relation to Key 18, The Moon. Since the *hierosgamos* symbolizes a marriage of sexual opposites, and since we associated red with the active masculine principle of sun and sulphur, and white with the passive, feminine element of moon, quicksilver, and salt, the apparel of the angel depicts a marriage of opposites, and even Waite acknowledges that the figure is androgyne, connoting the resolution of sexual opposites. Thus from silver and gold chalices we may infer the *coniunctio* of sun and moon, but even more than that the number fourteen is significant because the sun pours its light into the full moon on the *fourteenth* day of the lunar cycle. The flow between chalices suggests this, since the fluid does not fall down but is attracted on a diagonal from one to another. In the exoteric Marseilles deck, this passage of "water" is even more lateral. We are not to take the mysteries of the Major Arcana at face value when the laws of gravity are defied, so an "odic force" or spiritual essence is transferred from above, solar chalice, to lunar chalice, below, underworld, the female, receptive/passive realm of earth. The Marseilles deck also utilizes red and blue pitchers, blue having all the same associations as silver. Indeed, the Waite pack of ten years ago lined the upper half of the angel's red wings with a blue edge, whereas now the wings are purple, the union of red and blue. This current Waite deck also features not only iris, symbolizing the goddess of the rainbow, but an actual rainbow crowning the angel. As water and light in union, a rainbow suggests "above," and it has a relation to the peacock's tail in that the full spectrum of colors symbolized the *lapis'* manifestation. In Key 14 spirit (above) manifests as an angel on earth (below), the hierophant being the mediator on earth for spirit, its representative *below.* In keeping with his role his crown is gold, which we said symbolized the celestial order of the spiritual realm. Instead of a metallic crown, the angel bears on his forehead the symbol for both gold and sun, while a solar "crown" conjoins with the dual peaks of earth in the background. Thus the meaning of the marriage of four and three, square and trine on the angel's breast, is restated many times in this card, commencing with the angel's feet, one on earth and one in water (spirit); and moving up to the angel's crown, we see the head outlined by a golden nimbus like that surrounding the head of the hanged man, whom we said was sun (spirit) descending to earth (nigredo, Physis), Keys 13-15. In Drawing 15, the solar crown (One) of Key 14 is "swallowed" by duality, the feminine Dyad of matter, in the same abyss to which the fool descends in Key 0, and in the same way in the adjacent card, Key 13, that the sun sinks between the two pillars of the pairs of opposites and appears to be swallowed by the "crocodile" miter of the clergyman. Facetiously we may say that church dogma engulfs the spiritual essence of a religion, but this is playing with words, perhaps justified in that Tarot is playing with cards.

At all events the sequence of crowns is most interesting; for in "Death" the emperor (of Key 4) loses his crown. Note the sprawled body with fallen crown. The miter of Key 13 which swallowed the sun becomes the golden crown of the hierophant, he being the mundane representative of spirit on earth, as gold is the material manifestation of the sun (spirit). But gold is spirit fixed, and the spiritual sun craves liberation from the leaden bonds of Physis, Key 15. The alchemical fire in the athanor (oven) is the means of separating the king and queen, Key 16, "The Tower," or the

DRAWING 15.

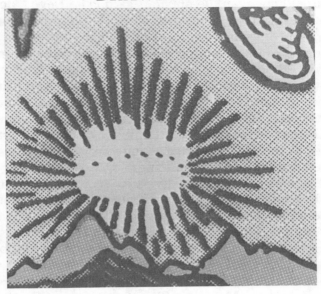

One from the two, or the king from the wolf (devil) who has devoured him, as in the previous card, The Devil. Alchemically the most common metaphor of this process is the separation of gold from lead, and "The Tower" in both Waite and Marseilles presents a crown dislodged from the material edifice. Waite obviously equates his golden crown with the solar principle separated from matter and restored to spiritual autonomy. Thus in the tale the crowns alone tell, we may read the descent of spirit to matter, above in union with below. After this liberation in Key 16, henceforth no figures of the Major Arcana require crowns, garlands and the red feather of truth sufficing.

Let us move on to the next vertical sequence, Keys 6 and 15, which introduce the theme of "Opposition"; thus there is a relation to the column of Keys 2, 11, and 20. Six consists of two and four (feminine and masculine, priestess and emperor); five and one, the mediation of above and below attained in five (man) now canceled by new duality as the One seeks another, more transcendent form. This opposition is manifest in the Marseilles Tarot in the personifications of Virtue and Vice, ugly and comely maidens between whom the lover must choose. In a way, the Tarot reader is inserted into the card in the form of the Lover. Above his head is Cupid, his arrow about to fly. Cupid's presence substantiates our attribution of Keys 4-6 to Venus, goddess of love. Waite substitutes an angel for Cupid, and Paul Foster Case, the American mentor of the Golden Dawn, defines the angel as "Raphael, angel of air, the element attributed to Gemini."[148] Gemini is of course the zodiacal sign of The Twins, themselves at once complementary and antagonistic. The glyph for Gemini presents a symbolic picture of the two pillars of Key 2, Boaz and Jachin. These pillars recall *all* the pairs of opposites because they are light and dark. In Key 6 Waite cleverly converts them to "the Tree of Life, bearing twelve fruits, and the Tree of the Knowledge of Good and Evil,"[149] that is, the Tree of Death, since eating its fruit brought expulsion from the eternal paradise. The opposition/antagonism theme of Key 6 is repeated in its vertical companion (6 + 9 = 15), since Key 6 depicts Paradise and Key 15 Hell. Although at first glance Key 6 seems to introduce a Biblical theme very far afield from alchemy, this is not the case. The liberation of King and Queen which occurs in the next series (7 + 9 = 16) has a definite alchemical relation to the lovers and their bondage in Key 15. According to Jung, "Like the King and Queen, our first parents are among those figures through whom the alchemists expressed the symbolism of opposites."[150] Indeed, Adam is known in alchemy as the first Adept, which links him to Key One, which we described as the adept/alchemist. Further, Adam has a parallel to Hermes/ Mercurius, since he is androgyne, bearing Eve from his own body.

But the theme of column 6 and 15 is not the same as the series of Key One, being opposition not unity. As Adam (One) bears Eve from his body, the One bears Two, the feminine Dyad of multiplicity—hence the correlation to Keys 2, 11, and 20.

These "Opposition/antagonism" columns have also a horned motif in common, horns appearing in none other of the vertical columns. "The High Priestess" contains the solar/lunar crown as well as the Taurean horns, while "The Devil" is of course crowned with goat horns, and the damned Adam and Eve now wear horns. The significance of the horned motif will be more apparent in our astrological perusal of the Major Arcana, but the connection with the Gemini myth of duality has to do with the polar opposites of summer and winter solstices, spring and autumn equinoxes. Horns symbolize the crescent moon, and the lunar/chthonic antagonism to the solar/spiritual principle. The equinoxes represent the points of descent/ascent to and from the underworld by the sun. Key 6 portrays the sun at the meridian, equivalent to the then summer solstice in Leo. Key 15 is the polar opposite, Capricorn as devil with the firebrand inverted, symbolizing solar fire at the abyss of the nigredo. Alchemically this "devil" is *sol niger*, lead, in which gold is immanent. The horned god Hermes/Mercurius—in that he integrates all opposites—is equally at home above or below in the underworld, and as such is the appropriate guide for the human soul.

Key 6 also contains the alchemical opposites of earth and air, Raphael being the angel of air, depicted by Waite as emerging from clouds, while the mountain in the background symbolizes the earthly opus, replete with all the planets in the earth (metals) necessary to accomplish the alchemical transformation. Cirlot notes that "In alchemy... the reference is nearly always to the hollow mountain, the hollow being a cavern which is the 'philosopher's oven.' The vertical axis of the mountain drawn from its peak down to its base links it with the world-axis. . . . As in the case of the cross or the Cosmic Tree, the location of this mountain is at the 'Centre' of the world."[151]

From meridian to abyss, the world-axis is the line of descent of the Fool and of the sun from summer to winter solstice. The root of the mountain is in Hell, as the *prima materia* for the gold is lead. In psychological terms, the tip of the mountain protruding above the surface may be likened to the ego, whereas the unfathomable depths below are akin to the unconscious. Quite simply put, mountain unites above and below, and since this union is a prerequisite for accomplishing the Great Work, mountain is an apt symbol for the opus.

Besides the horn motif, the "Opposition/antagonism" columns have another common element. In unity there is no necessity for choice since all is harmony, all opposites flowing into one another, as in the chalices of the angel in "Temperance." With separation comes a consciousness of distinctions, and judgments must be made. This theme underlies all five cards of the "Opposition" columns.

In Key 2 duality appears in the pillars and the lunar priestess contraposed to the solar centre wherein there is only Oneness. The "Law" which she holds is the message of Tarot, the necessity of finding equilibrium between the pairs of opposites by bringing them together in marriage or *hierosgamos*. Justice, we again remind the reader, was changed from Key 8 to 11 by Waite, and the propriety is demonstrated by its place in the judgment theme of Keys 2, 11, and 20.

Key 6 presents the mythic picture of what was perhaps man's first judgment, that in the Garden of Paradise. The conscious decision to obey the serpent and disobey God (Yahweh or Ialdabaoth, since we have equated the serpent with the Hermetic God) leads to the negative judgment of damnation upon the Lovers (6 + 9 = 15). Paradise may be likened to free will, and Hell to the no-choice situation portrayed in Key 15, the five-pointed star of man inverted to denote subservience of the conscious will to the devil.

But if Raphael appears in God's stead in the esoteric version of "The Lovers," what are we to make of the equivalence of Raphael and serpent in Origen's "Diagramma of the Ophites" cited in his attack against Celsus. The seventh archon was Ialdabaoth, "child of chaos," who had the form of an ass. Chaos, or the abyss of the nigredo, is the nadir represented by Key 15, so there is a correspondence between this devil and the God of the Old Testament. As we know, three of the other archons correspond in form to three of the apostles, their symbols being lion, bull, and eagle. Since Raphael is the angel of elemental air, his relation is to Aquarius, representing the fixed sign for Air. Therefore, in Key 6, serpent and angel may stand for chthonic and celestial aspects of this one principle which has an evolutive effect on the primal parents.

Besides his androgynous nature, Adam has other similarities with Mercurius. The name Adam adds to 360, the number of degrees in the zodiac, suggesting his relation to the Anthropos, or universal man. Too, he is created from the four elements, and like Mercurius is both good and evil, the latter characteristic symbolized by horns and tail in Key 15. Jung tells us that "According to a Rabbinic view Adam even had a tail."[152] This integration of opposites equates Adam with Mercurius; yet the real significance of this is the identification of both with the lapis, or transforming substance, which is the end product of the opus. This brings us to the relation of Key 6 to Key 7, the seventh step in the alchemical process and the last "step" of the Stairway of Planets. Besides The Chariot, Key 7 has been called "Victory," that is, the attained goal, which is the arcane substance. Interestingly enough, another esoteric title for Key 7 is "The Chariot of Antimony." Alchemically, antimony works upon lead to release the gold. If Adam = the arcane substance, then his release from the devilish grip of Saturn (lead) is the victory of antimony, Key 7, in which Adam/Mercurius may appear as the charioteer. According to Jung, "Adam, being composed of the four elements, either *is* the prima materia and the arcane substance itself, or he brought it with him from paradise [Key 6], at the beginning of the world as the first adept. Maier mentions that Adam brought antimony (then regarded as the arcane substance) from paradise."[153]

To the uninitiated eye, The Chariot is a veritable hodge-podge of perplexing signs and symbols. But let us follow the path from Keys 6 and 15 and the meaning of Key 7 becomes readily apparent. To begin, at the center of the chariot is a winged globe, the "*aurum aurae* as the end-product of the opus."[154] This symbol appears quite frequently in connection with the number seven and the seven planets. In the pictures at right we see two alchemical representations of the *aurum aurae* from 1625 and 1675. In the latter, the intersecting lines are drawn from paired suns and moons above and below, so that the fiery and watery trines are formed, symbolic of the union of spirit and matter, sun and moon, above and below.

Earlier we called attention to the graphic design of Key 7, a trine within a square, numerically a three and four combined. In Drawing 16 we see a square and triangle drawn on the *aurum aurae* with the numbers four and three. Jung's description of this picture is "Hermaphrodite on the winged globe of chaos, with the seven planets and the dragon."[155] Chaos and the abyss are synonymous for Saturn's realm, also known as the *prima materia*, *nigredo*, and *massa con fusa*. Simply said, it is that which has *yet* to be transformed. The winged Devil of Key 15 corresponds to the dragon/ruler of chaos, but he is also the dark side of Mercurius, as serpent was Raphael's chthonic aspect. In an alchemical text by Zosimos which Jung cites in *Psychology and Alchemy*,[156] the relation is seen of Key 7 as the "Chariot of Antimony" and the vanquished antagonist/devil of Key 15.

"Antimimos, the imitator and evil principle, appears as the antagonist of the Son of God [Adam as arcane substance = Christ]: he too considers himself to be God's son. Here the opposites inherent in the deity are clearly divided. . . . The alchemical parallel to this polarity is the double nature of Mercurius, which shows itself most clearly in the Uroboros, the dragon that devours, fertilizes, begets, slays, and brings itself to life again. Being hermaphroditic, it is com-

176

DRAWING 16

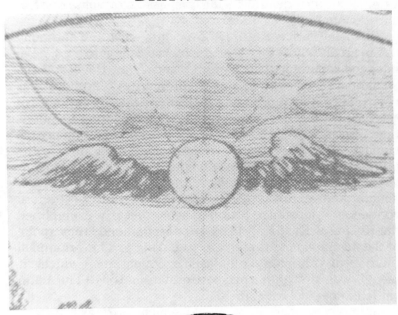

pounded of opposites and is at the same time their uniting symbol: at once deadly poison, basilisk, scorpion, panacea, and saviour."[157]

The point is that Antimimos as antagonist and antimony as the arcane substance that transforms lead into gold, devil into god, are linked in Keys 15 and 7, as Devil and the "Chariot of Antimony." Like Mercurius, antimony has chemical combinations that associate it with the darkness of the devilish nigredo, and the liberated sun. Jung mentions that "Antimony is associated with blackness: antimony tri-sulphide is a widely used Oriental hair-dye (kohl). On the other hand antimony pentasulphide, 'gold-sulphur' (*Sulphur auratum antimonii*) is orange-red. . . . The antimony compounds known to the alchemists (Sb_2S_5, Sb_2S_3) therefore contained a substance [sulphur] which clearly exemplified the nature of Rex [King] and Leo [Lion], hence they spoke of the 'triumph of antimony' . . . referring to The Triumphal Chariot of Antimony of Basilius Valentinus, which, it seems, was first published in German in 1604. The Latin edition appeared later, in 1646."[158]

Antimony appears in many alchemical texts as the *lapis,* the transformative philosopher's stone, and since we have made the equation lapis = Mercurius = serpent = Christ, the *Symbola aureae mensae,* 1617, by Michael Maier is of partic-ular import to our argument. Christ is analogous to the *filius regius,* or king's son, a frequent alchemical personification for the descended spirit, who calls out, "Who shall deliver me from the waters and lead me to dry land?"[159] These waters are the same abyss to which the fool, sun, and Mer-curius descend as embodiments of spirit, just as the arcane substance is spirit restored from the abyss of the nigredo (matter) at the end of the seven steps of alchemical process. As Christ as spirit took on form to become man, so Adam as the first man is the spiritual descendant of his Creator, com-posed of the four earthly elements. Key 15 represents "the darkest depths of matter" to which all the embodiments of spirit descend, and this is where the Maier text reveals the most esoteric meaning of antimony, "The Chariot." According to Jung, "For him [Maier] the *filius regius* or *Rex marinus* . . . means antimony, though in his usage it has only the name in common with the chemical element. In

178

reality it is the secret transformative substance, which fell from the highest place into the darkest depths of matter where it awaits deliverance."[160]

Deliverance comes from above, in Key 16, in the form of the lightning-like Logos. Rescue from "below" is akin to the fire in the tower (athanor) created by the alchemist. In this sense the alchemist's role parallels that of the divine King/Father/Logos, who comes to the rescue of his Son, spirit entrapped in matter. "At the end of the process, says Paracelsus, a 'physical lightning' will appear, the 'lightning of Saturn' will separate from the lightning of Sol, and what appears in this lightning pertains 'to longevity, to that undoubtedly great Iliaster.'"[161] The separation of Saturn from Sol is simply lead from gold. It is also the separation of Sol and Luna, since King and Queen must be purified (Key 17) before the final marriage of Key 18.

Recalling our Stairway of Planets, in which the next step up from Saturn is that of Jupiter, in a footnote to the above lines, Jung tells us "There is only *one* flash of lightning, which changes the darkness of Saturn into the brightness of Jupiter."[162]

The deliverance of Key 16 and the "Victory" of Key 7 are thus in our "Resolution" column—resolution, that is, to the problem of opposition/antagonism posed in Keys 6 and 15. The relation of Keys 7 and 16 to the other column of Resolution is one of symbolism uniting above and below, basically triadic concepts since below = 2, and above = One. The numbers two and six, being even, pose an antagonism of duality which the addition of One (as spirit) resolves in Keys 3 and 7 and their vertical equivalents. The empress is said to be pregnant; she is earthly matter about to bear spirit, resolving above and below as does the waterfall. Beneath The Empress, Key 12 depicts the myth of the descending Son/sun/spirit. We may add that there is a relation of Son/sun/spirit and antimony because the symbol on the shield of the empress is that of antimony reversed. In the conclusion of this series, Key 21 squares the circle, elevates the four elements to the celestial sphere, and intersects above and below in the form of the mandorla.

The Chariot continues the "Resolution" theme of above and below in that the charioteer's vehicle combines the cubic shape of matter (below) with the starry canopy of above. In other ways as well, The Chariot is a card of resolution of opposites. For example, the red and white lingam-and-yoni symbol beneath the *aurum aurea* is a *hierosgamos* of male and female, Sol and Luna. The sphinxes are a variation on the yin/yang oppositions of Boaz and Joachin in Key 2. These entailed life and death, as did the two Trees of Key 6, and are resolved in the crescent epaulets on the charioteer's shoulders. One lunar face frowns, the other smiles, equivalent to the waxing and waning—or dying and resurrected—moon.

A curious feature of the Waite "Chariot" is that the charioteer is not standing in a cube-shaped box; rather his body appears to be *emerging* from the stone. The perspective in this card presents a slightly downward view of the top of the chariot, which has a completely solid form. Our interpretation of this is that since the *seventh* card parallels the last step in the alchemical process, it is as if the spiritual Man, the resurrected Adam, the spirit Mercurialis, is born again or liberated from the stone. Further, we may liken the human figure emerging from the stone to the *lapis* and the human, healing personifications it is given to connect it with Hermes.

The principle alteration which Waite has made with the Marseilles' "The Chariot" consists in the substitution of black and white sphinxes for red and blue horses. In simple terms both color pairs are antithetical, suggesting resolution of polar opposites. Waite goes tradition one better in that the sphinx—like Mercurius—is a symbol for the harmony of all opposites, being even androgynous because it possesses feminine breasts, and unites the four elements and the four fixed signs of the zodiac; thus space above and matter below are united.

The charioteer's scepter denotes his autonomy, resulting from the resolution of above and below, the commandment stated in the upraised wand of the magician reconciled with his gesture below. In a personal reading, Key 7 indicates the individual autonomy resulting when the inner and outer contraries are harmonized.

As to the remainder of symbols in Key 7, only the eight-pointed star is of import to us, since it appears in our next column in Key 17, "The Star." Keys 8 and 17 belong with Keys 4, 13, and Zero in the "Completion/termination" category. The odd-numbered, previous series of "Resolution" comes to numerical rest in completion. The One is added to three and to seven. A manifest connection in Key 8 is the lemniscate of Key 1 appearing again after Key 7.

To one viewing the Major Arcana for the first time, Key 8 must appear very strange indeed; for one does not play with lions, so this card is not to be taken at face value. But the exoteric Marseilles also has a woman with Lion (Key 11). Whereas some sort of literal meaning may be attached to most of the Major Arcana, "Strength" defies literal interpretation. We must conclude that it is wholly symbolical. What is more, the actual source of this card lies in the many alchemical depictions of virgin and lion, or virgin and unicorn. (See Drawing 17.)

The lower picture—in its many variations—is often titled "The Tamed Unicorn," whereas in some Tarot decks "Strength" is titled "The Tamed Lion." According to Jung, "In the *Chymical Wedding* of Rosencreutz, a snow-white unicorn appears and makes his obeisance before the lion. Lion and unicorn are both symbols of Mercurius."[163] In the 17th century Ripley *Scrowle* we encounter a lion lying in the lap of the queen. Jung notes that the lion has replaced the unicorn, "but that did not present any difficulty to the alchemist, since the lion is likewise a symbol of Mercurius. The virgin represents his passive, feminine aspect, while the unicorn or the lion illustrates the wild, rampant, masculine, penetrating force of the *spiritus mercurialis*. Since the symbol of the unicorn as an allegory of Christ and of the Holy Ghost was current all through the Middle Ages, the connection between them was certainly known to the alchemists, so that there can be no question that Ripley had in his mind, when he used this symbol, the affinity, indeed the identity, of Mercurius with Christ."[164]

In keeping with the color symbology of sun, sulphur, and Mercurius' active side, Waite has colored his lion red (orange in some more recent decks). Bedecked in garlands of flowers to equate her with the virgin of the alchemical tableau above, the white woman represents the feminine aspect of Mercurius, with associations to moon, quicksilver,

DRAWING 17

VIII

STRENGTH.

and salt. To one who has not made these connections, A. E. Waite's "explanation" of this card only serves to preserve the mystery. He perseveres in his determination not to reveal the reasons for changing positions of Keys 8 and 11. It is worth repeating: "A woman, over whose head there broods the same symbol of life which we have seen in the card of the Magician, is closing the jaws of a lion. . . . For reasons which satisfy myself, this card has been interchanged with that of Justice, which is usually numbered eight. As the variation carries nothing with it which will signify to the reader, there is no cause for explanation. Fortitude, in one of its most exalted aspects, is connected with the Divine Mystery of Union; the virtue, of course, operates on all planes, and hence draws on all in its symbolism. It connects also with *innocentia inviolata*. . . ."[165]

As we have seen, the "Divine Mystery of Union" is the mercurial *hierosgamos*, combining and resolving all pairs of opposites, symbolized by the lemniscate, a symbol for infinity in that the universe is thought to devour and *regenerate* itself like the uroboric serpent. Of course the Eastern version is the *t'ai chi*, the yin-and-yang serpents.

Waite continues: "These higher meanings are, however, matters of inference, and I do not suggest that they are transparent on the surface of the card. They are intimated in a *concealed* manner by the chain of flowers, which signifies, among many other things, the sweet *yoke* and the light burden of Divine Law, when it has been taken into the heart of hearts."[166] The italics are mine. One can only wonder if Waite spoke as flowery as he writes. We may infer that the chain of flowers makes another figure-eight behind the woman; otherwise, we cannot consider it a chain by which she leads him, as Waite tells us earlier in his explication. Cirlot, in defining garland tells us as follows: "It has been said that everything in the universe is linked as in a garland," which symbolizes "tokens of bonds or connexion."[167] Despite Waite's flowery words about "light burdens of Divine Law" and "heart of hearts," the garland appears in order to demonstrate that lion and woman are but two *halves* of one being, Mercurius. He includes the lemniscate as a clue to the fact that this tableau is a representation of the same figure who appears in Key 1, the alchemist-magician. In the background, another clue: the mountain standing for the Opus of alchemical process.

In the exoteric Tarot, neither mountain, garland, nor lemniscate are present, but Waite makes one other alteration in the card, totally different from all other decks, revealing the alchemical persuasion of the Golden Dawn's Tarot pack. The woman's hands are placed above and beneath the jaws of the lion to indicate that she is closing rather than opening them, indicating that she "has already subdued the lion."[168] This aligns Waite's card more precisely with the "tamed" motif of the virgin and unicorn as a tableau of Mercurius. Furthermore, just as there is a progression in alchemical process, lion and woman are prefigurations of the *coniunctio* of sun and moon in our next column, Keys 9 and 18. The idea to remember regarding this *hierosgamos* is that King Sol is swallowed by Queen Luna, that is, the active masculine is subdued by the feminine half of the "marriage," which Waite anticipates by having the white woman close the lion's jaws.

Now as to connections between Keys 8 and 17, accounting for Waite's switch of 8 and 11, we said earlier that the great central star in Key 17 symbolized the Gnostic Ogdoad, the sphere of the fixed stars which the ascending soul attained upon successful transit through the realm of the planetary archons. Since they are seven in number and the Ogdoad the *eighth* sphere, one sees the relation of this card to Key 8. In this journey, Hermes/Mercurius is said to be the guide for the individual soul.

However, there is another interpretation for this card which does not negate necessarily the preceding meaning. In personified form, Mercurius frequently appears between King and Queen as offspring of the union. Where an actual sun and moon appear, Mercurius is symbolized as a star between them. Silberer notes that "this star is always placed in such a way that it receives the double radiation of the male sun ☉ and the female moon ☽ ; its light is thus of a bisexual nature, androgynous or hermaphrodite."[169] Now since Key 8 symbolizes the solar and lunar aspects of Mercurius, "The Star," Key 17, represents this star of Mercury.

184

Key 17 presents yet another clue linking it to Hermes/Mercurius. As offhandedly as possible, Waite says, "Behind her is rising ground and on the right a shrub or tree, whereon a bird alights."[170] The rising ground leads up to another hill or mountain, symbol of the Great Work, as in Key 8. The bird is perched in a single tree atop a hummock, a sort of mini-mountain with the same meaning. Significantly, the bird is red, connecting it to the active aspect of Mercurius, and perches in a tree atop the hill, thereby linking World-Tree and Opus, Macrocosm and Microcosm. But even more telling is the bird's beak, shaped like that of a wading bird, perhaps an ibis. In the *Hieroglyphica* of Horapollo, chapter ten, we read that the ibis is sacred to Mercurius.[171]

Very often the bird undergoes a color transformation similar to the alchemical stages of *nigredo, albedo,* and *rubedo,* as we saw in the *Chymical Wedding.* According to Jung, "The Chinese cousin of the *avis Hermetis,* the 'scarlet bird,' moults in a similar way. . . . As regards the origin and meaning of the *avis Hermetis,* I would like to mention the report of Aelian that the ibis is 'dear to Hermes, the father of words, since in its form it resembles the nature of the Logos; for its blackness and swift light could be compared to the silent and introverted Logos, but its whiteness to the Logos already uttered and heard, which is the servant and messenger of the inner word.' "[172]

The "swift flight" of the spirit/Logos, or the *spiritus mercurialis,* accounts for the many analogies with birds in alchemy: dove, pelican, eagle, crow, swan, cock, and phoenix, as well as peacock, which we mentioned earlier. There is a correspondence by color between birds and the planet/metals as follows: crow/Saturn-lead, swan/Jupiter-tin, cock/Mars-iron, pelican/Venus-copper. Mercury is tied to the dove in the parallel to Christ and/or Holy Ghost. Sometimes it is the eagle in its most sublimated form, since the eagle ascends higher than any other bird. But it is with the phoenix that the *lapis/spiritus* is linked most frequently, phoenix being an *increatum* like the uroboros because it is reborn from its own ashes. Ashes also call to mind the fire of alchemical transformation, and whiteness the salt that is both *prima materia* and *lapis,* beginning and end, Alpha and

Omega, like Magician and Fool. The phoenix, therefore, embraces polar opposites like Mercurius, and we shall explore these in our astrological run-through relevant to the opposition of lead-gold, Saturn-Sun, Aquarius-Leo.

Finally, our Tarot series has run its course and we arrive at Key 9, nine being the number of completion and fulfillment. If we have learned well our alchemical lesson, we are able to detect the beginning in the end, the *prima materia* in the *lapis,* and numerically speaking, the root of nine in the one and zero. Just as one and zero have a relation, so nine has connections with Keys 1 and Zero.

First of all, all three Keys combine "Above and Below" in their symbology. Significant details are the gesture of the magician, and the height and abyss configurations in Keys 9 and Zero. As Key 9 concludes the numerical cycle, and the top line of our Magic Nine arrangement, so Key Zero concludes the entire Major Arcana, and in a sense also commences the series, being the formative no-thing out of which number and form evolve. Because of their relation, the figures in Keys 0 and 1 are youthful, while the hermit is ancient, nine the "oldest" number of the sequence 1-9. Key 1 is the hermit as a youth.

Secondly, above and below are combined in the fire-water trines of the hermit's lantern, as we have mentioned. The alchemical prototype for this picture was reproduced in the section of this volume which dealt with Waite's known alchemical treatments as the basis for our thesis of imputing an alchemical symbology in the Major Arcana. But let us examine the lantern in the Marseilles' version of "The Hermit." (See Drawing 19.)

We note that there are three panels to the lantern, relevant to the number nine, since it is said to be a complete image of the three worlds, body, soul, and spirit. The horizontal lines in two of the red panels number *nine.* Most important of all are the colors red and white, which we associated with the pairs of opposites, sulphur and salt (or quicksilver), sun and moon, spirit and soul (or body). Through the use of the fire-water trines, Waite has conveyed the same alchemical meaning, with the addition of associations of active/passive and above/below; thus, Key 9 comprises a *coniunctio* like Key 18, "The Moon."

This being the case, we may look now for the relations of this our third column of "Union" to the first column, Keys 1, 10, 19, and to the second column, Keys 5 and 14. They should be manifest to the reader.

Although I prefer to touch lightly on divinatory attributions, in order that the reader not be hamstrung by "authority," impeding his own free-associations, Key 9's meaning is not ascetic isolation, nor is it a *quest* for value. Waite makes this clear. "But this is a card of attainment . . . rather than a card of quest."[173] The numerological interpretation of the number nine is the reason for this card's being attainment and fulfillment rather than quest for these values. The hermit is not seeking; he has arrived. Waite adds also, "His beacon intimates that 'where I am, you also may be.' "[174]

Now as to the other divinatory attribution of "The Hermit" to the path of the seminary or nunnery of traditional religion, the hermit's "way" is that of alchemy and Rosicrucianism. The latter may be inferred from the relation of nine as a combination of five and four. Graphically four is symbolized by a cross, five by the five-petaled rose of Key 5, The Hierophant. Further, we recall that "rose garden" represented both Rosicrucianism and the alchemical process. The "rosy" cross symbolizes the Rosicrucian movement, being a *five*-petaled rose hung, nailed to, or growing on a cross. Thus five plus four = nine, The Hermit, whose name stands for the hermetic path and not the way of the monastery.

As we said in the introduction, in Hermeticism God is thought to be within; therefore, divinatory attributions to Key 9 have relations to the Jungian concept of the Self, the god within the psyche. Furthermore, as Keys 1 and 0 have symbolic relations to Key 9, they and Key 9 may be interpreted as the Self. Just as the Self is the goal of the Jungian process of individuation, so too Key 9 is the goal of the numerical series 1-9. The Fool is a symbol of the Self in that it is an image of totality. The Magician is the Self in that he unites above and below, conscious and unconscious minds, a prerequisite for selfhood.

According to dream symbology, particularly that of the Jungian approach, the Wise Old Man represents the Self because his wisdom transcends all knowledge. This image of the Self parallels that of the concept of god as "Ancient of Days," the One who proceeds all temporal beginnings. Clearly The Hermit suggests the Ancient of Days.

We have seen the connections of Christ with the philosopher's stone, the *lapis*. The Father is often linked to the *lapis* as well as the Son. The One is of triune nature, the Holy Trinity, so he at once is the Son in the womb of the Virgin and the Father/Creator. The mystery of Key Nine's meaning is inherent in this concept; for he is simultaneously ancient and youthful, eternally regenerative. Again, we see the link to Keys One and Zero, and the regenerative uroboros. Keys One and Nine also have a relation to the sick king and his son of alchemy. According to Jung, "A similar idea appears in the Grail tradition of the sick king, which has close connections with the transformation mystery of the Mass. The king is the forbear of Parsifal, whom one could describe as a redeemer figure, just as in alchemy the old king has a redeemer son or becomes a redeemer himself (the lapis is the same at the beginning and at the end)."[175]

Furthermore, Jung tells us, "The contrast between *senex* and *puer* touches at more than one point on the archetype of God's renewal. . . . 'The Ancient of Days in his sublimity, dwelt as a babe in the womb.' 'Thy Babe, O Virgin, is an old man; he is the Ancient of Days and precedes all time.' "[176]

Another alchemical text tells us, "The stone is first an old man, in the end a youth, because the *albedo* comes at beginning and the *rubedo* at the end."[177] Thus the babe of Key 19, the rubedo, offspring of the union of spirit and matter, *coniunctio*, and hierosgamos. And finally the youth of Key Zero, end of the Major Arcana.

The Fool and The Magician represent two aspects of one principle, the Divine One as ineffable and formless in the case of The Fool, and with form as The Magician. This one principle is referred to as the Monad in Pythagorean philosophy, the Pythagorean tetractys bearing a remarkable relation to the foregoing pattern in the Magic Nine. The cycle we have delineated involves numbers 1-4 initially, and 5-8 subsequently, with final union occurring in Keys 9 and 18. The tetractys is rendered in the figure at right.

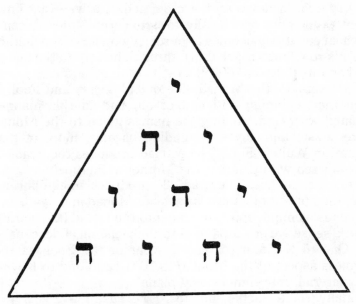

THE TETRAGRAMMATON.

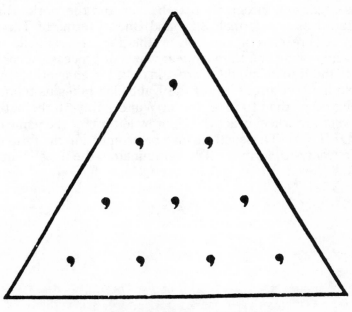

THE TETRACTYS.

The dots in the above figure may be related to the archetypes of numbers one, two, three, and four, but in the Pythagorean scheme they are defined in a way that links them even more specifically to our Tarot Major Arcana. Such an equation becomes a source of wonder as to whether Tarot's roots may reach down through history to the age of Pythagoras (born ca. 600 B.C.).

For example, the Monad, like our Magician and Fool, is both the beginning and end of all, and in this manner equated with God. Among the names given to the Monad were chasm and abyss, reminding us once more of that feature in Waite's Fool. The Monad produces the dyad—2 —associated with polarity, the Mother archetype, and goddesses such as Isis. The triad—3—produces an equilibrium from the opposition or *combination* of Monad and dyad, and descends as mind, spirit, or soul into the tetrad (the world). In this sense we see a parallel to the alchemical descent of the One to the four, or the descent of the Fool (as the formless aspect of the Monad) to 13 (Death) and to Key 4, the material, four-dimensional plane.

Finally, the tetractys adds to 10, because $1 + 2 + 3 + 4 = 10$, ten, the decad, being a perfect number to Pythagoreans because it integrates both heaven and the world, that is, formless and formal, Zero and One in terms of Tarot. Key 10 presents a concept of the formless angelic or heavenly plane and the manifest wheel of process. According to the Kabballah, there are said to be ten emanations out of Nothing. A discussion of the Kabballah takes us too far afield, other than to note that in Waite's Key 10 the outer circle of the wheel bears the Hebrew letters for the name of God, I H V H. These letters may be arranged in the form of the tetractys to form the Tetragrammaton, the Great Name of God.

CHAPTER VII

THE HERMETIC WORLD-PICTURE
IN
THE "WHEEL OF FORTUNE"

Waite's Key 10 is packed with meanings vital to the line of investigation we have pursued so far. First of all, "wheel" (Latin *rota*) is an anagram for Tarot, and in order to comprehend the full meaning of the Tarot pack, one must realize that on one level the wheel in Key 10 is the sun rolling through the sky. Waite has clarified the symbology latent in the Wheel of Fortune by elevating the wheel to the heavenly realm. This he does by surrounding the wheel with clouds on which recline the symbols of the four apostles, which also are equivalent to the four fixed signs of the zodiac, Taurus, Leo, Scorpio and Aquarius. These same figures grace the four corners of Key 21, The World, in traditional exoteric Tarot. The esoteric meaning latent in both cards is that human life and destiny in the mundane "world" interacts with influences transcending the mundane. Fundamentalist philosophy equates this influence with God and His Word, the Bible; hence, a fundamentalist need look no further for his meaning of Key 10 than the four evangelists, Matthew, Mark, Luke, and John.

However, since Hermetic teaching and alchemy place the divine within, we must examine more closely Waite's Key 10. Indeed, before we are through a totally different world picture shall stand. Frequently, the World Tree appears in esoterica's shorthand as the caduceus, the staff representing the tree's trunk, while the spiral serpent stands for the ascending and descending path of the sun through the year. Waite presents both elements in the Wheel of Fortune, but amplifies the symbology to extend its significance to still-richer dimensions. The Hermes/Mercurius staff is lengthened to double as one of the spokes of the eight-spoked wheel in Key 10. The serpent is made golden and moved out to the reader's left—or the involuting side—of the wheel. The effect is to equate the serpent with the sun's descent from the meridian to the underworld, the sun's golden journey being equivalent to the individual soul's journey to the underworld. Waite gives us the *serpens mercurii,* guide to the underworld, and *also* an Egyptian underworld figure, the red figure evoluting, which we shall discuss later. Again, we must not forget the connection Key 10 + 9 = 19, since ROTA equals the Wheel of the Sun, and like the sun, the soul of man returns to flight from its underworld journey.

Furthermore, the eight-spoked wheel of alchemy combines the four points of the alchemical polar opposites with macrocosmic opposites, that is, the zodiacal signs for the equinoxes and solstices. Waite presents this concept by means of four spokes pointing in the four directions of these signs, bull, lion, eagle, man, while placing symbols for alchemical pairs of opposites on four spokes of the wheel. Thus Above and Below interpenetrate symbolically in Waite's masterful depiction of the Wheel of Fortune. In the same way, the human plane and the divine are thought to interact for good or ill, but in terms of Hermetic science, the cause of the destiny must be located within. At the center of the wheel, therefore, is the mesocosm, the soul of man, around which turns the world and the universe. This point of light, rendered as the Monad, One, reminds us of the underlying unity behind all apparent pairs of opposites. Finally, we shall explore in our last chapter the relation between Key 10 and Key 1, the return to the Monad by means of a spiral journey through the Major Arcana, an *anodos* that reflects the visual form of the caduceus.

But for now, "Let therefore the tree be planted and its root be ascribed to Saturn. . . ."[178] So we read in Gerhard Dorn's *Theatrum chemicum,* 1659. As Jung points out, the World Tree has a connection with the seven planets through the seven metals;[179] and in its branches coils the *serpens mercurii.*

We shall see that this World Tree reconciles opposites of above and below, chthonic and celestial, heavenly and demonic, good and evil, divine and natural, axis and process about the axis; that is, the rotation of planets about the pole has its microcosmic equivalent in the *rotatio* of metals in alchemy, corresponding to the transformative process in man the mesocosm. This "goldmaking" represents as well "the opus, which we know coincides with the seasons."[180] The World Tree "links earth and heaven: rooted in darkness its crown expands into light. The trunk of the World Tree is the central pivot on which the world turns."[181]

"Ultimately all creation takes place at this point, which represents the ultimate source of reality . . . the 'navel of the world,' 'Divine Egg,' 'Hermetic Egg,' 'Hidden Seed' or 'Root of Roots'; and it is also imagined as a vertical axis . . . which stands at the centre of the Universe and passes through the middle of three cosmic zones, sky, earth and underworld. It is fixed at the heavenly end to either the Pole Star or the sun, the fixed points around which the heavenly bodies rotate. From here it descends through the disc of the earth into the world below."[182]

From the earlier geocentric point of view, as opposed to the heliocentric Copernican, a golden serpent often symbolized the sun in its movement about the pole and up and down through the signs of the zodiac, pursuing on its annual journey a spiral course. Or, the sun was thought to roll through the heavenly zodiac like a giant wheel; hence the relation of the Great Work, *opus*, to a wheel.

Thus World Tree and Wheel, like the caduceus, are symbols which connect various planes of value or consciousness. The anagram ROTA for TARO may be this wheel, with Keys 1-15 representing the descending, *materializing* impulse of opus, wheel, or World Tree. Keys 16-21 ascend in a spiritualizing direction. The way down the Tree (involution) comprises a death of the spirit; yet without it there can be no birth of matter (evolution); thus the two directions are cosmically complementary, Fall and Incarnation one and the same. From the view of earlier World Tree mythologies, Christ's cross is a tree of crucifixion and yet the means of His (and man's) resurrection and reunion with spirit; "a tree sacrifice is the way in which a god (Attis, Osiris, or Odin) is united with his transcendent immortal self. . . ."[183]

In the picture below, we see a rendering of a specific cosmic moment, with the World Axis depicted as a trunk of a tree, the branches of which are the signs of the zodiac, whereon hang the fruit or planetary rulers of those signs. Such a world-picture is important to us, since the Tarot Major Arcana are a reflection of this moment, circa 2,000 B.C., when Moon and Sun are together at the midheaven (summer solstice or top of the "tree"), because Tarot presents the *hierosgamos* of Keys 18 and 19. Further, as we examine this picture, we note that the descending (left) side of the tree has the sequence ☿ , ♀ , ♂ , ♃ , and ♄ (Mercury, Venus, Mars, Jupiter, and Saturn), the same order of planets in our correlation with the Keys 1-15. Thus the sun, or spirit, descends to the nadir or underworld of the devil/Saturn.

DRAWING 21

SUMMER SOLSTICE

WINTER SOLSTICE

We now turn our eyes from the mundane sphere of metals to gaze above at the celestial sphere of gods. Standing between the two as mesocosm, man attempts to transform his own dull lead into gold of the sun, in order to join the gods in their immortal realm at the end of mortal life. This desire of man manifests in Tarot in the leading out of "The World" to "The Fool," Key Zero, the number of infinity.

Heretofore, we have defined the microcosmic relations. Now we must focus on Tarot's macrocosmic implications. Since each metal also stands for a planet, we are once again on the Stairway of Planets. In "The Heaven," Chapter XI of an 18th-century alchemical text, we read: "You shall take seven pieces of metal, of each and every metal as they are named after the planets, and shall stamp on each the character of the planet in the house of the same planet. . . ."[184] In becoming "clothed" materially, the descending soul takes on the metallic qualities of the planets, until at the abyss of the nigredo the soul's condition is "leaden."

In ascending, the soul sheds the planetary conditions imposed by the Archons during the descent; or in other versions, passes safely these "custom-stations" through *gnosis* (knowledge) of secret passwords and magic talismans designed to appease these cosmic jailers bent upon holding the soul in bondage. In still other variations, the sun-god's journey through the planetary house blazes a trail which the human soul may follow.

At all events, the ascent involves a *transmutation* of the soul's material qualities, along with a corresponding *transformation* of consciousness, until one has attained the *hierosgamos* of soul (moon) and spirit (sun), or has transcended even these and reached the eighth sphere beyond the cycling universe. As to the earliest origins of this concept of the ascending soul, the Egyptians placed within the mummy's sarcophagus a papyrus ritual entitled "The Book of the Gates, concerning the manifestation unto the Light." These gates led to the palace of Osiris (the sun-god) and numbered 21, the same as our *numbered* Major Arcana. We cannot say that this is the origin of the Major Arcana, because Tarot as we know it today bears little resemblance to the invocations addressed to each deity guarding those gates. As in Tarot, it may have been that the seven planets were assigned a triad, so that a planet's sphere of influence extended to three gates. Leaving speculation to others, we can say that many of the macrocosmic world-pictures of the early religions of initiation bear a resemblance to the Stairway of Planets which we have discovered in the Major Arcana. This was especially true of Mithraism, a Near Eastern religion that flourished circa 2,000 B.C. We read in Cirlot, "In Mithraism, the ceremonial steps were seven in number, each step being made of a different metal (as was each different plane of the ziggurat in a figurative sense). According to Celsus, the first step was of lead (corresponding to Saturn). The general correspondence with the planets is self-evident. Now, this idea of gradual ascent was taken up particularly by the alchemists from the latter part of the Middle Ages onwards. They identified it sometimes with the phases of the transmutation process."[185]

Also, in Zosimos the seven steps of ascent bear a relation to the Stairway of Planets, as we noted earlier, and Zosimos himself called alchemy the Mithraic mystery. In due course we shall touch on some of the elements of Mithraism, but beyond the aforementioned correspondences, the points (or Gates) of descent and ascent bear a profound relation to the Major Arcana. In our picture of the World Tree, Capricorn (Key 15) is at the bottom, and Cancer at the top. According to Macrobius, "The soul on its descent from the One and Indivisible source of its being in order to be united to the body, passes through the Milky Way into the Zodiac at their intersection in Cancer and Capricorn, called the Gates of the Sun, because the two solstices are placed in these signs. Through Cancer, the 'Gate of Man,' the soul descends upon Earth, the which is *spiritual death.* Through Capricorn, the 'Gate of the Gods,' it reascends up into heaven."[186]

Thus these "Gates" are the solstices of winter and summer, with Cancer and Leo on the cusp of the latter in 2,000 B.C., the cusp of Aquarius/Capricorn being the point of the winter solstice. Selecting from these signs the polar-opposite fixed signs, Leo fixed fire, Aquarius fixed air, the macrocosmic picture is completed by the addition of fixed water, Scorpio, and fixed earth, Taurus. The symbols for these are lion (Leo), man (Aquarius), scorpion or serpent (Scorpio), and bull (Taurus), which have Christian equivalents in the symbols of the four evangelists, which appear in "The World" in practically all Tarot versions, the Marseilles included, and are added by Waite to Key 10, "The Wheel." The correspondence of evangelists to signs is lion, Mark; eagle, John; man, Matthew; and ox, Luke. Henceforth, we shall refer to this arrangement of figures as the four fixed signs. Frequently they appear as a four-headed being in one body known as a tetramorph. Or, Christ may appear as the mystic "Centre." Waite's "Wheel of Fortune" has an actual centre, of course, and the meaning of that card has to do with the corresponding cycling of the universe and alchemical process, as we have seen. Therefore, the four fixed signs have meaning beyond the evangelists as being seasonal points along the path of the wheel (process, *opus*). Furthermore, since the four fixed signs represent the solstice and equinox positions on the World Tree, they are not to be interpreted only in a traditionally Christian sense. Another argument in favor of our thesis is the conspicuous absence in the Major Arcana of Fish and Lamb, symbols for Christ, but also relevant to the vernal-point sign of Christ's historical period. The Arian age (Ram) ends at A.D. 1, and the Piscean age (Fish) commences with Christ's birth. Christ and Adam have a connection, Christ being the Second Adam. Adam's composition of four elements relates him to the Gnostic Anthropos, and as such he is a kind of tetramorph.

Whatever sign appears at the vernal point is the sacrificial animal which symbolizes the god of that religious period. For example, the Last Supper consisted of fish, bread, and wine, the Body and Blood of Christ. In the period 4,000–2,000 B.C. the bull appears in most cultures as the sacrificial animal and the symbol of the god, from the Egyptian Osiris/Apis to the Celtic Hu. The bull also has a unique relation to the "Centre," being the animal in the middle of the labyrinth in the Cretan culture, both Christ and bull appearing as saviors to be slain in order to deliver the world from death, which the labyrinth represents. (The equivalence of dragon with Mercurius as both poison and healing *lapis* conveys this same meaning.)

Since we have delineated the alchemical theme in Tarot, and since alchemy's roots are in the pre-Christian period, our equation is justified of the four fixed signs with the macrocosmic picture of 4,000–2,000 B.C. Regarding this earlier period, we may see the roots of Christian symbology. According to Cirlot, "Another four-part grouping of animals is to be found in Sumerian art, composed of a lion, an eagle, and a peacock mounted on the back of an ox. *The Book of the Dead,* on the other hand, mentions a group of three beings with the heads of animals and a fourth being with a long-eared human head (like the heads in some Romanesque paintings). Likewise, Ezekiel's vision contains the lion, the eagle, the ox and man. Oriental iconography must have had a great influence upon Ezekiel's vision and Egyptian images must have been specially influential."[187] Subsequently Cirlot identifies peacock with Man (Aquarius): thus the Sumerian four-part grouping corresponds to our macrocosmic picture.

Finally, we must not forget that the *hierosgamos* of alchemy, the conjunction of sun and moon, occurs at that point in time when the cusp of Cancer (ruled by Moon) and Leo (Sun) are together at the midheaven. This occurred in 2,000 B.C. Archeologically, it was the period of the Megalithic peoples, those builders of giant structure such as Stonehenge, macrocosmically oriented in the stone alignments which have proved to be calculators primarily of sun and moon positions, *particularly their "wedding" in the phenomenon of eclipse.* In the *hierosgamos* of Key 18, The Moon, we noted that the sun is swallowed by the moon, to be reborn again in Key 19, The Sun, as in the analogy of Gabricus and Beya. According to Cirlot, "Megalithic culture, possibly reflecting some obscure tradition of remote antiquity, was given to expressing the struggle of the gods against the monsters that, from the beginnings of creation, sought to devour the sun. When they formed the cosmos out of chaos, the gods, in order to safeguard what they had created, placed the lion on the celestial mountain and posted four archers (at the Cardinal Points) to ensure that none might disrupt the cosmic order."[188]

The ascendancy of the sun from the sea, or from the abyss of chaos, may be read as a metaphor of human differentiation of consciousness, the separation of ego from the abyss of the unconscious. The sun's "journey" had great import for the peoples of our Megalithic era, as a kind of god-journey which reflected their own higher aspirations, the midheaven and tops of mountains being the traditional abodes of gods. Thus, the seventh step in the Stairway of Planets is made of gold, the Sun-door through which the released soul attained the eighth gate, equivalent to the Gnostic Ogdoad, in which the influence of the planetary spheres is transcended.

There is an important connection between lion and bull which manifests in the difference between the calendar year, commencing January 1, and the zodiacal year, which has its onset at the spring equinox. At the time of the Megalithic peoples the bull is "breaker of the year," the animal sacrificed to death (the underworld from fall to spring equinox) in order that the sun-god might attain the midheaven of the solstice. Or the bull *is* the sun-god who dies and is resurrected. Or the bull and his horns (crescent moons) indicate the lunar death-goddess of eternal natural process, the feminine aspect of himself whom he weds in order to be reborn from her. "The lunar bull becomes solar when the solar cult supplants the more ancient cult of the moon."[189] Alchemy's concern with "gold of the sun" as the goal of the opus, and the view of the heavens in which the sun-god attains the heights of the solstice, reflect once again the correspondence of above and below. Hence, in our following investigation, we shall treat the mythologies of the sun-god in his many forms, the cosmic order of the four fixed signs—as in Tarot—and the sun-god on the celestial mountain.

For our purposes, Mithraism is a perfect amalgam of astrology and alchemy. In the 2nd century, Celsus tells us, "Those things are obscurely hinted at in the accounts of the Persians, and especially in the mysteries of Mithras, which are celebrated among them. In the latter there is a representation of the two heavenly revolutions: of the movement of the fixed stars and of that taking place among the planets, and of the passage of the soul through them.

"The representation is of the following nature. There is a ladder with lofty gates, and on the top of it an eighth gate.

The first gate consists of lead, the second of tin, the third of copper, the fourth of iron, the fifth of a mixture of metals, the sixth of silver, the seventh of gold."[190]

Certain Mithraic structures reflect the macrocosmic picture, such as the mosaic floor at Ostia. Known as the "Seven Spheres," it depicts seven gates and seven planets, the entire design encircled by the signs of the zodiac. One cannot fail to see in these the correspondence to the World Tree of metals and planets. But it is the final stage of the Mithraic initiation which is of interest to us. ". . . Lion, Incense, Fire, Bough were all linked, even identified. A holocaust with incense burning symbolized the sacrifice [who] was also himself the victim, who died to be reborn. The rite thus expressed a fire-transmutation, turning the initiate into sun-gold."[191]

Thus we may read Key 16, The Tower, as a necessary sacrifice, perhaps not as willing as that of The Hanged Man but, nevertheless, liberating, since it commences the ascent. That which was inflexible has begun to bend. The accoutrements of Mithraic sacrifice, boughs and incense, have further significance. "In the Egyptian system of hieroglyphs [a bough] means 'to give way' or 'bend.' "[192] In Key 16, nigredo, Key 15, gives way to Logos, the higher will, Below yielding to Above. The relation of above and below is also indicated by incense, in the Mithraic rite, and the smoke issuing from the tower, for "smoke is a symbol of the valley-mountain [abyss-solstice] antithesis, that is, of the relationship between earth and heaven, pointing out the path through fire to salvation. According to Geber, the alchemist, smoke symbolizes the soul leaving the body."[193] Thus the soul is freed from the grip of Physis in Key 16, the following card representing the apotheosis of the eighth sphere. "The soul in its ascent was thought to give back the qualities it had absorbed at each stage of its descent. Thus each halt was a sort of transmutation in terms of the relevant metal; after the seventh change came the absorption into the luminous bliss of the eighth sphere."[194]

We also linked Key 17, The Star, to the star of Mercury, the eight-pointed star frequently shown with the sun and moon, and they are together in Keys 17, 18, and 19. As Hermes/Mercurius/Thoth once led us into the underworld, now he is our guide for the ascent aloft. As to his duality, the chthonic and heavenly aspects, this can be explained by the shift in religious viewpoints from an afterlife in the underworld to ascension to the sphere of the fixed stars. In this sense, Tarot's Major Arcana is a model "Book of the Dead." In Key 1, Hermes demonstrates by this gesture that the path aloft must encompass below, else wholeness cannot be attained. The Jungian criterion, of course, is the reconciliation of conscious and unconscious. In Key 10's wheel the descent takes the form of a golden serpent, while the ascending figure is Hermes/Anubis, devil-Typhon *and* human element in one. The two crosses within the wheel (spokes) interpenetrate, one a vertical axis, such as the World Tree, and one a horizontal, the mundane plane. The other cross's four points indicate the four fixed signs and their *macrocosmic* correspondence to equinoctial and solstitial points, since the figures are resting on clouds. In the eight spokes we have the eight-pointed star of Mercury. The next vertical card is "The Sun," so we have been guided aloft as if along a vertical axis comprised in Key 1 by Mercurius' spine, encircled at the waist by the uroboric serpent; down the vertical axis of the World/Tree in Key 10, with the glyph for Mercury set squarely on this axis; through the abysmal waters of dissolution below (♒); to the shining glory of Key 19, and Mercurius in this reborn form as child of the *hierosgamos*. But his descent again is inevitable, for 19 reduces numerically to 10, and 10 to 1; hence the One who assumes the many forms of multiplicity but remains indivisible.

This first vertical sequence of the Major Arcana has an even more esoteric interpretation, for which I must thank Jack Lindsay. His *Origins of Alchemy in Graeco-Roman Egypt* was recommended to me by Gilles Quispel, the eminent Gnostic scholar, who provided recommendations in that field. As one reads the following paragraph from Lindsay, the important thing to keep in mind is that Tarot has been attributed to Egyptian sources not only as the Book of Thoth but also because *Ta-ro* is said to mean royal road in Egyptian, whether by language or by pictograph has never been made clear. However, even if this attribution is incorrect, Lindsay's discussion of the "Royal Highway" of

203

Kundalini yoga may be applied to the wand/spine of The Magician, the World Axis/Tree of Key 10, and the sun of the midheaven which culminates this vertical sequence in Key 19.

The rod or staff can be linked in a general way with the sacred Tree, Mountain, or Djed-pillar that are prominent in Egyptian mythology and ritual; and much light is cast on the inner meaning of these symbols by Indian ideas. There we find the idea of an invisible canal called *nadi* in Sanskrit (from *nada,* movement). Various translations have been made of the term: subtle canals (tubes), luminous arteries, psychic canals or nerves. There were many *nadi,* but three chief ones: *Ida, Pingala,* and *Susumna.* The last-named, the most important, corresponded to the vertebral column, *Brahma-danda*: 'the microcosm of the macrocosm.' It was the great road for the movement of the spiritual forces of the body; and around it were twined, like the two snakes on Hermes' staff, the two other *nadi, Ida* on the left, female and passive, and *Pingala* on the right, male and active. On the top of *Susumna,* at a point corresponding to the top of the skull, shone the Sun. Along the central axis were located six main centres or *cakras* (circles, wheels, represented in the shamanist rituals of Central Asia by the six cuts made in the Tree before which the shaman falls in his possessed fit of initiation and which in turn represent the six heavens through which he ascends, with mimed episodes at each stage). At the base of the spine, like a snake coiled into spirals, sleeps *Kundalini,* the 'igneous serpentine power,' which awakens during the initiation and rises up, from base to top, through the various *cakras* till it reaches *Sahasrara,* located at the suture on the crown where the two parietal bones meet. This aperture, the *Brahme (Brahme-randbra),* is the place where 'the Sun rises.' The original text thus expresses the imagery: 'The Bride *Kundalini* entering into the Royal Highway [the central nadi] and resting at certain spots [the six *cakras*] meets and embraces the

Supreme Bridegroom and in the embrace makes springs of nectar gush out.' A Brahmin of Malabar, speaking of the Dravidian caduceus, said, 'The snakes that enlace represent the two currents that run, in opposite directions, along the spine.'

But can we definitely transport these notions into ancient Egypt? It seems that we can. Take such a representation as that from the tomb of Ramses VI of a staff on which stands a mummified figure; between him and the staff-top is a pair of horns, and wriggling across the staff, lower down, in opposite directions, are two snakes. The dead man, at the last Hour in the Book of the Underworld, leaves his mortal remains, sloughs them, and is reborn as the scarab Khepri. A stele sets out the idea: 'Homage to you, mummy, that are perpetually rejuvenated and reborn.' The horns on top of the staff are called Wpt, 'summit of the skull, to open, divide, separate'—that is, the parietal bones are thought of as opening to release the reborn dead-man. Wpt also means the Zenith of the Heaven.

We see, then, in ancient Egyptian thought a system closely analogous to that of India which we discussed. The individual spine and the world-pillar are identified; there is a concept of life-forces moving up and down this axis; the skull top is also the sky-zenith; the new birth of the life-force is one with the rising of the sun. The microcosm-macrocosm relationship is very close to what we find in alchemy, but with the latter the whole system operates on a new and higher level of philosophic and scientific thinking.[195]

Germane to our macrocosmic picture of the four fixed signs, we must note that the Egyptian zodiac has in the place of Cancer, the crab, the scarab beetle Khepri. Furthermore, this sign is on the cusp with Leo at the solstice of 2,000 B.C., that is, the "Zenith of the Heaven." To the Egyptians this sign stood for the sun (instead of Leo); thus, the "breaker of the year" for the vernal point is ninety degrees away, or Ammon-Ra, the sun-god in the form of Ram.

As we look once more at our other cards for the "Union" series, Key 5, and beneath it Key 14, and, Keys 9 and 18, we see that at "the summit of the skull" of the angel of "Temperance" shines a sun which follows the vertical line made by the hierophant's white cloth, itself in the exact position of his spinal chord. Then, too, the hermit's staff has at one end the light of sun and moon in union (symbolized by the two trines), while at the other end there is the actual conjunction of sun and moon. Although *yoga* means "union," I do not mean to imply a conscious intent on Waite's part, however remarkable may be the appearance of the sun at the "*Wpt*/Zenith" of Keys 19, 14, and 18. Rather, the connection of the alchemical caduceus to the Kundalini system makes one wonder if the roots of alchemy lie further back than even Egypt, perhaps in a Sanskrit yoga discipline that made its way to the Near East in 4,000 B.C. or earlier. Mithraism itself was a combination of Persian Zoroastrianism, a solar mythology, and Chaldean astrology. Transmutation by fire (sun) may have been linked to the Stairway of Planets and to *ascent* to the sun at the midheaven. Indeed, Alexander Wilder, in his *Philosophy and Ethics of the Zoroasters,* states that "Mithras is the Zend title for the sun, and he is supposed to dwell within that shining orb."[196] Mithras is said to have both a masculine and feminine aspect: "As *Mithra,* this deity represents the feminine principle; the mundane universe is recognized as her symbol. She represents Nature as receptive and terrestrial, and is fruitful only when bathed in the glory of the solar orb."[197] In all of our sun-bull cults of the pre-Christian period we shall see many striking similarities, not the least of which is the fact that "the Apis [Egyptian solar bull] . . . comes into being when a fructifying light thrusts forth from the moon and falls upon a cow in her breeding season."[198]

For now, our interest is in the relation of alchemy to Mithraism. According to Manly Hall, "The Mithraic cult is a simplification of the most elaborate teachings of Zarathustra (Zoroaster), the Persian fire magician."[199] We recall the fiery tortures of *The Vision of Zosimos,* who called alchemy "the Mithraic mystery." A Mithraic candidate for admission was tested by twelve trials, called "The Tortures," which took place in a cave especially constructed for that purpose. Like the ascent of the eight steps, these twelve trials are symbolical of the signs of the zodiac through which the sun-god (Mithras) passes in his macrocosmic initiation. The twelve labors of Hercules parallel this myth, and "initiation" by the Major Arcana includes the cyclical descent to the winter solstice, followed by an ascent to the midheaven of the summer solstice. Similarly, a journey to the four quarters of the world (the four fixed signs of the zodiac) may symbolize the initiatory experience of attaining wholeness, that is, encompassing all opposites.

Mithras and Mercurius have many common elements, such as the masculine and feminine aspects, solar and lunar. As *anima mundi,* Mercurius must be liberated from *prima materia,* and as *spiritus mercurialis* he is freed by fire from stone. Similarly, Mithras was born from a rock. "In works of art he is shown emerging as a naked child from the 'Generative Rock' *(petra genetrix),* wearing his Phrygian cap, bearing a torch, and armed with a knife. His birth is said to have been brought about . . . 'by the sole heat of libido (creative heat).' "[200] The alchemist provides the flame for Mercurius' emergence from stone, whereas Mithras provides his own.

Just as Mercurius mediates between underworld and heavenly realm, and incorporates good and evil, so too, "while Ormuzd and Ahriman are struggling for control of the human soul and for supremacy in Nature, Mithras, God of Intelligence, stands as mediator between the two. Many authors have noted the similarity between Mercury and Mithras. As the chemical mercury acts as a solvent (according to alchemists), so Mithras seeks to harmonize the two celestial opposites."[201]

Joseph Campbell notes that in the first stage of the Mithraic initiation, "the neophyte was known as 'Raven' *(corax),*"[202] the peacock without its feathers. In our color symbology, black is associated with the metal lead and the planet Saturn. In the *Viatorium spagyricum* of 1625, there is a picture of a dying old man on whom perches a crow or raven. He is *Mercurius senex,* the Saturnine aspect of *Mercurius* as *nigredo.* The raven carries the same meaning.

Blackness is always the initial condition, representing unevolved matter, and therefore an apt color for the primary stage of the Mithraic initiation.

"The red man and the white woman, called also red lions and white lilies, and many other names [in Tarot, red lion and white woman, and also red roses and white lilies], are united and cooked together in a vessel, the Philosophical Egg. The combined material becomes thereby gradually black (and is called raven or ravenhead), later white (swan); now a somewhat greater heat is applied and the substance is sublimed in the vessel (the swan flies up); on further heating a vivid play of colors appears (peacock tail or rainbow); finally the substance becomes red and that is the conclusion of the main work. The substance is the philosopher's stone, called also our king, red lion, grand elixir, etc.... In the stage of projection the red tincture is symbolized as a pelican."[203] The pelican's association with the rubedo is because of a curious misunderstanding of the bird's pouch, which it uses to feed its young by opening its bill. In alchemical depictions, the pelican is seen rending its breast, its blood showering on its young; hence, a parallel was made to the sacrificial blood of Christ. However, besides the pelican, the phoenix and red ibis are thought to be Mercurial birds, as is the eagle because it flies highest, that is, closest to the sun.

In the Tarot Major Arcana a cosmic sacrifice appears in the Keys of descent, 1-15, and quite specifically in "The Hanged Man," as we have noted. The cosmic dragon that becomes the stuff of the universe also has its equivalent in the Gnostic uroboros, and in the figure zero, which resembles a serpent biting its tail. And in the tableau of the fool, as Waite depicts him, the sacrifical descent to the abyss engenders all the forms of matter, just as Nothing, the Unmanifest, Zero, is the source of all the multiplicity of forms of life. From out of the *no*-thing evolved the One, and from out of the One, the Many, as we saw in our numerical runthrough.

The plane of the macrocosm may be detected in Tarot in the Keys of the ascent to Above, 16-21, and in Zero. These cards were assigned to Moon and Sun on the Stairway of Planets. It is also apparent that the Keys of the third tier,

19-0, are all macrocosmic. Each of these depicts its primary symbol in the sky, the fool being on a peak but *filling* the heavenly backdrop behind him as if his body were composed of stellar points like a zodiacal man. Indeed, this seems to be Waite's meaning, for the ten "wheels" on his garb suggest the turnings of the heavenly spheres, three of which comprise a descending trine of water/spirit, which were also indicated in the nipples and navel of the child in The Sun. The ten wheels also suggest Key 10, The Wheel, and thereby The Fool's relation to the Monad, $10 = 1 + 0 = 1$.

By means of its spiraling movement, the serpent suggests the cycling of the cosmos; hence, the primordial serpent embodies all the ideas of the rhythmical process of the macrocosm, expanding and contracting (in terms of our modern astronomers), uncoiling and coiling, winding up and winding down, descending and ascending, dissolving and coagulating (in terms of the alchemists), involuting and evoluting, disappearing as the fool into the abyss, appearing again as the magician in a "now-you-see-it-now-you-don't" performance that boggles the sense-oriented intellectual mind. This rhythm may also be likened to a dance of illusion, Maya as the Hindus name her, manifest in Key 21, The World, which is to say, the forms of the world appear as the dance of Maya.

In the East form is not taken for reality, whereas Western man has built an altar to materiality, the scientist being the high priest of such a faith. For the purpose of comprehending the philosophical system behind the enigmas of the Major Arcana, it is absolutely necessary that we understand the alternative view to materialism. In order to do this, we must view the macrocosm from the perspective of so-called primitive man in the pre-Christian era. As we shall see, the macrocosm is not merely materiality turned "out-there," distant matter, but rather the macrocosm is a sphere or plane of higher consciousness of which the earth and all forms within the universe are but *expressions* thereof. Therefore, God may express Himself as a man, and man may discover his divinity. Expressed alchemically, this is the realization that we are "gold of the sun."

Obviously there has been a movement away from this

kind of thinking, which encompasses Hermeticism and the Great Myth, which I mentioned in the beginning. To the scientist an evolution of ideas has taken place, to the Hermeticist such a reductive turn of mind seems to be an *involution.* To the reductionist, existential mind, man is utterly separate from the macrocosm, itself regarded as nothing but a projection of mundane myths and ideas, a reading into Above by Below. There can be no cosmic influence on man, according to this argument, since "out-there" is nothing but dead matter; thus there can be no spiritual influence nor even an astrological effect. A great deal of scientific *hubris* is involved in this stance, since the alternate sees the material world (and man) as projections of the cosmic plane.

Tarot, of course, presents this alternative point of view. All the tableau of the Major Arcana, the pictorial forms, patterns, and colors, like the world itself, are expressions of archetypal Ideas, themselves the formative powers of the Macrocosmic plane. To the student of philosophy, the familiar ring of Plato is present here. Hermeticism perhaps goes one step further by postulating a higher plane of Consciousness *without* formal being. This is an important distinction from the reductive view, which cannot countenance consciousness without some sort of physical brain to facilitate self-awareness. But the physical brain may have become a trap of consciousness. What the abyss of the nigredo is for spirit, so too the brain may be for consciousness. With our material propensity for measuring, we now know that different states of thinking manifest in different brain waves. Seemingly certain psychic potentialities have been forsaken in the evolution (or involution) of the brain towards more sense-oriented abilities. Split-brain research points to the dichotomies of spirit and matter. Earlier thought suggests that man reflected an angelic or spiritual plane, the brain then being more open to the macrocosmic influence, or perhaps even a direct *channel* of communication.

Why man turned from the macrocosm and became so hamstrung spiritually that he could not perceive anything beyond the evidence of his five senses is best answered by a myth from Zoroastrianism, the forerunner of Mithraism.

Ahriman, the Antagonist of Light, severs man's vision into the Macrocosm by restricting his consciousness to "the three dimensional world of measure, number, and weight. Ahriman wishes to mislead man into regarding the sense-perceptible world of physical existence as the only reality. But for the intervention of Ahriman, the spiritual power underlying the forces of nature would never have been veiled from man."[204]

Tarot presents to the modern, sense-soddened mind that alternative viewpoint. Although we may now sanction— from our enlightened point of view—the reality of "spirits" from the collective unconscious (the Jungian archetypes), we do not allow that the uroboros extends to bite its own tail, that is, that "within" extends to "without," where spirit may exist as consciousness without physical form. Lacking terminology for all that is not either mundane or psychological, we have only the term Macrocosm to serve us. In terms of Tarot, and the *Emerald Tablet,* we call this "Above," and sanction its formative power as it manifests "Below."

The descent of Above to Below may be seen as a sacrifice, spirit fixed on the cross of matter. In the Heddernheim relief of Mithras slaying the bull, his cloak flies out in the wind like wings, "thereby equating the hero and the victim with the celebrated alchemic marriage of the volatile with the fixed."[205] In the same way, Gabricus (sun) devoured by Beya (moon) is a sacrifice and a *coniunctio.* The same union of volatile and fixed is represented by the interpenetrating trines lighting the hermit's lantern. His cloak is worthy of explication here. As Cirlot tells us, "Within the symbolism of garments, the cloak is, on the one hand, the sign of superior dignity, and, on the other, of a veil cutting off a person from the world . . . isolating him from the instinctive currents that move the generality of mankind."[206] The hermit's isolation is two-fold, terminating the numerical sequence and standing alone on an icy peak. But his isolation is completely self-sufficient, as the symbol of the *hierosgamos* indicates. Beneath him—in our vertical sequence— sun and moon shine in severe isolation.

Presently we shall deal with the polar opposition of bull

and serpent, or bull and dragon, in relation to the equinoxes of Taurus and Scorpio, but for now the dragon—as the bull —is of interest to us as the animal to be sacrificed. The point is that Scorpio and Taurus, leading in and out of the labyrinth of the Underworld, have associations of symbology relating to death and rebirth. In alchemy, the winged dragon symbolizes the volatile, whereas without wings the fixed is connoted. Earlier we noted that Key 16, The Tower, is a card of sacrifice, whether willing or unwilling. Key 16 appears below Key 7 in our vertical arrangement. The symbolic relations between the two cards are quite esoteric and require further explication. First of all, Waite specifies a trefoil crown on the king, three spikes to the crown, one at each side and one in the middle, the top being rounded. Waite leaves no doubt about his intention because he also places a trefoil crown on the head of the falling queen. Quite obviously the trefoil has connotations of the divine Trinity, and was a common symbol thereof in the Middle Ages. But Waite's orientation is alchemical. How then, we may ask, is a trefoil crown of import? The answer lies in the nature of Christ's sacrifice. As we have seen, Christ and *lapis,* the stone of the philosophers, are frequently equated in alchemy, and the production of the lapis is either the seventh, or last, step in the alchemical process, or follows immediately thereafter. In Key *Seven,* The Chariot, Waite substitutes the yin/yang sphinxes for the two serpents which usually appear with the *aurum aurae* or winged disc. Let us hear again from Cirlot on this symbology, the italics being mine. "The 'winged disk' is one of the most widespread of ancient symbols . . . in the profoundest sense it represents matter in a state of *sublimation* and transfiguration. The two small serpents which are often to be seen next to the disk are those of the caduceus, alluding to the equipoise of opposing forces."[207]

Vertical Keys 7 and 16 define, in the most esoteric way, the release of the spiritual or volatile from the fixed *prima materia* by means of the sacrificial fire of sublimation. Now the meaning of the fiery tower of Key 16 becomes clearer, cremation being "the consummation of sacrifice through fire, and, from the mystic point of view, any kind of cremation, are all symbols of sublimation, that is, of the destruction of what is base to make way for what is superior; or, in other words, salvation of and through the spirit."[208] But this view of sublimation is Christian. From the alchemical standpoint the *alchemist* is the saviour since he frees the spirit/Nous from the fixating grip of Physis. Then given the appearance of the lapis, it acts—whether psychical or physical—as the healing panacea for all woes, similar to the Saviour's role; thus the divine *Gnosis* requires the personal sacrifices of the alchemical process. Waite places the trefoil crown atop a tower, which is a symbol of ascent, as we have seen. But the tower itself extends from the top of a mountain. Here, then, the meaning of the trefoil crown: "When it is located upon a mountain it comes to signify knowledge of the divine essence gained by hard endeavour, through sacrifice or study (equivalent to ascension)."[209]

Ascension is up the World Axis, along the Stairway of Planets, and Key 16 commences the ascent. Earlier we called attention to smoke as symbolical "of the relationship between earth and heaven," Above and Below. The thunderbolt which frees the crown from the foursquare material world (the four-sided tower) unites the volatile and fixed, the fiery and earthly. According to Cirlot, "This image of the Logos piercing the darkness is universal. The *vajra,* the Tibetan symbol for both 'thunderbolt' and 'diamond,' is also connected with the world-axis."[210] When we mention the world-axis, the four fixed signs of Keys 10 and 21 again come to mind, and with them the sacrificial animals of the equinoxes. Certainly the black and white sphinxes of Key 7 represent these polar opposites, but they stand as well for *all* opposites.

Since the element of sacrifice figures so prominently in The Tower, we may look for indications of Scorpio or Taurus. The Christian equivalent of Scorpio in the four fixed signs is the eagle, or St. John. There are three noteworthy points in The Tower which link it to the eagle. First, the thunderbolt is symbolic of the eagle, and in many cultures, including our own national insignia, the eagle clutches thunderbolts in his talons. Secondly, instead of this, "the eagle is depicted carrying a victim. This is always an allusion to the sacrifice of lower beings, forces, instincts and to the victory [Key 7] of the higher powers (i.e., father principle, *logos*)."[211] Again the accent is on sacrifice, the dominant principle of the equinoxes. Thirdly, we have equated cremation (Key 16) with sublimation and volatilization. In alchemy, either phoenix or eagle is "the symbol of volatilization. . . . The victory of spiritualizing and sublimating activity over involutive, materializing tendencies."[212] So whether a dragon or eagle is utilized, Scorpio relates to both.

As we have seen, polar opposites partake of their antitheses. Sacrificer and victim merge with one another, as in the tableau of Mithras slaying the bull. The scorpion attacks the bull at the point of his greatest vulnerability, the masculinity for which bulls are known, but which must be sublimated to the spiritual fertility of the life-giving grain, the transfigured blood that shall become bread, as Christ's Body and Blood changed to bread and wine. The solar logos of Mithras' blade enters the bull at the throat (ruled by Taurus) just as the lightning logos pierces the tower, freeing the pairs of opposites, volatile and fixed, from the grip of matter. If one understands the deeper meaning of The Tower and the Mithraic tableau, the sense of deliverance of both is apparent; for the bull's link is to the underworld and the horned gods who rule there, and Tarot's sacrifice is of the prima materia, the underworld of the horned god of Capricorn, whose metallic equivalent is lead.

HORNS

We shall speak now of the meaning of horns as they appear in Tarot and traditional mythology. Symbolical associations are many, so our task is not easy; however, if we keep in mind the following overview we shall have our horns in proper place:

1. Because of spiral shape, horns usually connote the world of cyclical process, death and rebirth, over which the lunar goddess holds sway, her horns being the waxing and waning crescent moons.

2. This goddess is associated with duality (Key 2), since

214

God the Father, the Logos, is One, a unity thought to be indivisible until spirit and matter separate.

3. Because of the separation and duality, the horned goddess is frequently regarded as the antagonist to the solar/masculine principle. As such she may become an underworld goddess seeking to eclipse his "light" (life), Gabricus and Beya. Or a third principle may be introduced as the antagonist, a horned god of the underworld, who seeks to separate the lovers (sun and moon), marry the sun's bride, and rule in the sun-god's stead. Whichever the case, in this latter sense the horned god and the spiral signify the labyrinth of the underworld, from which one enters and departs at the autumn and spring equinoxes.

Given all the foregoing, it is proper that a horned animal—the bull—stands at the spring equinox, in the period of the four fixed signs, for by his sacrifice the solar logos is reborn from the underworld. Finaly, then, the spiral horn is an apt symbol of the macrocosmic journey of the sun, winding up and winding down from solstice to solstice.

Our guide entering and leaving the underworld is Hermes/Mercurius/Thoth, whose *origins* are in the period 4,000–2,000 B.C. when Taurus was the sign of the vernal equinox. The symbol for Taurus may be seen in the High Priestess' crown in Key 2. Combining the solar orb with the crescent moon, Taurus' glyph is like that of Mercury's. If we think of the underworld (night) as the moon's realm, and day the sun's, then these symbols reconcile the two kingdoms, and Taurus is the proper sign for the equinox, since the sun then breaks free of the dark lunar influence and moves on to the zenith of the solstice. Astrologically, although Venus rules Taurus, the Moon is exalted in Taurus. Considering the bull's correspondence to the sun god in the pan-Mediterranean area, we can see how Taurus' glyph comprises a *coniunctio* of sun and moon.

The underworld from which the sun emerges has an equivalence to the labyrinth whose most common symbol is the spiral, of which the caduceus of Hermes is a variation.

Setting our glyphs together on one line, the similarities tell us a great deal about the relations between Taurus and the prototypes of Hermes/Mercurius/Thoth.

In the above glyphs we see that Mercurius combines the cross of matter with solar and lunar symbology; thus he mediates on the mundane plane between the lunar under-world (Scorpio to Taurus) and the "light" half of the year from Taurus to Scorpio. But a deeper meaning is implicit in Mercurius' glyph; for he possesses both devilish and godly qualities, as we saw in our alchemical run-through. There-fore, he reconciles heaven and hell (underworld); guides us below and guides us above; and harmonizes protagonist and antagonist, the dark element which must be sacrificed (bull) before ascent may commence. Now we may begin to under-stand the empathy which the god feels for the sacrificial animal, the antagonist part of himself which is put to death so that a new wholeness may be attained, an integration of dark with light, good with evil, below with above. In psychological terms, the bull is the personal shadow, those dark, undesirable aspects of the personality which have fallen from light (consciousness) into the darkness of the un-conscious, and which the ego must acknowledge as one's own before shadow transformation may take place and a new wholeness be attained. The solar god's eventual *hierosgamos* at the solstice with the feminine antagonist, the lunar underworld goddess, is but a variation on this same theme.

By now it should be clear that Tarot, with its accent on descent to the underworld and ascent to the zenith; its sym-bology of volatilization, that is, *sacrificing* the grosser elements of the body in order to free the spirit body; and finally its judgment of the dead (Key 20) is nothing less than what was known in the Tibetan and Egyptian early cultures as a "Book of the Dead." To be sure, there is no verbal instruction for the corpse, but the path along the Stairway of Planets is clearly marked, and the thread of Hermes/Mercurius/Thoth is there for us to follow. Tarot presents a profound moral and psychological system as well, which instructs the quick on how to prepare for resurrection in the spirit. Let us look again at vertical sequence 2-11-20, yet another reason for Waite's switching of Keys 11 and 8. Our guide the magician gestures, and descent to the underworld commences at the portals Boaz and Jachin, guarded by the lunar goddess. Unity (Key 1) is lost in duality (Key 2), and life beset by the pairs of opposites. In Key 11, another judging figure sits between two portals, and it is only when we recall that Boaz and Jachin are called "Severity" and "Mercy" that Justice has great significance in its position beneath Key 2, for the right pillar (beneath "Severity") is fronted by a sword, whereas the pillar beneath "Mercy" is fronted by the scales. "Mercy" carries the day, since in "Judgment" the resurrection of the dead takes place. The symbology is precise, and our Magic Nine arrangement places it in the proper perspective, but there can be no doubt of Waite's conscious intent.

MITHRAIC SYMBOLS IN TAROT

Elsewhere, in one of Waite's last books, *The Holy Grail,* he speaks of the four Tarot suits of the Minor Arcana as the four symbols of the legend of the Holy Grail. "The canonical Hallows of the Grail Legend are of course the Cup, the Lance, the Dish, and the Sword. I am wondering now how many critical works have been written on the Holy Grail and yet it has occurred to no one that its hallows may be somewhere else in the world than in old books of Romance. They are in the Tarot. The reason for these Hallows also being in the Tarot reposes in certain secret records now existing in Europe."[213]

In *From Ritual to Romance,* Jessie L. Weston sees the origin of the Grail symbols in pre-Christian Mithraic rites. I

217

think we have established quite solidly the fact that alchemy is "the Mithraic mystery," and that alchemy is the main persuasion of the Major Arcana. From this we can assume that "the reason for these Hallows [Grail symbols] being in the Tarot" is that they were passed down from the Mithraic mysteries to Hermetic secret societies. C. W. King substantiates this theory, although without mentioning Tarot. "The importance into which the Mithraica had grown by the middle of the second century may be estimated from a fact mentioned by Lampridius, that the emperor himself (Commodus) condescended to be initiated into them. Nay more, with their penances, and tests of the courage of the neophyte, they may be said to have been maintained by unbroken tradition through the secret societies of the Middle Ages, then by the Rosicrucians, down to that faint reflex of the latter, the Freemasonry of our own time."[214]

The sacrificial mysteries involving the bull in ancient Egypt and Britain are of such importance to an understanding of the Major Arcana as a "Book of the Dead" that we must give them some consideration at this time. According to Cirlot, "The precise meaning of the horn-symbol was understood as far back as Egyptian times. In their system of hieroglyphs, the sign of the horn indicates 'what is above the head' and, by extension, 'to open up a path for oneself' [out of the labryinth of the underworld]. . . . It is a striking fact that the signs which initiate the cycle of the Zodiac (Aries and Taurus) are both represented by horned animals."[215] To this we may add that the sacrifice in the god's stead of the horned animal is offered to the powers of the underworld at the portal of departure, the vernal equinox. We shall see this same rite enacted on the other side of the world in offerings of tusked boars to the Devouring Ghost of the underworld.

The spiral horn reflects both Above and Below, macrocosm and underworld, the unwinding of the solar year and the winding down to the opposite pole. In Manly Hall we read, " 'In Zoroaster's cave of initiation, the Sun and Planets were represented, overhead, in gems and gold, as was also the Zodiac. The Sun appeared, emerging from the back of Taurus.' "[216] That is to say, the sun-god is reborn at the vernal equinox in the sign of Taurus, the bull then becoming the sacred vehicle for the sun-god's spirit life.

In the Mithraic tradition, "Ormuzd had produced by his *Word* [Logos-Breath] a being the type and source of universal life for all creation; this being was called *Life,* or the *Bull* (the same word in Zend stands for both)."[217]

"As the sign rising over the horizon at the vernal equinox constitutes the starry body for the annual incarnation of the sun, the bull not only was the celestial symbol of the Solar Man but, because the vernal equinox took place in the constellation of Taurus, was called the *breaker* or *opener* of the year. For this reason in astronomical symbolism the bull is often shown breaking the annular year with his horns. . . . The most important of all symbolic animals was the Apis, or Egyptian bull of Memphis, which was regarded as the sacred vehicle for the transmigration of the soul of the god Osiris."[218]

After a period of twenty-five years, the Apis bull is drowned. Lament for its death continues until a new Apis is found, whereupon it is said that Osiris is again resurrected. The drowning of the Apis may be thought of as the solar bull's descent to the underworld in the waters of Scorpio, rebirth taking place in the earth sign Taurus, which as a symbol of fertility was said to plough the fields.

Whatever interpretation we put upon the bull, we must always recall the polar opposite, Scorpio. Those cultures in which a winged bull appears undoubtedly had the eagle—or a similar bird—as the symbol for Scorpio; for the fabulous monsters of mythology are generally amalgams of two opposing signs of the zodiac, the most famous example being the chimaera, with head of lion, body of goat, and fish's tail, or Leo combined with the mergoat Capricorn. The dragon is probably a variation of Scorpio as the gigantic starry serpent of the astrological House of Death, the portal into the underworld. The dragon must be slain by the sun-god so that his "rebirth" is possible at the opposite pole, when the bull is offered in sacrifice. In *The Hermetic Tradition,* G. C. Evola notes that "dragons and bulls" are the animals fought by sun-heroes (such as Mithras, Siegfried, Hercules, Jason, Horus, or Apollo). . . ."[219] This is no coincidence, but points to the significance of the period 4,000–2,000 B.C. as the macrocosmic cradle of much of our present mythology.

THE CULT OF THE DEAD

Now the bull sometimes has a serpent form in the mythology of ancient Britain. In *The Secret Societies of All Ages and Countries,* Charles Heckethorn, describing Druidic temples, says: "Their temples wherein the sacred fire was preserved were generally situate on eminences and in dense groves of oak, and assumed various forms — circular, because a circle was the emblem of the universe; oval, in allusion to the mundane egg . . . ; serpentine, because a serpent was the symbol of Hu, the Druidic Osiris. . . ."[220]

Actually Hu appears as often in the form of a white bull, identified with the sun, and an interesting source for this mythology is Lewis Spence's *Mysteries of Britain,* pertinent to our study of the Major Arcana as a Book of the Dead because Spence defines the mythology of what he calls the Cult of the Dead.

> That the Iberian race from North-West Africa were the original disseminators of this tradition, carrying it to Britain on the one hand and Egypt to the other in the guise of the Cult of the Dead has, I think, been demonstrated, especially in its historic aspect as associated with 'Iberian' Neolithic culture and its introduction to the British Isles. The voyages of early New Stone Age and Bronze Age men to our shores, and the erection by them of stone monuments, leads to the assumption that they must also have imported their religious and occult beliefs. The long barrow men were traders, voyaging from Spain to Britain, at a period generally placed at about 2,000 B.C., and they had embraced the Cult of the Dead is proved by their burial customs. Other races followed them, but although their religious beliefs have left certain traces, the aboriginal absorbed all others of later introduction, the Keltic peoples embracing its principles and grafting their mythology upon it to a great extent. This it was which rendered the faith of

220

Britain unique in Europe, and caused the peoples of the Continent to regard it as the exemplar and prototype of the ancient faith of the West. The argument that it is 'absurd to argue that the Western barbarians taught the Egyptians and Cretans the Cult of the Dead' was countered by the theory that it emanated from a common centre in Iberian North-West Africa. . . ."[221]

Further on, Spence notes that the Druidic Cult of the Dead was a "Kelticized" version of the earlier Iberian, but what is more important, in Britain it passed through stages similar to those of its manifestation in Egypt. Spence's overview of these mythologies is that they point to a "Secret Tradition," in his words, the same which C. W. King sees in the Mithraic mysteries, which then were disguised further in the form of alchemy, and "maintained by unbroken tradition through the secret societies . . . down to . . . our own times."[222] As we have said, the Golden Dawn was the direct inheritor of this essentially Hermetic tradition. The Keltic mythology of Hu bears a relation to our macrocosmic picture of the four fixed signs, because of Hu's journey through Caer Sidi, meaning "Circle of Revolution" (Zodiac), and Annwn, the Underworld. In the Egyptian equivalent of this myth, Osiris rules as judge of the Underworld after his descent. Further, there is a symbolic parallel between Arthur's ship, in his descent to Annwn, and the barque which Osiris used to navigate Amenti, the Egyptian Underworld. Seemingly the Arthur of myth — not later Romance — has his origins in Hu, the *twelve* knights of the *round* table being Caer Sidi, the zodiac. Also, the Grail has a prototype in the Cauldron of Pwyll, the Head of Hades.

But what [Spence asks] of Arthur's connection with this myth of initiation and of the Harrying of Hades? It is plain that he, like Osiris, is the god of a mystical cult who must periodically take a journey through the Underworld, not only for the purpose of subduing its evil inhabitants, but of learning their secrets and passwords in order that the souls of the just, the perfected initiates, will be enabled to journey through that plane unharmed. This Osiris did. By

221

this agency through the spells and passwords given in his books, the dead Osirian, the man of his cult is franked safely through the gloomy region of Amenti, the Egyptian Annwn, to the golden realm of the divinity, so that he may live forever."[223]

Again, we see how the Keltic and Egyptian initiations reflect the Gnostic stress on acquisition of *Gnosis,* knowledge of the proper words to say to the planetary Archons as the ascending soul passes through their "customs stations." Tarot is silent, like the alchemical *Mutus Liber,* but in the imagery the way in and out of the underworld is clearly defined. One wonders if there were ever a written instruction to go with the Major Arcana, or whether it reflects an oral teaching of the Secret Tradition. And again, the uncertain origins of Tarot plague us. If we take its *appearance* in 14th-century Europe as its actual beginning, we may be reducing its history by thousands of years. There would have been little reason for anyone to pass on to another generation anything as expendable and worthless as a pack of cards, unless of course they were valued spiritually, in which case they must have been passed on secretly to avoid persecution. One card bearing the name and image of The Devil would have been enough for an indictment. Recognizing this I think we must opt for much earlier origins than 1390.

The question is, where do Arthur, Annwn, alchemy, and athanor all come together? The common element is a rite of initiation. The disturbing problem: is it the same initiation in many forms from one ancient origin, or are we seeing only parallels between disparate traditions? The reader will have to supply his own answer. But the beauty of Tarot is that it may be read forward or backward, that is, forward as a tool of psychological validity in the 20th century, as I demonstrated with the Jungian Spread in *Tarot and You,* or backward to the macrocosmic picture of 2,000 B.C.

Exploring celestial counterparts for the Grail, it may be likened to Annwn, that half of the zodiac below the horizons; thus the link to the Cauldron of Hades. This semicircle also corresponds to the zodiac below the equinoxes. An alternative interpretation likens the Grail to earth itself, since earth is the "vessel" for the descending spirit. Such a picture presents a panorama of Sky above and Earth below, the cosmic parents of creation myths. Earth, then, may be likened to a chalice which receives the fertilizing Logos in the same way in which the legendary Grail caught the blood of Christ, and the earth was made fertile by the blood of the Mithraic bull which immediately turned to grain. Hu's spouse in the Keltic myth is Keridwen, her Cauldron being "the great teeming Mother of Nature,"[224] as Spence calls it.

Let us look now at the Ace and Two of Cups, in the Minor Arcana, as reproduced below.

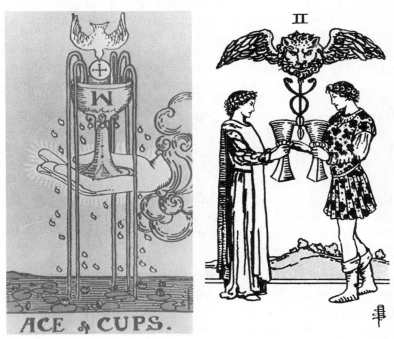

ACE of CUPS.

Waite's description is as follows: "a dove, bearing in its bill a cross-marked Host, descends to place the Wafer in the Cup."[225] There is no question that Waite intends the Grail for the Ace of Cups. Since the spirit Mercurius also took the form of a dove, the Christian meaning is quite similar, as the dove is the descending Holy Ghost. Turning again to *The Emerald Tablet*, the parallel is remarkable.

"The wind has borne it in its body. Its nurse is the earth." Wind/Breath/Word/Logos, these are manifestations of the Deity's act of creation. As in the myth of Sky-father, it is the act of Above on Below, the Earth, the mother goddess. Waite's chalice bears the letter M. Is this for Mary, the feminine principle in the creation of Christ? Mary is akin to The Empress, The Hanged Man being the solar Logos that descends through her and saves The World (3 + 9 = 12 + 9 = 21).

Cirlot writes that "M is the initial letter of the Virgin Mary, and also a sign of the *Millennium,* that is, of the end of this world."[226] I have noted that The Fool appears at the end of The World, the penultimate Major Arcanum. By intuition I had placed The Ace of Cups after The Fool, designating it the first of the Minor Arcana. This sequence I utilized in the ordering of the deck that proceeds the total of *nine* shuffles and cuts I designated in preparation for a Jungian Spread reading. Waite's sequence for the Minor Arcana commences with the King of Wands and concludes with the Ace of Pentacles. This 1969 intuition of placing Fool and Grail together is corroborated by a current discovery, Cirlot's observation that "as Blavatsky observes, M is the most sacred of letters, for it is at once masculine and feminine and also symbolic of water in its original state (or the Great Abyss)."[227] Thus the symbol of the abyss in *two* cards signifies the same meaning, the descent of spirit to the formative Abyss of creation.

Without wishing to explore further the Minor Arcana, I must call attention to the next sequential card, the Two of Cups, in which appears a caduceus and winged red lion. To be sure, there are once more suggestions of ascent and descent because of the caduceus; yet the winged lion bears the same meaning, "fixed" sulphur made volatile by the aerial symbology. Waite's secrecy is worth quoting. "It is a variant of a sign which is found in a few old examples of this card. Some curious emblematical meanings are attached to it, but they do not concern us in this place."[228] One wonders why he thought his readers bought his book, if not for the meanings of the cards!

While we are on possible relations of Tarot to the Grail theme, let us examine the four knights, recognizing that playing cards of today have only three court cards for each suit, knights having been dropped. It seems rather odd that pages (jacks) should have supplanted them. Out of this I perceive that society has become more concerned with subservience than sacrifice, which is what knighthood symbolizes. Zosimos told us of the tortures and ordeals of the *prima materia.* I suggested that many fairy tales have disguised alchemical import. The four knights as Waite colors them have a relation to nigredo, albedo, and rubedo, the colors for particular steps in the alchemical process. Keys 13-15 were the nigredo, 16-18 the albedo, and 19-21 the rubedo. Cirlot sees the knight as "the master, the *logos,* the spirit which prevails over the mount (that is, over matter)."[229] We saw how alchemy is a simultaneous process in alchemist and matter, transformation of psyche in the former and transmutation of metal in the latter; thus if the color indicates the state of matter, then when the horse is of the same color as the knight, we may infer more than casual correspondence. Let us begin with the black knight, the Knight of Cups, with a prefatory glance at Key 13, Death. In this Key the whole process of transmutation of the prima materia occurs as if in a flash: from left to right, the nigredo, Death as a *black* knight, astride a *white* horse, the albedo, with the sun (rubedo) at right.

Waite presents the black knight of the Knight of Cups bearing a golden chalice, thus indicating the beginning and end, as well as the golden potential within the nigredo. His horse is the darkest of all the knights' steeds, leaden in color. Significantly this horse is not moving, a forefoot pawing the air while his head bows submissively. Cirlot tells us, "black is associated with sin, penitence, the withdrawal of the recluse, the hidden rebirth in seclusion, and sorrow: thus the Black Knight stands for him who undergoes the tribulations of sin, expiation, and obscurity in order to attain to immortality by way of earthly glory and heavenly beatitude. . . ."[230] Although Cirlot's general description is of the medieval knights of legend, it is an accurate rendering of the figure of the Grail knight seeking immortality. Next comes the Knight of Swords, astride a light mount, although not snow-white like Death's horse, riding furiously through a windblown landscape, perhaps indicating that Swords connote the airy element as Cups may indicate water. White, Cirlot says, is associated "with innocence (natural as well as that regained through expiation), illumination, open-heartedness, gladness; thus the White Knight (Sir Galahad) is the natural conqueror, the 'chosen one' of the Evangelists, or the 'illuminated one' emerging from a period of *nigredo.*"[231]

Now with the knights of the next stage, rubedo, Waite becomes really cute in his inventiveness: an orange horse, with a knight decked in yellow finery! Such is the Knight of Wands. The steed no longer has the loose rein of the former card, the knight pulling him up short on his hind legs. Atop the knight's helm, an orange plume waves like a flame, and over his yellow garb, a series of salamanders are displayed. Obviously Waite wishes the Wands suit to be associated with the fiery element; for in Cirlot we read, "in alchemy, the salamander signifies fire—which in fact constitutes its general significance."[232] To this I would like to add that Waite presents us with the salamander as uroboros since the tails touch the mouths, making a complete circle. A more profound reading of the salamander, which dovetails with Waite's depiction of it as uroboros, links it to Mercurius as the world-creating spirit concealed or imprisoned in matter. The King of Wands is an interesting card because of the solitary salamander by the King's throne. The King's cape is golden, embroidered with salamanders. The back of his throne is covered with emblems of lions and salamanders, the lion being fiery sulphur, or the golden, solar principle imprisoned in matter.

The number of feet which the horses have on the ground also reveals something of the card's meaning. One foreleg raised in the Knight of Cups signifies the onset of the process, nigredo as beginning, the first step about to be taken. All four feet are off the ground apparently in the "airy" knight, perhaps to suggest flight. The steed is more controlled in the Knight of Wands, the hind legs planted. By the last knight, all feet rest foursquarely on the earth, suggesting solidity, permanency, and perhaps even the four fixed signs of earth, air, fire, and water.

Orange is a combination of yellow and red, so that the "reddening" commences in the Knight of Wands, and by the Knight of Pentacles it appears that both knight and mount have been bathed in blood. According to Cirlot, "the Red Knight is the knight sublimated by every possible trial, bloodied from every possible sacrifice, supremely virile, the conqueror of all that is base, who, having completed his life's work, is fully deserving of gold in its ultimate transmutation—glorification. Knighthood should be seen, then, as a superior kind of pedagogy helping to bring about the transmutation of natural man (steedless) into spiritual man."[233] Thus by the end of the alchemical (and knightly) process, elemental earth (pentacles) has been transformed into gold; for the knight holds the golden pentacle and a golden dawn lights the sky.

CHAPTER VIII

THE BOOK OF THE DEAD

What are the implications of the descent to the Under-world in the traditional sense of a Book of the Dead? First of all, it is apparent that ascent to a higher plane is not possible without prior experience of the mystical/death plane. The "treasure hard to attain," the cauldron of Keltic myth, is wholly symbolic, like the alchemical *lapis.* Returning to the myth of Hu, Lewis Spence continues, "Again, the spell, so to speak, by aid of which man escapes from death, triumphs over it, consists in power derived from knowing the whole of its cause. That is, the secrets of death must be plumbed and accurately understood before the soul can triumph over it. This throws some light on the allegory of the descent of Hu, or his other form Arthur, into the depths of Annwn. Not only did he penetrate thither for the purpose of seeking the cauldron of inspiration, the source of life, which was naturally located in the gloomy abyss whence life in its early forms was thought to have sprung, but he also sought to gauge the secrets and mysteries of death, the opposite of life, and that this knowledge was part of the initiation of the brotherhood of the Secret Tradition we can scarcely doubt."[234] Quite obviously there is a relation to the Egyptian *Book of the Dead* and the concepts therein, knowledge of which permits the soul to attain immortality. From our exploration of the Major Arcana, Tarot is in the mainstream of this Great Myth.

Alchemy and the Great Myth come together in the Major Arcana. In Osirian alchemy, the "embalmed," dead metals in the earth were transmuted—like the human corpse—yielding up an elixir of life-giving properties. We recall that this is often the offspring or new birth of the *hierosgamos* of above and below, sun as the celestial god, and moon as goddess of the underworld. In terms of the personal soul, the new birth is resurrection, reunion with the sun-creator, but *only* after assimilation/initiation through the dark antagonist. Presently we shall see how the initiation in the underworld has its universal parallel in the attempt to solve the labyrinth.

As we gaze upon the mysteries of the Major Arcana, too often our eyes are clouded with the veil of literalism, and we do not recognize that the images of Tarot were designed to evoke awareness of psychic planes which the soul had already traversed, and would again. To the modern eye, The Devil evokes repugnance or rejection, seldom recognition of the dark antagonist within and without, who as Death will enfold us and terminate all positivism. Without a proper Book of the Dead, the living cannot respond joyously to life, since absent are the awe, wonder—and finally—courage, with which the universe must be faced. Intellect and evidence of the senses solely have led us down a spiritual blind alley, Sartre's "No Exit," in which all life and all choices—even to live or die—are equally ridiculous. Tarot is an anomaly in the modern world, a relic, perhaps, of a culture in which soul-life was given a place, the body being animated for a time only by the spiritual dimension, then given up on the altar of the Dark God or Goddess, while the evolving soul proceeded on its homeward journey. This allegory of the complete cycle of the soul's journey, as well as of the sun's death and resurrection, and the macrocosmic serpent of the universe's spiraling regeneration, comprises the mystery of the Major Arcana as a Book of the Dead.

So far we have treated this journey as if the completion were always assured. What of those souls that become "stuck" in the Underworld, unable to evolve of their own accord? The equivalent may be found among the living. The three-dimensional world and the five senses constitute a very real hell, from which liberation is possible only through a cosmic "kick in the pants" akin to that of Key 16, the lightning-struck tower. Further, such persons may not have known·or been capable of giving the proper response to the challenges of their lives. Somehow it seems always that the spirit finds the proper means of education—a guru, book, or crisis—when the life is amenable to change. Before then, nothing of value comes to one, for the life is viewed as valueless. The "No-Exit" syndrome has its earlier counterpart in the labyrinth, both an image of the underworld and the macrocosmic spiraling of the sun on its journey down to death (winding down) and back to life (winding up to the zenith).

The period of the labyrinth in mythology is oriented to 4,000–2,000 B.C., when the horned bull was the emblem of the equinox's sacrificial redemption. Although our concept is of a labyrinth of right angles, we shall examine the experience of the labyrinth with regard to the symbols of the spiral, spiral horns, the crescent moon, and the spiraling serpents of the caduceus, all relevant to Tarot's descent and ascent—the uroboros again—and the macrocosmic picture of Bull, Lion, Eagle, and Man, the four fixed signs as they appear in Keys 10 and 21.

THE LABYRINTH

We recall that at the center of the Cretan labyrinth stood the minotaur, a monster half-bull, half-human. This figure corresponds to the devil/antagonist of Tarot's descent. In a sense, the labyrinth is a projection onto a flat plane of the vertical cycle of ascent/descent, the sun or soul's journey, the center of the labyrinth corresponding to the abyss. At this critical point, regeneration must take place, the new light be ignited, for it is the time of the birth of the messiahs. From the Jungian perspective, the descent into the unconscious may yield an encounter with the shadow/antagonist; but if the mystic center is attained, one then knows this "devil" to have been the self in disguise, the higher will *antagonistic* to the ego's weal. Ariadne's thread indicates a path leading to the Father/Creator. As a variation on the journey to the underworld, the labyrinth thus may be viewed as an initiatory problem to be solved. We have noted that Key 15, The Devil, presents a theme of bondage of the soul to matter. Cirlot tells us that "Mircea Eliade has made a special study of the symbolism of knots

231

and ties as they concern the tangle of thread which has to be unravelled in order to solve the essential basis of a problem. Some gods, such as Varuna or Uranus, are shown holding a length of rope, signifying their prerogative of supreme power. Eliade notes that there is a symbolic relationship between loops and bonds on the one hand and threads and labyrinths on the other. The labyrinth may be regarded as a knot to be untied, as in the mythic undertakings of Theseus and Alexander. The ultimate aim of mankind is to free himself from bonds. The same thing is to be found in Greek philosophy: in Plato's cave, men are fettered and unable to move (*Republic,* VII). For Plotinus, the soul 'after its fall is imprisoned and fettered. . . .' ''[235]

The soul's salvation may be found in the acquisition of *gnosis,* knowledge, which corresponds to finding the path or way. Such esoteric instruction is the stuff of a Book of the Dead, liberation of the soul's bondage being the goal of the instruction. The expression of this freedom is projected by Tarot's The Fool, in which all the earthly possessions may be carried on a single stick, the fool heedless of where he steps, even the abyss holding no terrors since he has conquered death.

The abyss is synonymous with chaos and Chronos (Saturn), whom we equated with the underworld, Keys 13-15. Descent presents a gradual progression of bondage, the hanged man being held by a coil of rope. We recall that he symbolizes the sun/Light/Logos descending to the abyss of the nigredo, darkness, disorder, Saturn's kingdom, chaos, the antithesis of the Logos. As to the significance of the hanged man's being bound by the foot, it is the foot that touches earth, and hence the whole relation of spirit to matter may be seen in the form of the hanged man's bondage.

Next come the three Keys of the abyss. In Death we see the earth holding the bodies, the concept of the grave as a prison for the soul. Temperance presents the amplified vision of the descent, a necessary tempering of matter with spirit so that it shall not be dead, but animated with divine presence and capable of resurrection. Key 15 is the depths, ultimate concretion and subservience. The lovers are chained to a cube of matter, and the five-pointed star of man is

232

upside-down, indicating Above now Below, head over heels, thought inverted. Interestingly enough, thought is one definition of Logos; so we see that Logos by all its definitions is entrapped and bound. Perhaps now it is possible to sense the horror which the Gnostics felt for the descent of the soul into life. Logos is order, and abyss is chaos. In the next card, divine purpose asserts itself, Logos as lightning effecting release from bondage, the "stuck" soul gainsayed paradise. The student of mythology will find interesting the comparisons between Tarot's The Tower, and concepts of divine intervention in both the Tibetan and Egyptian Books of the Dead; however, they are beyond our scope here.

SPIRAL HORNS

Below are pictures comparing various types of horns with spirals. From the side, a ram's horn or boar's tusk may make one or more complete turns. A straight horn when viewed from the tip may be thought to wind or unwind from the center, as such an image of the solar system or a spiral nebulae. And a bull's horn, when faced head-on the way a *torero* may see him, presents the semicircle of the crescent moon.

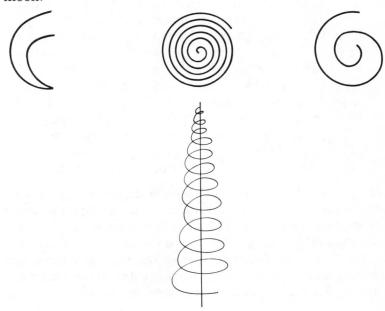

If the middle picture above is shown with a central axis and viewed from the side, it corresponds to the World Axis/Tree, around which spins the universal energies.

The caduceus and World Tree are similar, as we have seen. In his book *Alchemy,* Titus Burckhardt has written very perceptively on the relation between the two.

> When the immutable Divine Act which governs the cosmos, is symbolically represented by a motionless vertical axis, the 'course' of Nature, in relation to it, is like a spiral, which winds itself around this axis, so that with each encirclement it realizes a new plane or degree of existence. This is the primordial symbol of the serpent or dragon, which winds itself around the axis of the tree of the world. Almost all the symbols of Nature proceed from the spiral or the circle. The rhythm of the successive "unrollings" and "rollings" of Nature, of the alchemical *solve et coagula* is represented by the double spiral: ◎◎ . . .
>
> Nature in her dynamic phase . . . is portrayed by means of the two serpents or dragons, which, in the form of the well-known model of the staff of Hermes or caduceus, wind themselves round an axis—that of the world or of man—in opposing directions. . . . This fable supplements the Hermetic myth of the Staff of Hermes. Hermes or Mercury struck with his staff a pair of serpents in combat with one another. The blow tamed the serpents, which wound themselves round his staff and conferred on him the theurgic power of "binding" and "loosing." This means the transmutation of chaos into cosmos, of conflict into order, through the power of a spiritual act, which both discriminates and unites.[236]

Regarding the above, we may place two interpretations on binding and loosing. First of all, as psychopompos Hermes unties the knot that is the labyrinth, for he "solves" it by guiding us safely in and out of the underworld. Secondly, binding and loosing correspond to dissolution and coagulation, the latter process represented in the Major Arcana by Key 17, The Star. Hermes' act of binding has a parallel to The Tower, since the nigredo of The Devil and the chaos of The Tower are transmuted into cosmos, a star being the sun or polar axis around which gravitate the planets of a solar system. We recall that the Logos is the antithesis of chaos; thus the shaft of lightning in The Tower corresponds to the staff of Hermes and the magician's wand (Key 1).

SPIRAL LABYRINTH

Now, our traditional concept of the labyrinth is of a square or rectangular design composed entirely of right angles. By far the more common are spiral labyrinths, which according to Cirlot "should be interpreted as diagrams of heaven, that is, as images of the apparent motions of the astral bodies . . . because the terrestrial maze, as a structure or a pattern, is capable of reproducing the celestial."[237] Further, he notes that "the maze had a certain fascination comparable with the abyss . . . because both allude to the same basic idea—the loss of the spirit in the process of creation—that is, the 'fall' in the neoplatonic sense—and the consequent need to seek out the way through the 'Centre,' back to the spirit. There is an illustration in *De Groene Leeuw,* by Goose van Wreeswyk (Amsterdam, 1672), which depicts the sanctuary of the alchemists' *lapis,* encircled by the orbits of the planets, as walls, suggesting in this way a cosmic labyrinth."[238]

This concept of spirit falling into a labyrinth of planets is exactly what we examined in the theme of descent. The abyss was located in the signs of Saturn's dual rulership, Capricorn and Aquarius, connected with the winter solstice. The fifteen steps (and Keys) down proceeded through the domains of Mercury, Venus, Mars, Jupiter, and Saturn. Corresponding to Ariadne's thread, ascent is back the way one came, culminating in the conjunction of sun and moon at the zenith, the offspring of which is the child of The Sun, the reborn spirit, Mercurius, analogous to the *lapis* in that it bestows immortality, which may be seen as the resurrection in Key 20 following The Sun. There is a further relation between the spiral labyrinth and the Major Arcana in that the cycle from fool to magician, and back again, is like a spiral (the uroboros) which descends to the abyss of Key 0, from which the One is reborn, cosmos from chaos.

Of import to the symbol of the spiral labyrinth is the concept of regeneration or rebirth. Mircea Eliade tells us that "the essential mission of the maze was to defend the 'Centre'—that it was, in fact, an initiation into sanctity and immortality . . . equivalent to other 'trials' such as the fight with the dragon."[239] The center of a spiral labyrinth may be likened to the maw of a dragon/serpent/crocodile in which the spirit/soul is devoured. But the way back is through the center; thus *to be devoured is to be reborn,* and we find this theme in fairy tales throughout the world. If I may be forgiven a pun, a labyrinth is a form of Recycling Center.

Since The Devil in Key 15 has not devoured Adam and Eve, we may ask how this theme applies to Tarot. First of all, at the abyss or center there is always a fabulous beast, often a composite of human and bestial characteristics, symbolizing the lower element that must be slain or sacrificed so that the ascent of spirit/consciousness may proceed. Hades (darkness as antithetical to light) represents "the belly of the whale" of the Major Arcana, a term Joseph Campbell utilized in describing the many instances of this experience in mythology (in his book *The Hero With a Thousand Faces*). Of course, being swallowed is only another form of the descent to the Underworld, so the labyrinth is not only a diagram of heaven but also a map of the underworld. In this way Above and Below are united in the one symbol.

Being swallowed corresponds alchemically to those steps in the process known as putrefaction and dissolution. Key 13 depicts the former, and the gruesome strewn parts of the Marseilles' Death illustrates the way in which the body as *prima materia* is taken apart so that the *spiritual* body, the *lapis,* may be born. Rebirth is symbolized violently by The Tower, suggesting the birth trauma of psychology.

The highest conception one may realize about the labyrinth is that the known boundaries of space/time constitute a cosmic labyrinth through which one's own soul proceeds, its changing forms "devoured" periodically, but the thread of spirit to which the soul clings is never lost. In essence, this is the meaning of Key 10, The Wheel, the cosmos as a spiral labyrinth. Viewed not from the side but lying flat on the earth, the wheel resembles the great circle at Stonehenge, which was designed to reflect and calculate the celestial order of 2,000 B.C. In connection with the picture "The Sanctuary of the Lapis," which Cirlot cited from a 17th-century text by van Wreeswyk, we find many parallels to Waite's The Wheel, if the wheel is seen as lying flat on the earth reflecting the cosmic labyrinth. For those who wish to see this illustration, it is reproduced as Figure 51 in Jung's *Psychology and Alchemy*; but for our purposes here a description will suffice. The walls of this labyrinth consist of an earthwork or hedge, circular, with the glyphs for the planets indicated on these pathways. At the center is a small structure resembling a chapel, marked by Mercury's symbol and overhung by sun and moon. Jung describes this "Sanctuary" as "surrounded by the planetary orbits," but he neglects to mention the most conspicuous glyphs, sulphur and salt, which we noted symbolized spirit and matter. The impression one gathers from this picture is of a giant mixing bowl in which spirit and matter mesh, obviously the alchemist's athanor as microcosm of the macrocosmic mixture of spirit and matter. What interests us in relation to Tarot is that the same glyphs—sulphur and salt—are in evidence within Waite's wheel in Key 10. Also present in Key 10 are the symbols for Mercury and dissolution/abyss, which we just now associated with the labyrinth.

At the entrance to van Wreeswyk's cosmic labyrinth are a frolicking bull and cow, reminding of Taurus in the four fixed signs, and the fact that the *rota* or *opus circulatorium* commences in the spring, sun/gold reborn at the vernal point when it leaves the abyss of the *nigredo*. Representing the four fixed signs, the elliptical wreath is yet another version of the labyrinth. Thus, The World may be interpreted as the passage of the world (earth) through the labyrinth of space/time (cosmos) as a kind of mundane/celestial initiation which ultimately frees the divine essence, *anima mundi*. In Jung we read that the alchemist Ripley "says that the wheel must be turned by the four seasons and the four quarters. . . . The Wheel turns into the sun [10 + 9 = 19] rolling round the heavens, and so becomes identical with the sun-god or -hero who submits to arduous labors and to the passion of self-cremation, like Herakles, or to captivity and dismemberment at the hands of the evil principle, like Osiris."[240] Here again we see the correspondence between the wheel and the labyrinth. In yet another variation, Budge in his *Gods of the Egyptians* presents Serapis, with head of bull and body of man, "the Tryer or Adversary who tests the souls of those seeking union with the Immortals. The maze was also doubtless used to represent the solar system, the Bull-Man representing the sun dwelling in the mystic maze of its planets, moons, and asteroid."[241] The Alexandrian Serapis is frequently depicted standing upon the sacred crocodile of the Nile, the devourer of souls in the Judgment of the Dead, thus also the abyss or dissolution. In Waite's The Wheel of Fortune he states, "I have, however, presented Typhon in his serpent form."[242] Typhon descends to the abyss, in Waite's Key 10, indicated by the glyph for both Aquarius and dissolution.

Serapis is said to be a combination word of Osiris and Apis, the god and his bull form, the animal to be sacrificed. Set, the Antagonist of Osiris, appears either as a black boar or as Typhon. By invoking Typhon Waite hints at the relation, indeed, the identity of god and antagonist, the lower form of himself; for the adversary is often a blood relation of the god.

CRESCENT MOONS

As we have seen, a spiral may stand for Above or Below. A good rule to apply in determining these is as follows: if the spiral unwinds from right to left the macrocosm is entailed; if the spiral is closing, as right to left, involution to the underworld is symbolized. Particularly as they appear in The High Priestess, it may be thought that crescent moons symbolize the macrocosm; since the spiral may symbolize the orbit of the moon as well as that of the sun. However, the moon partakes of much of the negative symbology of the Antagonist principle. Until the *hierosgamos* is attained, a polar opposition is in effect, involving *all* associated oppositions to the sun/macrocosm: cold, moist, dark, etc. Thus the chthonic realm, or death and the underworld, is indicated by the crescent moons that fluctuate between growth and decay. The crescent that points to the left is waxing, its opposite is a waning or dying moon. By contrast the sun has no phases. Like the Antagonist, the moon seeks to devour her spouse in the eclipse, but he is reborn in her; hence, the crescent moons express the same duality conveyed by the symbol of the spiral labyrinth. Going one step further, we may say that the crescent moons are another variation of the labyrinth symbol in that one quarter-moon is evolutive and the other involutive. These poles of waxing/waning, growth/decay, connote the same meaning ("Severity" and "Mercy") as the pillars Boaz and Joachin; therefore the utter propriety of the crescent moons with the pillars in Key 2. To drive home his point, Waite twice presents the crescents, in the headdress of the priestess and in the horns at her feet. They are the horns of the bull, so we are not to forget the significance of this animal, in relation to Taurus and the four fixed signs, as "breaker of the year" at the vernal point. The Isis' headdress of the high priestess incorporates the solar disc and crescent horns, symbolizing Osiris and Apis, the bull form to be sacrificed. The feeling of Key 2, therefore, is of the entrance to the underworld, and this interpretation agrees with the initial descent progression of the Major Arcana.

The crescent horn/moons appear again in Key 7, which is frequently the number of the last step in alchemical process. But the descent in the underworld continues beyond Key 7 to Key 15, the abyss, so we may ask what "victory" (the card's alternate title) is won before descent is completed. These moons, worn as epaulets by the charioteer, indicate rank, stature, or level of attainment. Since they are emblems of the phenomenal world of growth and decay, the card signifies that the charioteer has *conquered* these. He descends to the underworld with impunity because he is the same figure as that in Key 1, Hermes/Mercurius/Thoth. Indeed, it was said of Thoth that he wore a spiral moon as his headdress for having won five days each year from the moon goddess.

Let us look closely at two more details in Key 2 and then return to Key 7. Directly above the crescent headdress is a

239

pomegranate mandorla, drawn as two crescent-shaped pods enclosing the seed center. These are closed, whereas the headdress crescents and the epaulets of the charioteer turn outwards. Key 2 indicates, therefore, involution and evolution, or *the way in and the way out of the labyrinth,* as we shall see when we come to our spiral arrangement of the Major Arcana. Secondly, the foot of the priestess' gown is drawn to resemble water flowing down out of the picture; this detail has puzzled many. These are the waters of the underworld, traditional to many mythologies, leading down to the chthonic realm.

Regarding the underworld journey, the golden bough or magic wand which Aeneas bears with him in Virgil's description in the sixth book of the *Aeneid* "is his own counterpart, his spiritual 'double.' "[243] A variation of the staff of Hermes, the wand is carried by magician and charioteer. Symbolizing the Logos, the shaft of lightning in Key 16 transformed chaos into cosmos. Again the relation of Keys 7 and 16 comes to the fore. We recall that two intersecting circles constitute a mandorla, symbolizing the interpenetration of heaven and earth, Above and Below, the lightning bolt of the Tower was the action of Above on Below. We associated Key 16 with sacrifice. Thus the charioteer and his wand (as well as Key 1) symbolize the descending Logos whose sacrifice renews the regenerative force of the world. When crescent moons which point in are closed, they become a mandorla, signifying world renewed. Is this not the meaning of The World, with the wreath precisely like the two closed crescents of the moon? Just as Key 1 proceeds full circle to Key 0, Key 2 has a culmination in Key 21.

One last esoteric note on the crescent moons. Waxing and waning they are "Mercy" and "Severity," and are frequently depicted with smiling or frowning faces, as in fortune smiling or frowning on one. Waite has drawn a smile on the face of the dying moon in the charioteer's epaulets, a tribute to his utter indifference to life and death, his "victory" in the face of death.

240

THE LABYRINTH AND THE JOURNEY
TO THE UNDERWORLD

Perhaps the most incisive description of the labyrinth appears in John Layard's "The Malekulan Journey of the Dead," in which he quotes C. N. Deedes, who states, "the Labyrinth was the centre of activities concerned with those greatest of mysteries, Life and Death."[244] The Malekulan culture of the New Hebrides is of particular interest to our study because it is a megalithic culture largely untouched by the modern world. According to Layard, "It is now generally recognized that megalithic culture such as is found in Malekula is by no means an isolated phenomenon there, but forms part of a network of similar cultures diffused by means of maritime migrations which spread over a large part of the globe in the late neolithic or early Bronze Age times. . . . In the opinion of the natives, this megalithic culture was introduced from outside. . . . In South West Bay these immigrants are said to have been white-skinned, with aquiline noses."[245] The megalithic period, we recall, is the time of the creation of Stonehenge, and the macrocosmic orientation of the four fixed signs at the poles. Although Malekula has no taurean mythology, the sacred animal is the boar, whose tusks may curve into as many as three spirals, and whose sacrifice is made "in order to propitiate and thereby circumvent the destructive power of a cannibalistic Female Devouring Ghost, whose object is to 'eat' or annihilate the spirits of the dead and thus prevent them from accomplishing the long journey to the Land of the Dead."[246] The devouring theme of labyrinth and underworld journey is further dramatized by the fact that the entrance to the stone wall enclosing the ritual lodge is called "shark's jaw."

The dead achieve rebirth by means of the sacrifice; so rather than being devoured and reborn themselves, as in the traditional myth of the labyrinth, a surrogate is offered. Because of this the sacrificer must be aware of a close link between himself and the boar; indeed, "the central act of the whole Maki is the *self-sacrifice* of a man who symbolically immolates part of himself in the form of his tusked boars, these most precious possessions which he has spent his whole life in raising, with which he ritually identifies himself."[247]

Rather than being swallowed by Devouring Ghost, the dead spirit enters a cave—which is also a womb—through which it must pass on the journey to the Land of the Dead. At the entrance sits Devouring Ghost, and now we get the full impact of how the labyrinth is an initiatory rite. "She has drawn with her finger, in the sand, a geometric figure, and she sits beside it, waiting for the dead man to come. He sees her from a distance. He is confused at the sight of her and loses his way. When he regains his path and approaches the Devouring Ghost, she rubs out half the design. The dead man must know how to complete it. If he succeeds, he passes through the lines of the geometric design into the cave. If he does not succeed, he is devoured by this terrible ghost."[248]

Now, the "rebirth" is not restoration to the living, nor resurrection in the body as we understand in Christianity, but rather parallels the Egyptian underworld, in which the reborn Osiris presides over the Not-dead, a pantheon of ancestors judged worthy enough not to have been devoured by the crocodile. In effect, the path of the labyrinth guides the dead soul to that renewed life beyond the grave which the ancestors are already leading. The heroes of myth who emerge from the underworld signify, by analogy, the eternal life awaiting the human soul. And this is precisely the message of Tarot's Major Arcana, a descent to the underworld in the grand tradition of a Book of the Dead, and reunion of the individual soul with the sphere of divinity, the only difference being that Tarot's reunion is Above, whereas in the megalithic tradition the soul remains in the underworld for its eternal life. As Layard notes, there are some rather amazing similarities between the designs of the Malekulan labyrinths and "the megalithic tombs of the pre-Indo-Germanic peoples of the Mediterrean region."[249]

Below in the figure at the left we see one of the Malekulan designs, which are studied by the living in order to prepare for the initiation by Devouring Ghost. Beside the Malekulan labyrinth is what I have named the Caduceus Reading, a way of proceeding through Keys 1-18 in the form of a spiral. We shall examine this in greater detail subsequently. Keys

19, 20, 21, and 0 are not included because they represent the macrocosm.

Next we come to the "curiously embroidered" wallet (as Waite describes it) which the fool carries at the end of his wand. One should note its close proximity—or conjunction—to the sun. Also, it is to the *left* of the sun.

To understand this symbol we must return from the Pacific islands of the New Hebrides to the area of the Mediterranean. Here there are many examples of pig sacrifices, one of which is depicted on a 5th-century-B.C. Grecian vase, and is described by Joseph Campbell in *The Mythic Image*. The purpose of the pig purification is to appease the Furies, bent on avenging Orestes' murder of his mother.[250] Here the parallel is manifest to the terror inspired by Devouring Ghost, and its acceptance of the tusked boar in the soul's stead.

We have examined the bull as the dark, underworld aspect of the god. In the West there is also a pronounced tradition of the boar as Antagonist. Joseph Campbell notes, "the animal, which at first had been slain in the character of the god, comes to be viewed as a victim offered to the god on the ground of its hostility to the deity; in short, the god is sacrificed to himself on the ground that he is his own enemy."[251]

We have analyzed the meaning of horns symbolically, and in particular the sacrificial bull of the vernal equinox, that point at which day and night are equal. The esoteric value of that day is in the union of life and death, light and darkness, or mundane and underworld planes. In terms of the god, shadow and self become reconciled in the Reborn One. Because the boar bears horns (tusks), we may expect a similar mythology of the regeneration of the world/year as a result of the sacrifice. But the myths in which the boar is involved present an interesting switch. The boar changes roles with the sacrificer and becomes instead the one who metes out death to the god. No matter, for we have said that sacrificer and sacrifice are dual aspects of the one god. Attis and Adonis, vegetation gods of the vernal equinox, were gored to death by boars, as was Diarmuid of Irish legend. And the heroes Tristan and Odysseus carried scars of their encounters with boars, the curved tusks of which represent the spiral path to the underworld. Like the epaulets of the charioteer, the horns of the waxing and waning moon, these scars represent the triumph over death and mark the man who has journeyed to the netherworld and returned. To be fully appropriate, the scar should be spiral as well!

In our Major Arcana, the fool has descended to the abyss and yet returned again. The bag which he carries signifies all that he has acquired in his travels Above and Below. We are not to think of the contents as material possessions, but as acquisitions of the spirit, adventures in consciousness, adjudged truthful by the red feather of Maat. The design which Waite does not reveal, but which Paul Foster Case tells us is the Eye of Horus, leads us now to a discussion of the quaternity of Osiris, Isis, Horus, and Seth. Earlier we had said that the Antagonist may be the god's feminine opposite, the Two of the One, duality, darkness, and death. Or the pair may seek harmony and union, as lovers do, but are opposed by a third principle that works their separation and/or death. Whatever the variation, the One desires to return to unity from multiplicity, as we saw in our numerical run-through. It is my thesis that the One is equivalent to Light, and that the pair of lovers were originally Sol and Luna, Sun and Moon, in practically every mythology. In time the *hierosgamos* of the macrocosmic plane came to be read as human legend, with equivalent gods and goddesses for every culture. The Antagonist was macrocosmically that which occulted the light of Sun or Moon. On the human plane darkness and evil merge in the Antagonist of the abyss. From ancient Persia to the Pacific, God is light. In Zoroastrianism the first emanation of the eternal One was Light, from which issued the King of Light, Ahuramazda. The Malekulan creator is Taghar, the man in the moon as the principle of light. On the moon he begets human children who descend into their mothers' womb, in a primitive way rather like the Gnostic soul of light that becomes clothed through descent through the planetary spheres. And we have seen the importance of all the sun-bulls of the vernal equinox, that period when light emerges from the underworld. Small wonder, then, that the mega-lithic people would build an observatory to delineate the risings and settings of sun and moon, and that modern man would interpret Stonehenge as a place of bloody sacrifices.

Around the world, in the various myths of the divine pair, we find a pattern in which the bride is promised to a great king or lord, that is, affianced to Death as a metaphor of human fatality. The flight of the lovers, therefore, is simply the journey of sun and moon to escape their "eclipsing" by the antagonist. They "die" when he casts his dark shadow upon them. Since Death is Lord of Earth's Underworld, it is noteworthy that some eclipses are caused by the earth's shadow passing across the face of sun or moon. In many mythologies, a serpent or dragon devours the light principle. Here it is of interest that the Antagonist pole of the four fixed signs is Scorpio, often depicted as a dragon or serpent, and the autumn equinox is the time when the light enters the underworld and continues to the abyss of the solstice.

From this point of view, let us look again at Key 6, The Lovers. In the Marseilles' equivalent, the angel overhead is Cupid with bow and arrow. Behind him the sun blazes in multicovered rays of glory. Ostensibly the sun has nothing to do with the myth of Cupid; yet he is "the every-dying, ever-living god,"[252] son of the Great Mother as Venus or Aphrodite. The analogy to the descending and ascending sun-god is apparent. I suspect that earlier Tarot depicted in some way the connection between the lovers and the light principle, perhaps a masculine sun and feminine moon separated by an Antagonist or Third principle. At any rate, this is precisely what Waite represents in Key 15, The Devil; so the rendering of a glorious angel of light, with the sun as well, seems a restoration of the correct concept of The Lovers as sun and moon. Further, the Tree of Life is depicted in Key 6 with twelve flames or lights—the zodiac, which is the "life" of sun and moon, since they are sustained by their journey through the zodiac. This then is a reading of Adam and Eve as sun and moon, with the introduction of death into the Garden of eternal life being the same idea as death/darkness eclipsing the life of sun/moon.

If this theory is incorrect, then we must ask ourselves what the sun and moon are doing in a deck of cards that is concerned only with mundane marriage, for such Key 6 came to be called in the 18th century. No, it seems to me that the Major Arcana presents a clear statement—when the esoterica are unveiled—of the microcosmic *hierosgamos* of sulphur and quicksilver, and the macrocosmic conjunction of Sol and Luna. Undoubtedly in time the frivolous interpretation of The Lovers as marriage would predominate, for playing cards always had been playthings, and this came to be the protection of the esoteric doctrine within the Major Arcana. But our task is rather like that of the restorer of a painting which lies beneath several layers of other pictures added over the years. One has to know how much to rub away—and where to stop!

We can say with certainty, however, that A. E. Waite's deck proves our theory, since the Eye of Horus ties together all the symbolic threads. And here we must thank Joseph Campbell for his insight on the Eye of Horus in *The Mythic Image*. In the case of the Osiris myth, the divine pair are mother and son, Isis and Horus. Osiris was the first son of Geb and Nut, the primal parents as earth-god and sky-goddess. Set, Seth, or Typhon as the Greeks called him, was the jealous second son, who presented Osiris with an elaborate coffin and invited him to lie therein. It is a wonder that Osiris did not suggest to Seth that he was harboring a death wish for him; nevertheless, Osiris lay in the box and Set slammed shut the lid. Now since Osiris was the sun-god, the sequestering of the light symbolizes the night-journey of the sun, or the annual descent to the abyss. The latter is more likely since Plutarch notes the date as the seventeenth day of Athyr, when the sun was in Scorpio, then the sign of the death of the sun at the autumn equinox. Set as Antagonist assumed many forms. As Typhon he is frequently a serpent (Scorpio), although "often symbolized by a crocodile; sometimes his body is a combination of crocodile and hog."[253] As the latter he is the figure which devours the souls found wanting in the Egyptian Judgment of the Dead, the god of the abyss as devourer of light. And, also, we recall Oswald Wirth's depiction of the abyss as a crocodile in his Tarot card of "The Fool." It is in the form of a black boar that he next appears in the Osiris story, and here we must pause to recall that the boar—like the bull—is initiator of the labyrinthian journey to the underworld wherein rebirth takes place. In Malekula the boar was the sacrifice; in our Western myths the boar *sacrifices* the god. But sacrificer and sacrifice are one, as we shall see.

Osiris' coffin comes to rest in a distant land where Isis, his queen, finds it, only to have Set steal his body, and as a *black* boar rend it into fourteen parts, the days of the dying moon, from full to black. All of the parts are retrieved by Isis (see Waite's Key 2 for Isis as moon-goddess), except for Osiris' phallus which has been swallowed by a fish. But to be shut up in a coffin is to be resurrected; to be the dark moon is to be full again; and to be swallowed is to be reborn. Indeed, in Osiris' case, by means of the mystic *djed* phallus, he fathers a son—while dead!—Horus, who symbolizes the sun reborn from the abyss. Most myths stop here, since the son is clearly the father, just as Osiris lives again in the annual Apis bull. But since the father is born again in the son, there is really no reason why the son cannot resurrect the father, and that is what happens next. But first Horus must "slay the dragon," that is, death itself, the Antagonist of the abyss who slew his father-son. Joseph Campbell recounts the duel. "In a passage of *The Book of the Dead* (the chief Egyptian funerary text of ca. 1500 B.C. and thereafter) it is related that Seth, in the course of his battle with Horus, transformed himself in a whirlwind of fire into a black pig, which when Horus looked upon it burned out his left eye."[254]

In the conflict, Set loses a testicle to Horus. It is not quite an eye for an eye, but an eye for a ball at least. The symbology of the eye is rather complicated. To simplify and leave much unsaid, because of the eye's perception of light and the phallic shape of eye-beams, it may be a fertility symbol. Joseph Campbell continues, "And it was this sacrificed left EYE OF HORUS, when presented as an offering to the mummy of Osiris, that restored the deity to life—and eternal Life, beyond the cycle of death and generation: so that now, enthroned forever in the Netherworld, he reigns there as lord and judge of the resurrected dead."[255]

Let us again recall that Set is the Antagonist aspect of the One god, the dark aspect, while the sun is the light principle reborn. The eye that is offered and effects the resurrection parallels the phallus by which Osiris begot Horus. Therefore, the rebirth is really the result of the offered phallus *and* the won testicle, dark and light elements joined, as Osiris as Light (Sun) unifies the kingdoms of life and death, or on the mundane plane, Upper and Lower Kingdoms of Egypt. According to Cirlot, "the Egyptians defined the eye—or, rather, the circle of the iris with the pupil as centre—as the 'sun in the mouth' (or the creative Word)."[256]

Now, in the culminating scene following Osiris' resurrection, Joseph Campbell reproduces the scene in the underworld in which Set appears in his fourth animal representation with the head of an ass. We recall that Ialdabaoth, the Gnostic Antagonist, equated with Saturn and hence the abyss, appeared in the form of an ass. Joseph Campbell's description is as follows: "The figure with the head of an ass, stuck with knives and bound by his arms to a forked slave-stick, is Seth; conquered. The Minotaurlike figure behind Osiris is the god Serapis, a late, Ptolemaic (hence Hellenized) personification of the mystery of Osiris' identity with the sacred Apis Bull (the name Osiris plus Apis yields Serapis). . . . Serapis and Horus, on the other hand, are standing squarely on this earth, Horus with the head of a hawk and wearing the tail of a bull. His hawk's head is a reference to his daily flight as the sun bird, east to west, at the close of which he passes into the earth, to become, next day, reborn. He is thus the one who 'begets himself,' the son who is one with his father, and is consequently known as the 'bull of his own mother.' That is the idea suggested by the bull's tail, which unites him by association with the procreative pharaonic force symbolized in Serapis."[257]

THE FOOL'S WALLET

Now in The Fool there seem to be two different designs on the wallet, depending upon the period of the deck purchased, although all are Waite's doing. The alternate to the Eye of Horus is a falcon head, Horus as sun-bird, who flies east to west and "passes into the earth, to become reborn on the next day. He is thus the one who 'begets himself.'" The symbol is perfect for the fool, since he passes into the earth (abyss) and begets himself from the djed of the magician, or as the One, appears from the No-thing. In the circular flight of the sun-bird encompassing the earth from east to west, we may read the serpent uroboros engirdling the magician's waist. And in this transcendent flight, we are not to forget the feathering of the soul's own wings, else the example of the god be lost to man.

So it is in the Malekulan boar sacrifice that Joseph Campbell finds the explanation of the Eye of Horus. "Who would have expected . . . that an image given in *The Book of the Dead,* of Seth as a black pig that burned out the left eye (the lunar eye) of Horus, would be found in the New Hebrides— in the identification of the black body between waxing and waning crescent tusks of a boar with the 'new' or 'black' invisible moon at the time of its apparent death?"[258]

What is the meaning of the experience of the labyrinth and abyss, being swallowed by the Antagonist? Joseph Campbell speaks of the mythological death in the mystic sense "of an awakening to immortality through an act of psychological self-divestiture: and this second is the understanding symbolized in the eye, the EYE OF HORUS, by which the one thought to be dead is disclosed to himself and to all to be in fact alive eternally, both in himself and in the person of his son. And it was Seth, furthermore, the black boar—who was finally metaphysically consubstantial and so at one with both Horus and Osiris—who had provided the occasion for the lesson."[259] This "consubstantiality" is beautifully illustrated in the picture "The Birth of Horus," in which appears the mystical quaternity of Osiris, Isis, Horus, and Seth. "Here the newborn sun-god Horus-the-Child hovers in the risen solar disk above the mummy of his murdered father, which—like Vishnu on the cosmic snake—is couched on the crocodile-god Sebek of the abyss,"[260] from whom spring lotus buds symbolizing "resurgent life."[261] Now Sebek is not Set or Typhon, you may say, and you are correct; but Sebek as crocodile is the benign aspect of the abyss principle, death that supports life and even engenders it, for Sebek was god of the Nile from which the lotus grew.

As a corollary to what we have said, not to be swallowed is not to be reborn, both in the mythic and psychological senses. The crocodile abyss buoys up the sun on his back, just as the sun rises out of the watery abyss. Like the twenty-two mysteries of the Major Arcana through which Hermes/Mercurius/Thoth guides us, the "lessons" which Set and Devouring Ghost provide are initiatory in the highest sense, indicating the way of the soul's rebirth.

And now let us have another look at The Fool. "As symbolized in the imagery of myth, it is at the summit of the mountain, the zenith of the day, the solstice of the year, the top of the Stairway of Planets, the apex of the World Tree, where the opposite sides come together that the mystery of this coming together of *all* opposites is realized, recognized, and solemnized in the symbolic adventure of the sacrifice or its equivalent, a sacred marriage. . . ."[262]

Its power is perfect if converted into earth, as the *Emerald Tablet* tells us. Above is about to "marry" Below once more, the Light/Logos wedding with the Antagonist of the abyss. But what of the alchemical conjunction of Sol and Luna, and the macrocosmic *hierosgamos* of sun and moon? They are here, too. The left eye of Horus is the dark of the moon at the conjunction with the sun. Horus' bright eye is the sun; so Waite has placed the Eye of Horus to the left of the sun to symbolize the conjunction of sun and moon, the *hierosgamos*. (See Drawing 22 on next page.)

We noted earlier that Key 9 contains the *hierosgamos* in the interpenetrating triangles within the hermit's lantern. Furthermore, The Moon depicts this conjunction, and now we have seen that The Fool does also. The significance of this is that all three cards conclude their linear series. Whether alchemical, psychological, or macrocosmic—the soul's reunion with its Creator-Spirit—the resolution of opposites which the *hierosgamos* symbolizes is the apotheosis of all process; hence, Keys 1-9, Keys 10-18, and Keys 19-0. Since Horus' offering to Osiris restores the god to eternal life, Waite's embellishment of the fool's wallet with the Eye of Horus is entirely appropriate for the card whose zero number symbolizes eternity.

THE ECLIPSE OF THE LOVERS

To return to my theory of the origin of sun and moon as the lovers of legend and mythology, let us take a parting glance at the Osiris story. Horus' left eye is the moon, the

DRAWING 22

dark or new moon. The bright eye—the right—is his solar eye. Together they are a *hierosgamos,* which may explain the double spirals engraved on megalithic stones. These spirals may be the winding up and winding down of the sun's path in its annual journey, and at the same time the image of descent and ascent of the labyrinth. But these double spirals may be the lunar and solar eyes of a god, appearing as shown below.

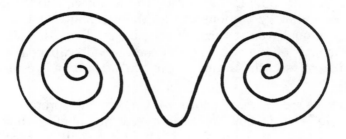

Now as a *hierosgamos,* these eyes are eclipsed by the Antagonist Set, since he puts out the lunar eye and causes the disappearance of Osiris, the solar eye. The correspondence to the eclipse of the lovers is manifest, as is the Celtic myth of Diarmuid and Grianne, promised bride of Finn McCool, Diarmuid's uncle. The lovers are pursued by Finn as Antagonist, bent no doubt on eclipsing their light; and to this day in the Irish countryside the great horizontal capstones of megalithic sites are known as "Diarmuid and Grianne's bed," while the vertical slabs are called "Finn's Thumb." Finn's Thumb casts a shadow on the sun or moon's light when rising or setting, while the "bed" is where the light lies. In view of the fact that so many megalithic structures have an astronomical orientation, as Hawkins has determined, it would be valuable to study these sites for orientations to eclipses and solar and lunar risings at the equinoxes and solstices.

THE FOOL

It is doubtful if anyone today, while playing poker with "jokers wild," stops to reflect that the joker—derived from the fool of Tarot—symbolizes the dying and resurrected sun-god. The tradition for this comes from Frazer's *The*

Golden Bough. Although he does not mention playing cards, there is an extensive mythology of the sun-king, with the death occurring near the vernal point and the renewal of the year being the result. The fool dies so that the sun-king may be reborn. There is no doubt that this myth is what Waite intends, because of the prominence of the sun and the zodiac design of the fool's garb. We saw the same myth in the esoteric meaning of The Hanged Man. The parallel is quite simple. The fool's journey to the abyss, and through all the initiatory stations of the Major Arcana, is like the sun's annual transit through the zodiac. Thus the sacrificial animal of the equinox and the human scapegoat play similar roles in the drama of the sun's death and resurrection.

Let us refer once more to Cirlot's interpretation of Oswald Wirth's The Fool: "an overturned obelisk—a solar symbol and also symbolic of the Logos—and a crocodile about to devour what must be returned to chaos."[263] In effect, then, Logos must be returned to the chaos of the abyss, for therein lies the renewal of the world (Key 21). As we have seen, the descent takes place on The Stairway of Planets, or the pole of the World Axis/Tree, which has its equivalent in the May Pole of the various calendar festivals, usually occurring on Whitsun, the *seventh* Sunday after Easter, celebrated as a commemoration of the *descent* of the Holy Spirit. According to Frazer's *The Golden Bough,* "A regular feature in the popular celebration of Whitsuntide in Silesia used to be, and to some extent still is, the contest for the kingship. This contest took various forms, but the mark or goal was generally the May-tree or May-pole. Sometimes the youth who succeeded in climbing the smooth pole and bringing down the prize was proclaimed the Whitsuntide King and his sweetheart the Whitsuntide Bride."[264]

Frazer points out that these kings and queens, or lords and ladies, represent the spirit of vegetation, that is, *the greening of nature associated with the sun's or year's renewal.* "At Hildesheim, in Hanover, five or six young fellows go about on the afternoon of Whit-Monday cracking long whips in measured time and collecting eggs from the houses. The chief person of the band is the Leaf King, a lad swathed so completely in brichen twigs that nothing can be seen of him but his feet."[265] Here we see a parallel to the May Pole (man as sacrificial tree, Christ's cross which in time came to symbolize his sacrifice), and to the festival of Cybele and Attis, celebrated at the vernal equinox. "On the twenty-second day of March, a pine-tree was cut in the woods and brought to the sanctuary of Cybele, where it was treated as a great divinity. The trunk was swathed like a corpse with woolen hands and decked with wreathes of violets, for violets were said to have sprung from the blood of Attis . . . and the image of a young man, doubtless that of Attis himself, was tied to the middle of the stem."[266]

Thus the May Pole is the god *and* the path (axis) of his descent down the World Tree. Often the Pole is pruned in such a way as to allow a bunch of foliage to remain at the top "as a memento that in it we have to do, not with a dead pole, but with a living tree from the greenwood."[267] The equivalence is apparent in the Christmas tree (the *ever*green lives when all other trees die), the Yule symbol of the Light/Logos/Savior. Incidentally, all of the wands depicted in Waite's Minor Arcana are pruned to permit some foliage to remain.

Other examples of the spirit of vegetation are Leaf King, Grass King, and Green George. In the more northerly latitudes these festivals may occur at Midsummer, since the vernal equinox is calculated for the equator, and the year's greening does not take place until much later. Midsummer is of course the summer solstice, which we associated with the sacred marriage of Cancer and Leo, and it is interesting to note the local mock marriages of young boys and girls who symbolize the macrocosmic pair.

The relation of these sun-kings to Tarot's fool becomes clear when we read in Frazer of the associated tradition of foolishness: ". . . a boy or lad is swathed in the yellow blossom of the broom, the dark green twigs of the firs, and other foliage. Thus attired he is known as the Quack and goes from door to door, whirling about in the dance, while an appropriate song is chanted and his companions levy contributions. In the Fricktal, Switzerland, at Whitsuntide boys go out in a wood and swathe one of their number in leafy boughs. He is called the Whitsuntide-lout (Pfingstlummel), and being mounted on horseback with a green branch in his hand he is led back into the village. At the village well a halt is called and the leaf-clad lout is dismounted and ducked. . . . Thereby he acquires the right of sprinkling water on everybody, and he exercises the right specially on girls and street urchins. The urchins march before him in bands begging him to give them a Whitsuntide wetting."[268] Three ideas are present in the Whitsuntide wetting, all of which have a relation to ideas we have discussed in connection with The Fool. First, wetting as *fertility*, matter impregnated by spirit, which has secondary associations of baptism by the Holy Spirit, symbolized in Tarot as the water triangle present in the arms and tunic of The Hanged Man and as one of the trines in the light (Logos) of The Hermit. The Whitsuntide-lout's dunking in the well corresponds to the fool's descent to the abyss, and this symbolic act bestows on him the right to "baptize" (save) others, in the same way that the fool's descent and return "points the way" of salvation for the individual human soul. At the same time, when we consider descending spirit in the form of the water trine, we should not forget the pattern of descending spirit symbolized in Key 1 by the magician's gesture, in Key 2 by the blue robe depicted as water flowing down, and in Key 3 by the waterfall. Of course, this idea appears as pouring water in Keys 14 and 17.

But, we may ask, why do myth and folklore associate fertility, greening, and renewal with madness? The nature-god Pan—and the derivation of the word *panic*—comes to mind immediately. Another reason goes back to our equivalence of fool and magician, Alpha and Omega of the Major Arcana; and fool as inversion of the king (4 + 9 = 13 + 9 = 22, or Zero). As to the origin of kingship, Frazer's theory is that the ancient tribal magicians and shamans became the kings of later societies because of their peculiar *mana*, or special powers. The madness of the shaman in performing his rite resembles that of the fool. So, too, the gyrating dances of the Sufis and Holy Fools reflect the macrocosmic spiral of the sun's path. The identification with the sun must be kept in mind always. Cirlot tells us that "the clown is the victim chosen as a substitute for the king, in accord with the familiar astrobiological and primitive ideas of the ritual assassination of the king."[269] This theory is given added weight when we consider the fool's sacrifice in relation to the scapegoat tradition. According to Manly Hall, "The practice among the ancient Jews of choosing a scapegoat upon which to heap the sins of mankind is merely an allegorical depiction of the Sun Man who is the scapegoat of the world and upon whom are cast the sins of the twelve houses (tribes) of the celestial universe."[270]

Again, the relation of The Fool to both sun and zodiac is apparent because of the prominence of the sun and the twelve lights of the fool's belt. Now the crucial times in the sun's passage through the twelve signs of the zodiac are the vernal equinox and the winter solstice. We may expect to find, therefore, festivals of fools oriented to the winter solstice to match those of the vernal equinox. These are the rites of the abyss, chaos and disorder, an inversion of the celestial order of the summer solstice where the sun reigns, just as the fool is an inversion of the king. Frazer cites the examples of The King of the Bean, Bishop of Fools, Abbott of Unreason, and Lord of Misrule, all festivals associated with this period in the Sun-king's journey when he fell ill and his strength (light) began to wane. Similarly, the sick-king of alchemy plays such a role.

The renewal of the year (the sun-king) through foolishness has its parallel in the magician/shaman's healing rites. That is to say, when the normal order is in peril, its antithesis may resolve the quandary; hence, society turns to the feet of the king for the king's salvation, which tells us that the fool is another aspect of the same principle. Fool = Magician, and Magician = the healer Hermes/Mercurius/ Thoth. Not only are we to think of this panacea as healing individual ills, but also the world is renewed and restored, and the celestial solar wheel enabled to proceed, the underworld spiral unwinding to the solstice. In the role of fool, the Sun Man serves himself as his sacrifice, thereby saving not only Himself but the world as well.

We have seen the associations of the winter solstice with chaos, and the astrological rulership of Saturn (Chronos) who *devours* his own children, the products of space/time. Also, the relations to death and the devil were delineated, often symbolized by a goat or an ass. According to Frazer,

"Among the buffooneries of the Festival of Fools one of the most remarkable was the introduction of an ass into the church, where various pranks were played with the animal. At Autun the ass was led with great ceremony to the church under a cloth of gold, the corners of which were held by four canons; and on entering the sacred edifice the animal was wrapt in a rich cape, while a parody of the mass was performed. A regular Latin liturgy in glorification of the ass was chanted on these occasions, and the celebrant priest imitated the braying of an ass."[271] The ass reminds us of the Gnostic archon/creator of the world, Ialdabaoth, who *inverted* cosmic order by his *evil* creation.

To conclude our brief study of the tradition of the fool, it is apparent that the import of this tradition is relevant to the themes we have delineated in the Major Arcana, particularly the Great Myth of descent and ascent, death and resurrection. Recalling that 1392 was the date of the first *recorded* appearance of Tarot extant today, we must realize that the folklore which Frazer recounts has its origins in that same period of European history. Therefore, not only are we justified in drawing on the folklore of the fool, but the Major Arcana cannot be explained adequately without bringing to bear this tradition, for the reader of today has only the most foolish and superficial associations with The Fool. A. E. Waite has certainly utilized the medieval folklore of the fool, but we must remember that all Tarot decks—no matter the period—include The Fool. Waite then has only restored these rich associations.

Finally, we must not forget the fool's connection with the sun in this tradition. Mindful of this, how else are we to interpret, except as we have done, the Major Arcana's The Sun and The Fool? They constitute the first and last cards of the third tier of our Magic Nine arrangement. The *Emerald Tablet* concludes, "What I had to say about the operation of the Sun is completed."

CHAPTER IX

THE CADUCEUS AND ASTROLOGY

Yet another symbol of the Great Myth is the sacred wand of Hermes, encircled with the evoluting serpents, linking rod and staff to World Tree, Stairway of Planets, and the numinous symbols of the East and Near East, Mountain, Tree, and *djed* pillar. Originating in the 4th millenium B.C. the concept of World Navel/Tree unites cosmic and mundane planes, or Above and Below. The spiral is the form which reconciles the two domains by means of both horizontal *and* vertical movement, analogous to a serpent's tree-climbing. Inherent in the symbology of World Navel/Tree is the sense of a Center, or Axis, which extends from the macrocosm, where the sun's serpentine course is from pole to pole during the year, to the microcosm, the cells of the human body which bear the spiral coils of DNA, carriers of genetic evolution. The true Fool may read in the caduceus symbol, therefore, his own initiation into the mystery dimension of cell and psyche, where Above and Below merge infinitely.

From the 4th millenium to the Christian era, the descent/ascent path of the soul itself undergoes a transformation, the Stairway of Planets becoming the tree of metals, or *arbor philosophica* of alchemy, retaining the correspondence of planets and metals. The point should not be missed that this is the pre-Christian "ladder of souls" in new form, less pagan perhaps to blunt accusations of planetary worship, but retaining analogies to the soul through the crystalline or glass transparency of the Hermetic "egg" refined within the "body" of the alchemical athanor. Just as the journey of the soul through the planetary spheres is a transformative process paralleling the refining of base metals in the alchemical process, we are dealing really with *transcendent* processes involving the evolution of spiritual consciousness.

In order to know where we stand in relation to these it is necessary to review the Hermetic perspective. To the lesser fool, the correlation of metals and planets is meaningless. However, secret societies have always made much of the fact that man's most precious gifts are utterly despised by the great mass of men. Thus in the "Tractatus aureus," "ascribed to Hermes and regarded as of Arabic origin even in the Middle Ages,"[272] the spiritual essence is described as "cast upon the dung heap."[273] Further, the alchemical gold is *aurum non vulgi,* that is, not common gold at all, but that which is to be reaped at the end of a spiritual process.

What is truly extraordinary is that in the marvelous coded economy of a deck of cards, we have the Great Myth of divine descent to the mundane plane, Word made Flesh, and then the elevation of the mundane soul to the plane of the divine. Now as I have said earlier, the sequence in the Major Arcana is of a descent from the divine plane (spirit) to the mundane, followed by an ascent to the divine, from Saturn to "gold of the Sun." As Jung notes, "in alchemy the ascent comes first and then the descent."[274] He then substantiates this by quoting from the *Emerald Tablet.* "It ascendeth from the earth to heaven, and descendeth again to the earth, and receiveth the power of the higher and lower things. So wilt thou have the glory of the whole world."[275]

At the same time, Jung notes that the probable Gnostic prototype first contains a descent, and *then* an ascent. Since Tarot commences with a descent, it is my conclusion that Tarot's roots must be earlier than contemporaneous with alchemy in the Middle Ages. Indeed the astrological system which places Saturn at the abyss is of the same consciousness that is demonstrated at Stonehenge and the Great Pyramid. Whereas alchemy is concerned with Mercurius, Tarot harkens back to Hermes, and even earlier Gnostic elements pervade Hermeticism. Therefore, alchemy appears to be a later form of Gnostic/Hermetic ideas of the last centuries B.C., preserved in the now legendary Books of Thoth. Jack Lindsay notes that they "certainly existed in Hellenistic–Roman times, if not earlier, since Clement of

Alexandria gives us an elaborate account of a procession in which they were carried:

> The Singer is the one opening the march, bearing one of the attributes of music. He must know by heart two of the Books of Hermes: the first that contains the hymn to the gods, the second that sets out the rules of the royal life. After the singer comes forward the Astrologer who holds in his hand the clock and the palm, symbols of astrology. He must know and have unceasingly on his lips the Books of Hermes treating of this science. These number four: one deals with the systems of stars that appear fixed; another on the meetings of the sun's and moon's light; the other two on their risings. In the third place comes the sacred Scribe with plumes on his head and in his hand a book and a rule, on which are set also the ink and reed he uses in writing. He in his turn is held to know what concerns the hieroglyphs, cosmography, geography, the course of the sun, moon, and seven planets. . . ."[276]

Four entire volumes on astrology! One book on eclipses and two on the risings of sun and moon: these are the concerns of the Megalithic peoples.

Thus, it seems that alchemy and the Hermes/Mercurius/Thoth myths are remnants of another Great Myth, circa 2,000 B.C., illustrated by Stonehenge's alignments, involving the journey of the sun through the zodiac, which is paralleled by the *rotatio,* or cyclical processes of alchemy. Mercury's proximity to the Sun and the tradition that has Prometheus lighting (at the wheel of the Sun)[277] the fire that he brings from the gods to man suggest that there may be an equivalence between these two gods, and, indeed, their functions are parallel.

In the circular symbology of the dragon or serpent biting its tail (uroboros), we are reminded of the zodiac, *zoe* (life) and *diakos* (wheel), which is, according to J. E. Cirlot, "the process by which primordial energy, once fecundated, passes from the potential to the virtual, from unity to multiplicity, from spirit to matter, from the non-formal world to the world of forms, and then returns along the same path. This," he continues, "accords with the teaching of oriental ontology, which holds that the life of the universe is split into two opposing yet complementary phrases; involution (or materialization) and evolution (or spiritualization). . . . As Jung notes, according to Manichean belief the demiurge builds a cosmic wheel, related to the *rota* and the *opus circulatorium* of alchemy and identical in that it signifies sublimation [that is, spiritualization] . . . this form of motion, rotation on the vertical plane—descending and ascending—echoes the Platonic theories of the soul's 'fall' into material existence and its need to find salvation by returning along the same path."[278]

I am concerned here with the connection between the functions and associations of Hermes/Mercury and the Major Arcana of the Tarot. In other words, the message of Tarot is Hermetic; therefore, if we specifically examine Hermes/Mercury's various roles and functions, we shall see a connection with Tarot *in every respect.* For example, Mercury was also a god of crossroads, and the statues, or herms, of the erect god convey the same transformative meaning as the lingam/yoni symbols of Tantra Yoga that unite sexual and spiritual energies. A crossroads is also a place of conjunction or coming together of opposites; in the same sense Mercury symbolizes the resolution of all opposites. On another level of meaning, a crossroad is not merely a two-dimensional, mundane crossing, but if we include the third dimension of a vertical plane, then the implication of spiritual ascent or descent is involved. Where this "ladder" or "Stairway of Planets" intersects with the mundane plane is known as the ecliptic. If we add the fourth dimension, of time, there are then certain points in time of specific importance in the intersection of the mundane and heavenly. These are of course the equinoxes and solstices, wherein the temporal and mundane stand still, so to speak. The etymology of solstice is as follows: "*sol*, sun + –*stitiu*, a standing still, from *sistere*, to cause to stand (still), to stand still (of *sist*)."[279] Sun/spirit and its equivalent the human soul "find salvation by returning along the same path" through the zodiac, or up the Stairway of Planets. Mercury, in his masculine, active, sulphurous aspect, symbolizes the sun/spirit/logos and, indeed, makes the same journey as the

Sun, yet stands at the crossing as "pointer of the way" for the human soul. In another aspect Mercury is feminine because its metal is white, identifying quicksilver with the moon astrologically, salt alchemically, and the passive *anima mundi* that has to be rescued or resurrected from matter. Union of Sun and Moon is the alchemical *hierosgamos,* which Mercury as androgyne also symbolizes.

Sometimes the figure is a *monstrum hermaphroditum,* an hermaphoroditic monster that contains fearsome quaities that one sees associated with medieval depictions of the devil. We must remember that as messenger from the sun (logos), Mercury passes through hell, or the nadir, the dark chthonic realm of superstition, but also of pure idea, wherein all duplicities and contraries are married, resolved. Again, such a symbol guides one into the mystery dimension of one's own psyche and its 'intersection' with the collective unconscious; thus Jung has seen Mercury/Hermes as a symbol of the individuation process.

To sum up the functions and associations of Mercury/Hermes/Thoth: he is a guide to the underworld, where he may manifest shadow/trickster/devil qualities associated with the chthonic world and the *prima materia*; yet he is *lapis*, philosopher's stone *in potentia*, and "pointer of the way" for the human soul who may follow him up the Stairway of Planets that intersects the heavenly and mundane planes, where he may mediate at the wedding of Sun and Moon, dual aspects of himself, or appear as the *anima mundi,* the feminine soul of the world, or as Logos, the spiritual Word of God. As scribe of the gods he leads the procession that culminates in the gold of the sun, the *solificatio* initiation in which the midnight sun is seen shining on high.

ASTROLOGICAL ELEMENTS

As Jung tells us, "One of the roots of the peculiar philosophy relating to Mercurius lies in ancient astrology and in the Gnostic doctrine of the archons and aeons, which is derived from it."[280] Since by Hermetic law Above and

Below correspond, we can see the reason for mundane replicas of the macrocosm, as well as stone structures that chart the movements of the sacred sun and moon, particularly to render aid through ritual magic to a dying sun at the solstice when its regeneration may have been in doubt.

The Major Arcana depict the descent from the macrocosm in many forms. Key 10 presents the involuting golden serpent, related to the Serpent/Saviour of the Gnostic sect known as Ophites. Key 12 is a graphic symbol for sulphur, which was thought to be the active fire of the sun. Temperance, Key 14, depicts an angel descended from on high, his wings still spread. The abyss of matter, Key 15, confines Eve and Adam, who is the Gnostic Anthropos or First Man. If we think once more of the 15 steps of descent of Zosimos, and the relation to the planetary picture circa 2,000 B.C., then the abyss or solstice occurs in Key 15, Saturn's domain, ruler of Capricorn. The descending path has been through Virgo, Libra, Scorpio, Sagittarius, and Capricorn (5 signs with 3 cards each, totaling 15 steps). The way back to the midheaven of the summer solstice proceeds in an evolutive direction up the right side of the planetary houses.

Next, we proceed through Sagittarius' opposite number, Pisces, governed similarly by Jupiter; up through Aries, opposite Scorpio, both ruled by Mars; next through Venus-ruled Taurus, across the stairs from Libra; and through Mercury's Gemini, opposite Virgo. In the Major Arcana, therefore, the ascent is along the same path as the descent, and since the planetary rulers and their sequence are the same, no redundant cards are needed to convey this idea. Most significantly, since no series of Keys has appeared for Queen Moon and King Sun in the sequence of Keys 1–15, when the ascent has reached the point beyond Gemini, then cards are introduced for Moon and Sun, the planetary houses of the midheaven of Cancer and Leo, Keys 16–18 being those for the moon, and Keys 19–21 the sun.

Our Magic Nine arrangement with Keys 19, 20, 21, and 0 on one plane indicates that the latter series stands for the macrocosmic or spiritual realm; moreover, this heavenly kingdom dramatizes the elevation of the mundane to it. In Key 19, The Sun, a horse appears, which Waite tells us is "animal nature in a state of perfect conformity."[281] Although I do not have in hand the first edition of Waite's *The Pictorial Key to the Tarot,* it is evident that in subsequent editions he revealed less than before, since Paul Foster Case, in quoting that first edition, tells us that Waite indicates the horse is a "symbol of solar energy."[282] A further equation of Keys 19–0 with the plane of liberation is manifest in another revelation of the first edition: "The child is fair, like the Fool, and like the Fool, wears a wreath and a red feather. The feather has the same meaning as that of the Fool. The wreath is of flowers, instead of leaves, intimating the near approach to the harvest of final realization and liberation."[283]

This final harvest of souls is present in the resurrection of Judgment, Key 20. Here the sense of Tarot as a Book of the Dead comes again to the fore (dead matter elevated to the angelic realm). Note that the bodies of the resurrected corpses are of the same grey color as the backgrounds in Keys 13–15, which we associated with Saturn and the abysmal signs of Capricorn and Aquarius, paralleling man's own dull lead. The Book of the Dead familiar to Western man is the Egyptian. Waite was steadfast in his rejection of Egyptian origins for Tarot, yet freely utilized Egyptian symbology where it suited his purposes (sphinxes in Key 7 and Typhon in Key 10).

From the astrological point of view, Tarot's Major Arcana presents the sun's annual journey through the zodiac, the Stairway of Planets. Sun and Fool are akin, aspects of the spiritual essence. The Fool is meant to signify this because his garb bears ten solar wheels of eight-spoked wheels, also symbolic of the *rotatio,* the alchemical process. The alchemists saw a parallel between the cycle of the sun's annual death and resurrection and the transformative process whereby man becomes gold of the sun. According to the *Emerald Tablet,* the perfection of the sun's work (*opus*) occurs when it returns to earth, ascent and descent being the spiral cycle from pole to pole during the year. In a moment we shall follow the serpent's path through the Keys of the Major Arcana.

What are we to make of the fact that all of the figures in Keys 19–0 are naked except the Fool? In Key 19, "The child is naked," says Waite, "in accordance with an old Qabalistic saying that spirit clothes itself to come down and divests itself of the garments of matter to go up."[284] Why then should the Fool be clothed? The answer is obvious. Clearly he is about to come down again, the abyss looming before him.

Earlier we indicated the correspondence of The Chariot, Key 7, to The Magician, Key 1, and to The Fool. The propriety of the Magic Nine was established—in part—by the relation of Key 10 (wheel) + 9 = 18 (sun), wheels being early solar glyphs. Cirlot notes that "The idea of the sun as a two-wheeled chariot is only at one remove from this."[285]

Since there are connections between Keys 1 and 7, the addition of nine suggests that we are to look for parallels between Keys 10 and 16. First of all, the import of Key 10's meaning is our astrological theme of ascent and descent. Descent is manifest in Key 16, the fall of king and queen, but ascent is cleverly disguised in some very esoteric symbology. However, since the exoteric Tarot also depicts a tower, we are safe in saying that our interpretation is not the result of Waite's esoteric additions, but inherent in original Tarot. Indeed, the tower bears a relation to the Stairway of Planets and the whole theme of ascent/descent; for the tower is symbolic of ascent "by the simple application of the symbolism of level (whereby material height implies spiritual elevation) . . . the same symbolism as the ladder—linking earth and heaven. . . . Since the idea of elevation or ascent, implicit in the tower, connotes transformation and evolution, the athanor (the alchemist's furnace) was given the shape of a tower to signify inversely that the metamorphosis of matter implied a process of ascension."[286] Even in the exoteric Tarot, the tower's dislodged peak bears a strong resemblance to a King's crown. But why a sovereign's crown? The second noteworthy feature of our card makes clear the reason for this. Key 16, we recall, is the beginning of the ascent to heaven. What is it that shatters the chains of materiality which bind the lovers of Key 15? It is the action of Above on Below. "The thunderbolt (or lightning) is celestial fire as an active force . . . related to dawn and illumination, symbolic of the spring princple and of the initial stage [ascent] of every cycle. The thunderbolt is held to be an emblem of sovereignty."[287]

Mundane autonomy is overthrown by the bolt from Above. The alchemical parallel is the separation by fire of the pairs of opposites (symbolized by king and queen) from the leaden-colored *prima materia*. In Key 16, the divine, therefore, descends to the mundane in the form of celestial fire, enabling commencement of the ascent back to the divine to take place.

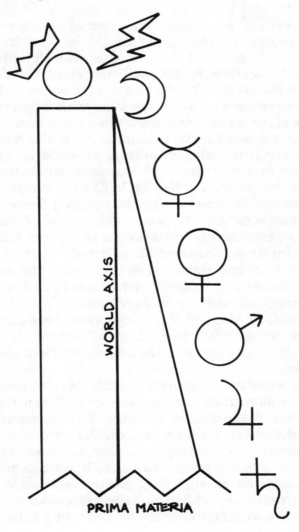

The picture above demonstrates the connection between Key 16 and the world-axis symbol of the Stairway of Planets. At the winter solstice, the abyss of the nigredo, some intervention is necessary from "above" to initiate the spiritual birth, to ignite the new light of the ascent phase. Significantly, Key 16 follows Key 15, the nadir. The structure of the tower presents a picture of undifferentiated matter *(prima materia)* at the base, and gold at the crown. This is the order of the planetary rulerships of the Stairway of Planets, and the order of transformation of the metals within the athanor, which the tower so closely resembles. The twenty-two yods of fire are the initiatory keys of the Major Arcana, transforming in effect, which lead the initiate to the spiritual height and liberation of The Fool.

Besides World Tree, Stairway of Planets, and Wheel, there is yet another archetype of meaning which conveys a sense of the macrocosmic spirit's descent to man, the theme of our astrological run-through. This is the inverted (or descending) triangle, in alchemy symbolic of water; yet these waters are cosmic and baptismal, akin to those being poured by the angel of Key 14. In Key 6, the angel's form is the graphic design of a triangle, touching the point of the mountain's earthly aspiration. The symbol of water links both ascent/descent, *prima materia* and divine, because the primal waters "contained all solid bodies before they acquired form and rigidity. For this reason the alchemists gave the name of 'water' to quicksilver in its first stage of transmutation and, by analogy, also to the 'fluid body' [spiritual] of Man."[288] Water also symbolizes descent and ascent in that it falls from "heaven" and thus involutes in the raining process, whereas by evaporation it evolutes to heaven.

The water trine appears graphically in many places in the Tarot Major Arcana but most obscurely of all in the nipples and navel of the child in The Sun. We have mentioned the triangle in Key 12, The Hanged Man; and whether it is interpreted as the glyph for sulphur, or as the water trine with the cross of matter above, both symbols signify the spiritual principle, equivalent in alchemy to active sulphur or quicksilver. According to Waite's first edition: "The nipples and navel of the child are the points of a water triangle, hinting at the letter Mem and the Hanged Man. For the stage of unfoldment represented by the Sun is the expression of the law the Hanged Man symbolizes."[289]

In describing Mem, Paul Foster Case tells us that it is "the second of the three mother letters of the Hebrew alphabet. Its name means literally 'seas,' but, like many plurals in Hebrew, it designates a general idea, in this instance, 'water.' In this connection, we may note that the alchemists call water [quicksilver] the mother, seed, and root of all minerals.' "[290]

This substantiates what we have said of Mercurius as uroboros, or beginning and end of process, Keys 1 and 0, lead and gold, dark-sun and Sun, *prima materia* and philosopher's stone; thus it can assume the form of active sulphur or quicksilver.

Case continues: "*Water,* the element represented by Mem, is the first mirror. Water reflects images upside down, and this idea is carried out by the symbolism and title of Key 12, which is a symbol of reflected life, or life in image, of life in the forms taken by the occult 'water,' quicksilver or cosmic substance."[291]

Thus the esoteric meaning of Key 12 is cosmic substance descending or involuting. The graphic design of this card, triangle and cross, conveys this meaning on an elementary level, as we saw in our first run-through. What Case fails to notice, and what our Magic Nine reveals, is that as water reflects the world upside down, Key 21, The World, is the mirror reflection of Key 12, in *number* as well as image.

Note that the right leg is rigid in both cards, and the left leg is bent behind. Waite enforces the mirror reflection of the two cards by adding a second wand to *anima mundi;* hence these form a triangle identical to that of The Hanged Man. (See Drawing 23.)

To whom or what does The Magician point to in Key 1? Drawing a line from his arm, we see that it indicates Key 0, The Fool, which cards have been linked, along with Key 7. If an equal angle is drawn from The Fool, it ends at Key 7, forming an inverted pyramid or water trine, with its base running from Key 1 to Key 7. Interestingly enough, the figures of Magician, Charioteer, and Fool, which define the angles of the trine and stand at its three corners, represent

DRAWING 23

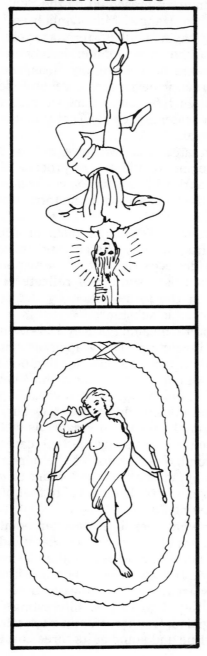

esoterically Hermes/Mercurius, the spiritual Monad whose descent is symbolized by an inverted trine!

But the relation of these three Keys does not end here. We recall that the descent to the four and the ascent to the Monad are simultaneous. This was discussed relevant to The Fool's descent vertically to Key 4, the elemental, mundane world of four dimensions, four directions, four elements, etc. The glyphs for salt and *lapis* being similar in some alchemical texts, we are to infer that salt is interpenetrated by spirit, and rendered thusly: ⊡ . In this glyph we see combined the square world of Key 4 and the circular cosmos of Key 0, demonstrating the "impossible" squaring of the circle, impossible because incommensurable planes are united, Above and Below, or the circle of the infinite, and the square of the bound world. Essentially the meaning of circle-squaring is also the meaning of the Incarnation, which is the Mystery behind the mystery of descent. Delving into this now would take another hundred pages. Suffice to say that the unique trine of Keys 1, 7, and 0 demonstrates the squaring of the circle, or the reconciliation of bound and Infinite, Below and Above, as surely as it is demonstrated at Stonehenge and the Great Pyramid. The demonstration lies in the relation of the numbers of the trine. Instead of zero, let us take 22 for The Fool, since it is the twenty-second Arcanum, which gives us 1, 7, and 22. If 7 is the diameter of a circle, then its circumference will be 22. The elusive principle sought by the ancients was *pi,* which is the value of 22. Seven is also the path of the Monad (1), the Stairway of *Seven* Planets to which it descends in its incarnation; hence $22/7 = 3.14$, *pi.*

If water symbolizes cosmic substance, or the spiritual essence of nature, and if "spirit clothes itself to come down," then this card of imminent descent presents spirit congealed in the form of ice, that is, water in the solid state.

Let us examine now the Fool card of Oswald Wirth, Waite's Fool, and the planetary houses. The icy peaks also suggest spiritual elevation, and on the Stairway of Planets, only the sun in Leo conjoined with the moon in Cancer are higher than Mercurius in Virgo. This *hierosgamos* is represented by a moon filling the right-hand side of the picture; for the way Waite cuts off part of the sun suggests to me the picture needs completing, as I have done above with part of the planetary houses. Mercury's twin, of course, is in Gemini. Although the Wirth card appears to be very different from the Waite Fool, the meaning is the same. Wirth's added features are the crocodile and obelisk, the latter a solar symbol, and the former signifying chaos or the abyss; so both cards convey similar meanings, albeit esoterically.

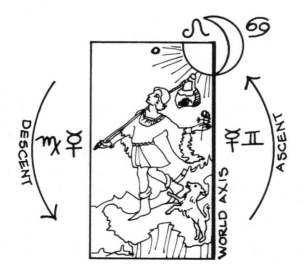

THE CADUCEUS READING

The spirit Hermes/Mercurius is in a sense the spirit of the Sun, the highest of the high; he is also the homunculus or offspring of the Sun. He brings with him the message of the gods, the Logos. In *Origins of Alchemy in Graeco-Roman Egypt,* Jack Lindsay notes:

> Hermes, the ancient soul-guide into the underworld, was given a celestial role with the swing of popular belief from the dark realm of Hades below the earth as the site of the afterlife, to the bright spheres of the star-world. . . . An epigram of the 1st century A.D. declares: "Wingfooted Hermes took your hand and led you on high to Olympus and set you to shine among the stars of the sky." The acquisition of Hermes as guide implied some sort of mystery-initiation. In a Mithraic catacomb on the Appian Way Hermes-Mercury leads the initiated before Hades and Persephone (Pluto and Prosperpine). Here, though in the service of astral religion, he reasserts his underworld-image; but he has to point upwards.[292]

Larousse notes that although "the functions of divine messenger and 'guide of souls' could, astrologically, be related respectively to a diurnal and a nocturnal aspect, they may also be the descending and ascending currents symbolized by the two serpents of the caduceus."[293] The nocturnal aspect of the god refers to his underworld function, *psychopompos* or guide of the dead, as was Thoth. In the serpents of the caduceus, one direction and function is involutive, from light, and the bearer of the "heavenly" message of eternity, towards darkness and concretion. Once there—in the underworld of Saturn's domain—the direction and function is evolutive, and Mercurius now functions as the "pointer of the way" that men may follow back to light and to the celestial realm.

We shall now examine the significance of the caduceus in relation to a *spiral* way of reading the Major Arcana which I call the Caduceus Reading. We have seen how the Magic Nine revealed the numerical and alchemical esoteric meanings of each Key. The lemniscate (or lazy eight because the figure lies on its side) symbolizes infinity in the symbols of numbers. From our study of the spiral, we have seen that like the experience of the labyrinth, its meaning is regeneration, the involuting and evoluting of the serpent-spirit uroboros. The lemniscate is symbolic shorthand for the caduceus, itself a depiction of the regenerating uroboros.

The initiatory experience of the Major Arcana has led us to the underworld and back, following our guide Hermes/Mercurius/Thoth, the mediator of Above and Below. Will a pattern emerge if we follow the spiral thread through the labyrinth of the Major Arcana? Eight is the number and shape of the serpent, so let us pursue the wisdom of the serpent. "Time and time again the alchemists reiterate that the *opus* proceeds from the one and leads back to the one, that it is a sort of a circle like a dragon biting his own tail."[294] In this Caduceus Reading, meaning derives not only from the *archetypal* interpretation of the number eight, but also from the actual shape of the number. We shall proceed from the one, represented by either 1, 10, or 19, since reduction again yields one. Let us begin with the number ten, Key 10, The Wheel of Fortune. This card symbolizes the cycle of descent and ascent, in terms of the human soul the reincarnation into world/body. A reading such as we shall pursue now is *macrocosmic* in perspective in that the scope is the descent of god/spirit/soul from the heavenly realm to the mundane, wherein it undergoes initiatory and transformative experiences and, having passed all tests, is reunited with its celestial origin. Therefore, the Caduceus Spread is nothing less than the Great Myth rendered in the form of the serpent/spiral of involution and evolution. There are two paths that we can pursue from the macrocosm Above. One path "proceeds from the One" in the form of Key 1, The Magician, and follows the descent indicated by his gesture Below. The other path follows the cycle of descent of Key 10. A rather amazing numerical synchronicity indicates the map we may follow, the sequence of numbers being eight and ten throughout our path. The former number is regeneration, the latter unity. The path from Key 1 follows a pattern of + 10 − 8 while descending, the return Above indicated by − 10 + 8. For example, 1 + 10 = 11, the second card of our station, while 11 – 8 = 3, the third card on our path, and *etc.*

The alternate path follows the sequence – 8 + 10, or 10 – 8 = 2, the second station, and 2 + 10 = 12, the third station. Now if the reader will examine the Caduceus Spread, he will see that it is the Magic Nine rendered vertically and without Keys 19, 20, 21, and 0. But instead of proceeding through the Keys sequentially, we shall follow the spiral of the serpent; hence the name Caduceus Spread.

The most telling point regarding the spiral reading of the Major Arcana is that it appears to encompass the common elements of most mythic cosmologies. In it Gnostic, Christian, Buddhist, and Hindu mythologies come together. Of course, each of these would interpret the individual stations of the soul's journey in their own specific ways, but the underlying structure, the bones beneath the serpent's skin, so to speak, are universally true to all mythologies.

Let us begin with The Wheel, Key 10, the symbol of reincarnation in the East, and of the cycles of descent and ascent in the Judeo-Christian tradition. Or, as the *Emerald Tablet* has told us, the One "comes down again from heaven to earth," commencing the cycle of regeneration. As I have said, 8 is the number of regeneration, and of the serpent who sloughs his skin (death), so let us subtract 8 from 10, the result being 2. Following the path of the involuting, materializing serpent, our descent is through the *even* numbers, whereas the ascending, dematerializing, and spiritualizing serpent follows all *odd* numbers. In connection with even numbers, we called attention to elements of fixity, stasis, and polar opposition. The descending spiral through even numbers is the down-tendency of the soul in response to the longing of Physis for Nous, and spirit for matter, the Ineffable for Form, plus countless other variations. All religions play upon this monomyth, akin to the eternally spiraling movement of the microcosm, and its signature is imprinted in the microcosm of our cells in the spiral structure of DNA.

The atom splits, the cell divides, and the Monad of divine unity becomes two by the process of regeneration (10 – 8 = 2).

Our reading of Key 2, The High Priestess, was extensive indeed; but if the archetype of 2 is recalled, the Unmanifest has generated a binary, and with it duality as the basic quality of natural process. The pillars in The High Priestess comprise a gateway, the point at which the Monad, soul, or spirit enters the world of polar opposition and tension. This tension may be followed in all of the subsequent even-numbered Keys, until ascent and resolution of tension commences with the odd-numbered Keys. The High Priestess' veil hides the mystery of the Unmanifest, which burgeons into life (the pomegranates) at the gateway of Boaz and Joachin, night and day, the dawn of the soul, dark and light, death and life. Waite calls her "the bright reflection." She is the One reflecting on itself through form, as sunlight may be thought to reflect itself by moonlight.

Proceeding through our spiral reading of the Major Arcana, the addition of 10 to 2 yields a sum of 12, The Hanged Man, symbolic of spirit's descent to matter, or active to passive, which we delineated in the color symbology of the hanged man's garb, and in the spiritual trine made by his arms and the cross of matter formed by his feet. In Key 12 God becomes Man by Incarnation. This messiah theme is prevalent in most mythologies, combining themes of spirit and matter, just as the number 12 combines the Monad and the Dyad of matter.

The presence of the Monad, spirit, or the divine should be retained in the reader's mind, during our spiral descent, by reference to Key 10, that is, the sun glyph is symbolized by a wheel, and in Key 12, the golden nimbus jogs our memory to Key 10, as will the angel's nimbus in Key 14.

We have now analyzed but three of the even-numbered Keys in the descent and manifestation; yet already we may discern a difference between those of return to unity ($+10$) and those Keys of regeneration (-8). These Keys appear at the left, for the former, and at the right for the latter. The Keys of return to unity (10 and 12) contain elements of the cosmic, and the divine, or the Monad, whereas Key 2 and the other Keys of Descent, 4, 6, and 8 are mundane and material. Pursuing this idea, we shall see that Keys 14, 16, and 18 on the left also contain elements of the Monad associated with the return to unity which results from the addition of 10. Of course, the whole process of ascent, which we shall follow in subsequent Keys by adding 8 and subtracting 10, constitutes a return to unity (the Monad); however, we have a minicycle within the greater cycle in each spiral of the serpent. Therefore, we can be completely predictive about the next station. For example, in the *regeneration* which follows Key 12, the material reasserts itself. 12 – 8 = 4, the number of earth, the four directions, four elements, four seasons, etc. Alchemically, a cube of salt bears the same meaning. The Emperor's throne in Key 4 symbolizes the autonomy of the mundane, *untempered* by spirit. But here we can be predictive again, knowing that in our minicycle there will be a return to unity, or that the grip of Physis on Nous will be lessened; thus 4 + 10 = 14, Temperance, wherein an angel appears, the golden halo of the Hanged Man shining once more, and the sun, symbolic of the spiritual source (wheel = sun in Key 10) radiating a crown of glory above the *dual* peaks. The exchange between golden and silver cups bears the same meaning—spirit tempering matter—as the sun's light reflecting in the silver moon (Key 10 – 8 = 2). Therefore, the material cube *does* contain a spiritual essence, alchemically the lapis, which is to be returned to unity by means of the alchemical fire. The esoteric shorthand for this is the graphic design on the angel's breast, the fire trine contained within the square (cube) of matter.

The next regeneration occurs when 8 is subtracted from 14, yielding 6, The Lovers. This is the regeneration of eros the sexual polarities exerting a tension that seeks resolution in union. In our graphics for Key 6, we called attention to the two trines of fire and water, aspiring matter and descending spirit, but the essence of this union is best presented by Tantra yoga, in which the partners in sexual embrace transcend—or burn away—their mundane selves and become god and goddess. In the West, sexual desire is linked through the guilt of the Garden to the Fall, and to ruin, which Waite indicates as the meaning of Key 16, 6 + 10 = 16. Key 6 does depict the serpent of the Fall, so the progression to Key 16 follows the monomyth of the West, at least.

Return to unity is symbolized by the shattering of polarities, king and queen, masculine and feminine, and by the material stone, akin to The Emperor's cubic throne. The solar crown again appears, and the lightning-like Logos reasserts the autonomy of the macrocosmic Monad, the apparent catastrophe resulting in a new regeneration, the harmony of opposites depicted in Key 8 (16 − 8 = 8). Here we may consider a medieval alchemical text, which tells us that the red lion must be touched by the white woman, that is, fiery sulphur must be tinctured by mercury to effect a stabilizing of disparate elements.

Key 8 is particularly important to the spiral reading of the Major Arcana for three reasons. First, it is the last card of *descending* regeneration, being followed by Key 18, the last card of return to unity. Eight being the number of regeneration, and this being Key 8, we may expect to find a link between the archetype of eight's numerical meaning and the esoteric symbology of the card. This is manifest in the lemniscate spiral above the woman's head, and also present in the garland, looped in a figure eight, linking woman and lion. The lemniscate signifies infinity, and we may infer that the cosmos is infinite by an alternating cycle of return to unity followed by regeneration, akin to the expansion/contraction theory of cosmologists in which all the matter of the universe returns to an infinitely dense point or centre (the Monad) and then blows up (regenerates) in one Big Bang. Now since the Monad is represented by Keys 10 and 1, ten reducing to one, it is significant that these cards of the return to unity also bear the spiral lemniscate. In Key 1, it appears over the magician's head, and is also symbolized by the serpent uroboros about his waist. In Key 10 the descending spiral serpent has associations with regeneration, while the wheel's centre, and all other symbols in the card, present the concept of return to unity, the World Axis. Indeed, Key 10 signifies the alchemical concept of squaring the circle, resolving all polarities, particularly sulphur and mercury, the glyphs for which appear within the spokes of the wheel, and which appear also in Key 8 as red lion and white woman.

The second point of significance in relation to Key 8 has to do with the Stairway of Planets. We recall that the *hierosgamos* at the summer solstice consisted of the two adjacent signs Cancer and Leo, ruled by Queen Moon and King

Sun. The first descending sign from this celestial pair was that of Virgo, ruled by Mercury. Key 8 is a tableau of the lion (Leo) and virgin (Virgo). In his book *The Pictorial Key to the Tarot,* Waite is as abstruse as possible in relating the woman to Virgo, saying only that the card "connects also with *innocentia inviolata*. . . ."[295]

Waite says also that the card "is connected with the Divine Mystery of Union,"[296] which we have explored as the *hierosgamos*. Significantly, for the third and final reason, the return to unity (8 + 10 = 18) is the *coniunctio* of Sun and Moon depicted in Key 18; thus, our descending spiral culminates most appropriately.

In terms of the monomyth of world religions, the union "here below" is of body and soul, spirit and matter, God and man, the incarnation of the divine in man. The dog and wolf, Gabricus and Beya, symbolize these concepts. In summary, therefore, we see that the five cards of return to unity (Keys 10, 12, 14, 16, and 18) all contain a symbolic clue to their origin card: Key 10, sun as wheel; Key 12, sun as golden nimbus; Key 14, sun as golden halo *and* crown; Key 16, sun as golden crown; Key 18, sun in *coniunctio* with moon, descent being through the lunar portals of Key 2.

By Key 18, the sun/spirit/gold has been swallowed in the abysmal depths of matter, but by reversing the path, as in the Stairway of Planets, the ascent to the Monad, the return to undivided, unpolarized unity, may be attained by the individual soul. This is clearly expressed in Key 18 by the golden path, which commences at the abyss and rises ever higher into the peaks of the distant mountains. Above, on one of these peaks, we may assume, stands the hermit, and above Key 18 in our reading stands The Hermit, his lantern bearing the "married" trines of spirit and matter, or Above and Below. He faces along the line of the Magic Nine in the direction of his quest, the One, or Monad, symbolized by the magician in Key 1 who makes the gesture "As Above, so Below." Let us recall again that nine is the number of completion, attainment, and fulfillment, the implication being that only when the earthly task is resolved may ascent commence for the individual soul to return to the Monad.

In ascending we reverse the sequence by *adding* 8 (regeneration) and *subtracting* 10 (return to unity). Our first

279

sequence is $9 + 8 = 17$, The Star. During descent the spirit had become clothed materially (the mantle of the hermit, perhaps). Now these vestments are forsaken, and the spirit will appear naked before its creator at the final judgment, which is presaged before the Monad by Key 11, Justice. But before the soul/spirit arrives there, various antagonists will seek to impede the return to the One, the creator, sun/light, or in Gnostic terms, the Ogdoad, the eighth sphere above the seven planets, represented in Key 17 by the eight-pointed star. The circular form of the Stairway of Planets is also depicted by the seven lesser stars.

We proceed to our next station, The Chariot, by the formula $17 - 10 = 7$. The chariot itself may be thought of as the vehicle for the soul's progress, just as the sun-god was sometimes shown in a chariot moving through the sky, but more likely it is symbolic of the journey itself; for the highly ritualized apparel of the charioteer and its esoteric markings—note the apron—present the *initiated* soul about to undergo a trial that will test it sorely.

This stage of the monomyth seems common to all religions; it is the challenge of Evil to Good, Duality to Unity, Darkness to Light, in short, the encounter with the Antagonist. In terms of Gnosticism, this figure is Ialdabaoth, creator of the physical world, whose archons or jailers seek to hold back the ascending soul. These planetary demons may be appeased by the right propitiatory words, the Book of the Dead memorized by each man while quick in order to vouchsafe his passage among the dead. Seven inscriptions hang from the charioteer's belt. Are these not the proper hieroglyphs or talismans to speed him on his way past the seven planetary demons? Through his ordeal he must not give in to his fears, but face woe or weal with equanimity, this idea symbolized by the faces in the crescent moons on his shoulders, one frowning, the other laughing.

If we gaze again upon The Star and look at The Chariot, we see that the starry sky has been transposed to the starry canopy above the chariot, and the eight-pointed star is placed at the charioteer's crown. It would be naive to assume that these are haphazard relations. Clearly the Caduceus Reading of the Major Arcana enhances what we have learned from the Magic Nine; for it is the journey through the

280

planetary spheres which the charioteer undertakes, and the Ogdoad, or eighth sphere, is his goal.

Next, the encounter with the Antagonist, $7 + 8 = 15$, The Devil. As to the chained figures, these may be thought of as uninitiated souls, those not saved by the teachings every religion professes to impart to its followers, these teachings being the *raison d'être* for the soul's salvation. Now in Key 15, an esoteric sign appears to contradict the Ogdoad quest, the liberation from the qualities which the planets imparted to the soul upon descending. At the forehead of the Devil is the inverted *five*-pointed star, the number for man made obeisant to the Antagonist's will. Note also the open palm of the Devil, on which is etched the Mark of the Beast. Look then at the crown and head of the Hierophant ($15 - 10 = 5$).

The Hierophant, Key 5, is the initiate who has successfully passed the test. The triple crown integrates in one symbol heaven, earth, and hell, and his gesture, as Waite tells us, "gives the well-known ecclesiastical sign which is called that of esotericism, distinguishing between the manifest and concealed part of doctrine."[297] An initiate who survives becomes himself an initiator; thus a hierophant is one who initiates others into the mysteries of life and death, $5 + 8 = 13$, Death.

In Key 13, the golden crown of the hierophant has become the black helm of the nigredo condition, suggesting that at this station of the journey the physical body returns to the nigredo (earth) as the soul journeys on. Key 13 also presents the banner of a white rose on a black field, a significant change from the *white* lilies of Key 5. Five, as the number of man, signifies a mediary condition, between Above and Below, or Heaven and Hell; and these dualities are represented by the red roses, for the active condition, and the white lilies, for the passive phase, as well as by the gold and silver keys. However, lilies do symbolize resurrection, or rebirth in the spirit; therefore, the five-petaled white rose is parallel in meaning to the Fool's white rose, "signifying the extinction of all interest in life and in the manifest world."

As mentioned before, Death, Key 13, also has another relation to The Fool in the symbol of the red feather, related to the spirit because of its associations with birds and the flight of the spirit or the *winged* soul. This combination of red and white hints at a *t'ai chi*-type blend of active and passive, that is, birth in death. Further, the feather signified truth and justice, in the judgment revealed in the Egyptian Book of the Dead, and we are nearing that judgment, Justice, Key 11, being the penultimate card in our Caduceus Reading. But the feather has symbolic connotations as the Word, the Logos, with which both gold and the sun are associated, gold being particles of the sun ripening in the earth, according to alchemy.

In Key 13, a golden crown lies atop the ground, while the sun emerges from the earth at sunrise, that is, the Logos reasserts its autonomy in the form of the sun emerging from the underworld. Key 13 may be likened to Good Friday and Easter in *one* tableau, for the resurrected sun suggests the vernal equinox, when the sun-god breaks free of the earth's six darkest months. If Key 13 depicts a sunset instead of a sunrise, then why does Waite utilize a golden dawn for the next three cards, Keys 3, 11, and 1? A further glance ahead also reveals significant changes in the crowns on our next three figures, gold ascendant once more, nigredo (Death's black helm) transformed. By Key 1, all material symbols of spiritual autonomy are forsaken, and the Magician's crown is purely a symbol, the lemniscate of eternity.

We recall that Key 3, and its vertical series, developed the archetype of three as the principle of heaven, the Empress being "clothed in the sun," or Logos. Her crown is that of the zodiac, twelve stars signifying the soul's *transitus* through planetary realms. This journey is thought to be circular, like the shape of the uroboric serpent with tail in mouth, or spiral, like the lemniscate, since the sun's journey about the poles is a spiraling descent and ascent. The Magician's staff is akin to the World Axis, and to the parallel system which links the Stairway of Planets and the magician's spine, for lemniscate and uroboros encircle him. Keys 3 and 1 are attained by subtraction of ten, $13 - 10 = 3$, $11 - 10 = 1$, and represent return to unity.

The final card of regeneration is Key 11, $3 + 8 = 11$, and the final way of the ascending soul, on its journey to reunion with the One, is blocked by the figure of Justice with sword in hand, recalling the angel Michael guarding the gate to Paradise. Indeed, Paradise has the same connotations as return to the Monad, for the soul is then no longer separate from its creator, no longer confronted by duality. In this final test or confrontation of the spirit, Waite calls attention to the fact "that the figure is seated between pillars, like the High Priestess. . . ."[298] Having told us that much, he then obfuscates his meaning by telling us what does not apply, as follows: "The law of Justice is not however involved by either alternative. In conclusion the pillars of Justice open into one world and the pillars of the High Priestess into another."[299] The latter sentence, however, is of extreme importance to our rendering of the Caduceus Reading, the clues to each world indicated by the nature of the veils between the pillars.

Auric readers may be familiar with the purple color; it is assigned the highest spiritual vibration. In Key 11, the color of this veil reveals that through these pillars lies the way to reunion with the Monad, spiritual apotheosis for the ascending soul, whereas palms and pomegranates of Key 2 connote the fruitional world, the material world which is entered through the pillars of The High Priestess. Should a negative judgment prevent the soul from passing, the rejected soul would have to return along the way it had come, reincarnating once more. A detail which Waite has added to Key 11, the two green strips of cloth hanging in front from the figure's cape, suggests the two serpents of the caduceus, or the two paths of our spiral reading. A very close look reveals a serpent's head.

With the last station safely passed, the soul attains the Monad, $11 - 10 = 1$, the One.

CONCLUSION

Reviewing the three treatments given to the Major Arcana, numerical, alchemical, and astrological, it should be clear to us now that all three of these postulate the existence—beyond natural reality—of a formative, nonphysical essence that animates life through its immanent power. In the realm of number, there is an archetype of meaning behind ordinary numerals, all number being emanations from the Monad. Furthermore, alchemy is the spiritual discipline that aims to restore the One, in its descended state of material adaptation, to its spiritual essence, sun/gold/lapis, etc. Astrology is yet another Hermetic art, the personal horoscope revealing the One's manifestation in man, one's configuration of planets reflecting the One's potential within the man.

Finally, through our spiral reading of the Major Arcana, we followed the path of the cosmic uroboros, expanding and contracting, regenerating and returning to unity, also the microcosmic double helix of DNA, preserver of our ancient psychic history, at once vehicle and pathway for archetype, god, and devil. The Major Arcana, as a contemporary Book of the Dead, reflect Western man's aversion to death and the material power which the Devil exerts over him through the credo that *his material form is the limit of his autonomy.* Thus the body is not easily forsaken, nor easily enjoyed during the lifetime, since the tenacious clinging to materiality is graceless because it is motivated by fear.

The Hermetic alternative view enables one to play the life as a kind of drama of one's own creation, a dream, perhaps, that the dreamer dreams. Mechanistic chance, cause and effect, are not operative in this view of the universe; hence, joy, vitality, and dynamic interplay between man and cosmos manifest in daily experience. When tragedy manifests, such a man displays his heroic potential, for he realizes the tragedy—like the joy—is his personal creation, a test for his further expansion of consciousness. Whether joyous or tragic, man and cosmos hold a dialogue in which the One grows in one, and one evolves in the One. This, then, is the ultimate sense of a Book of the Dead: return to the splendid, shining consciousness of the golden One, who during the lifetimes was being born within, or rather, maturing, since the One had created the egg/child/man. To die, then, is to exchange form for non-form, energy transformed or stepped up to a higher level. But mind, spirit, soul—call the Ineffable what you will—is that aspect of eternity which Divinity shares with us, and we with That.

And at the end of time, when the serpent uroboros grasps his tail in his mouth, then the infinite dimension of the cosmos shall be swallowed as if by a Black Hole, matter shall collapse, galaxy on galaxy, until All That Is is contained once more within the still point of the Monad.

LIST OF FOOTNOTES

1. Richard Roberts, *Tarot and You* (Vernal Equinox Press), Box 581, San Anselmo, California 94960
2. Titus Burckhardt, *Alchemy: Science of the Cosmos, Science of the Soul* (Baltimore: Penguin Books, Inc., 1971)
3. *Ibid.,* p. 41
4. Catherine Hargrave, *A History of Playing Cards* (New York: Dover Publications, 1966), p. 224
5. *Ibid.*
6. Arthur Edward Waite, *The Pictorial Key to the Tarot* (New York: University Books, 1959), p. 100
7. Jean Doresse, *The Secret Book of the Egyptian Gnostics* (London: Hollis and Carter, 1960)
8. Origen, *Contra Celsus*
9. J. E. Cirlot, *A Dictionary of Symbols* (New York: Philosophical Library, Inc., 1962), p. 20
10. C. G. Jung, *Psychology and Alchemy* (New York: Bollingen Foundation, Inc., 1953), p. 460
11. *Ibid.,* p. 57
12. Herbert Silberer, *Hidden Symbolism of Alchemy and the Occult Arts* (N.Y.: Dover, 1971), p. 368
13. Cirlot, *op. cit.,* p. 297–99
14. Paul Foster Case, *The Tarot* (Richmond, Virginia: Macoy, 1947), p. 13
15. Cirlot, *op. cit.,* p. 223
16. *Ibid.,* p. 198
17. *Ibid.*
18. Case, *op. cit.,* p. 14
19. C. G. Jung, *Mysterium Coniunctionis* (New York: Bollingen Foundation, Inc., 1963), p. 221.
20. *Ibid.,* p. 222

21. Case, *op. cit.*, p. 13
22. Jung, *Mysterium Coninunctionis*, p. 224
23. Waite, *op. cit.*, p. 152
24. M. von Franz, *Aurora Consurgens* (New York: Bollingen Foundation, Inc., no date), p. 4
25. Roberts, *op. cit.*, p. 10
26. Case, *op. cit.*, p. 52
27. Waite, *op. cit.*, p. 76
28. *Ibid.*, p. 80
29. *Ibid.*, p. 83
30. *Ibid.*, p. 80
31. *Ibid.*, p. 159
32. Hargrave, *op. cit.*, p. 224
33. Waite, *op. cit.*, p. 124
34. *Ibid.*, p. 95
35. *Ibid.*
36. Cirlot, *op. cit.*, p. 270
37. Waite, *op. cit.*, p. 104
38. Cirlot, *op. cit.*, p. 232
39. *Ibid.*, p. 352
40. *Ibid.*, p. 23
41. Case, *op. cit.*, p. 52
42. Cirlot, *op. cit.*, p. 318
43. *Ibid.*, p. 269
44. *Ibid.*, p. 194
45. *Ibid.*, p. 125
46. Case, *op. cit.*, pp. 57 and 59
57. Waite, *op. cit.*, p. 83
48. Cirlot, *op. cit.*, p. 118
49. *Ibid.*, p. 220
50. Waite, *op. cit.*, p. 161
51. Cirlot, *op. cit.*, p. 222
52. *Ibid.*
53. *Ibid.*
54. *Ibid.*
55. *Ibid.*, p. 223
56. Case, *op. cit.*, p. 12
57. Cirlot, *op. cit.*, p. 223
58. *Ibid.*, p. 207
59. Jung, *Mysterium Coniunctionis*, p. 185

60. *Ibid.,* p. 332
61. *Ibid.*
62. *Ibid.,* p. 185
63. *Ibid.,* p. 188
64. *Musaeum Hermeticum,* "Aquarium Sapientum" (Frankfurt, 1678), p. 84
65. C. G. Jung, *Alchemical Studies* (New York: Bollingen Foundation, Inc., 1967), p. 210
65a. Jung, *Psychology and Alchemy,* p. 304.
66. Jurain, *Hyle und Coahyl* (Hamburg, 1732)
67. *Ibid.*
68. Henri-Charles Puech, "Gnosis and Time," in *Man and Time: Papers From the Eranos Yearbooks,* IV. (New York: Bollingen Foundation, Inc., 1957), p. 67
69. Jung, *Psychology and Alchemy,* p. 295
70. *Ibid.,* p. 336
71. *Ibid.,* p. 338
72. *Ibid.,* p. 297
73. Emma Jung, *Animus and Anima* (New York: Spring Publications, 1957), p. 29
74. M. von Franz, *op. cit.,* p. 189
75. Joseph Henderson and Maude Oakes, *The Wisdom of the Serpent* (New York: MacMillan Co., 1971), p. 110
76. *Ibid.,* p. 113
77. C. G. Jung, "Transformation Symbols in the Mass," in *The Mysteries: Papers From the Eranos Yearbooks,* II. (New York: Bollingen Foundation, Inc., 1955), p. 331
78. C. W. King, *The Gnostics and Their Remains* (Minneapolis: Wizards Bookshelf, 1973), p. 228
79. *Ibid.,* p. 30
80. Jung, *Alchemical Studies,* p. 59
81. *Ibid.,* p. 60
60. *Ibid.,* p. 61
83. *Ibid.,* p. 60
84. *Ibid.,* p. 61
85. *Ibid.,* p. 64
86. *Ibid.,* p. 333
87. *Ibid.*
88. *Ibid.,* p. 62

89. *Ibid.,* p. 331
90. *Ibid.,* p. 63
91. Jung, *Mysterium Coniunctionis,* p. 231
92. Jung, *Alchemical Studies,* p. 63
93. *Ibid.,* p. 330
94. Jung, *Psychology and Alchemy,* p. 357
95. *Ibid.,* p. 408
96. Waite, *The Secret Tradition in Alchemy*
97. *Ibid.*
98. Waite, *The Pictorial Key to the Tarot*
99. Waite, *The Secret Tradition in Alchemy*
100. Jung, *Psychology and Alchemy,* p. 395
101. *Ibid.,* p. 431
102. *Ibid.,* p. 78
103. Manley P. Hall, *The Secret Teachings of All Ages* (Los Angeles: The Philosophical Research Society, Inc., 1962), p. CXLV
104. *Ibid.,* p. CXLVI
105. *Ibid.,* p. CXLV
106. Waite, *The Secret Tradition in Alchemy,* p. 169ff
107. Charles Poncé, *The Game of Wizards* (Baltimore: Penguin Books, 1975), p. 184
108. *Ibid.,* p. 185
109. Jung, *Psychology and Alchemy,* p. 337
110. *Ibid.,* p. 331
111. *Ibid.,* p. 329
112. Jung, *Mysterium Coniunctionis,* p. 25
113. Jung, *Psychology and Alchemy,* p. 413
114. Hall, *op. cit.,* p. XCII
115. *Ibid.*
116. Jung, *Mysterium Coniunctionis,* p. 149
117. *Ibid.,* p. 149
118. *Ibid.,* p. 147
119. *Ibid.,* p. 145
120. Cirlot, *op. cit.,* p. 80
121. Jung, *Mysterium Coniunctionis,* p. 147
122. *Larousse Encyclopedia of Mythology* (New York: Prometheus Press, 1966), p. 41
123. Cirlot, *op. cit.,* p. 105
124. Ralph Metzner, *Maps of Consciousness* (New York: Collier Books, 1971), p. 61

125. *Ibid.*
126. Cirlot, *op. cit.*, p. 263
127. Jung, *Mysterium Coniunctionis,* p. 146
128. *Ibid.,* p. 221
129. Cirlot, *op. cit.*, p. 249
130. Waite, *The Pictorial Key to the Tarot,* p. 76
131. Jung, *Mysterium Coniunctionis,* p. 21
132. *Ibid.,* p. 19
133. Jung, *Psychology and Alchemy,* p. 166
134. Cirlot, *op. cit.,* p. 71
135. Silberer, *op. cit.,* p. 400
136. Waite, *op. cit.,* p. 88
137. Silberer, *op. cit.,* p. 212
138. Waite, *op. cit.,* p. 75
139. Silberer, *op. cit.,* p. 185
140. *Ibid.,* p. 188
141. *Ibid.,* p. 187
142. Cirlot, *op. cit.,* p. 222
143. Case, *op. cit.,* p. 82
144. Cirlot, *op. cit.,* p. 223
145. *Ibid.*
146. Waite, *op. cit.,* p. 124
147. Cirlot, *op. cit.,* p. 314
148. Case, *op. cit.,* p. 87
149. Waite, *op. cit.,* p. 92
150. Jung, *Mysterium Coniunctionis,* p. 382
151. Cirlot, *op. cit.,* p. 209
152. Jung, *Mysterium Coniunctionis,* p. 408
153. *Ibid.,* p. 397
154. Jung, *Psychology and Alchemy,* p. 385
155. *Ibid.,* p. 372
156. *Ibid.,* p. 360ff
157. *Ibid.,* p. 372
158. Jung, *Mysterium Coniunctionis,* p. 332
159. Jung, *Alchemical Studies,* p. 145
160. *Ibid.,* p. 146
161. *Ibid.,* p. 152
162. *Ibid.*
163. Jung, *Psychology and Alchemy,* p. 436
164. *Ibid.,* p. 438
165. Waite, *op. cit.,* p. 100

166. *Ibid.,* p. 103
167. Cirlot, *op. cit.,* p. 110
168. Waite, *op. cit.,* p. 100
169. Silberer, *op. cit.,* p. 400
170. Waite, *op. cit.,* p. 136
171. Jung, *Psychology and Alchemy,* p. 452
172. Jung, *Mysterium Coniunctionis,* p. 195
173. Waite, *op. cit.,* p. 17
174. *Ibid.,* p. 105
175. Jung, *Mysterium Coniunctionis,* p. 281
176. *Ibid.*
177. *Artis Auriferae,* I, p. 390, Basel, 1593
178. Jung, "The Philosophical Tree," *Alchemical Studies,* p. 311
179. Ibid., p. 310
180. *Ibid.,* p. 314
181. Roger Cook, *The Tree of Life* (New York: Avon Books, 1974), p. 6
182. *Ibid.,* p. 9
183. *Ibid.,* p. 6
184. Jurain, *Hyle und Coahyl.*
185. Cirlot, *op. cit.,* p. 298
186. King, *op. cit.,* p. 346
187. Cirlot, *op. cit.,* p. 320
188. *Ibid.,* p. 319
189. *Ibid.,* p. 33
190. Jack Lindsay, *Origins of Alchemy in Graeco-Roman Egypt* (London: Muller, 1970), p. 35
191. *Ibid.,* p. 36
192. Cirlot, *op. cit.,* p. 31
193. *Ibid.,* p. 285
194. Lindsay, *op. cit.,* p. 35
195. *Ibid.,* p. 190
196. Hall, *op. cit.,* p. 23
197. *Ibid.*
198. Hawkins, *Beyond Stonehenge* (New York: Harper & Row, 1973), p. 232
199. Hall, *op. cit.,* p. xxiii
200. Joseph Campbell, *The Masks of God, Occidental Mythology* (New York: Viking Press, 1964), p. 260

201. Hall, *op. cit.,* p. xxiv
202. Campbell, *op. cit.,* p. 255
203. Silberer, *op. cit.,* p. 126
204. Trevor Ravenscroft, *The Spear of Destiny* (New York: Bantam Books, 1974), p. 253
205. Cirlot, *op. cit.,* p. 47
206. *Ibid.*
207. *Ibid.,* p. 79
208. *Ibid.,* p. 63
209. *Ibid.,* p. 48
210. *Ibid.,* p. 324
211. *Ibid.,* p. 89
212. *Ibid.,* p. 88
213. Waite, *The Holy Grail,* p. vii
214. King, *op. cit.,* p. 117
215. Cirlot, *op. cit.,* p. 144
216. Hall, *op. cit.,* p. 54
217. King, *op. cit.,* p. 31
218. Hall, *op. cit., p. 91*
219. Cirlot, *op. cit.,* p. 84
220. Hall, *op. cit.,* p. xxiii
221. Lewis Spence, *Mysteries of Britain* (London: Rider & Co., no date), p. 235
222. King, *op. cit.,* p. 117
223. Spence, *op. cit.,* p. 127
224. *Ibid.,* p. 253
225. Waite, *The Pictorial Key to the Tarot,* p. 224
226. Cirlot, *op. cit.,* p. 177
227. *Ibid.,* p. 176
228. Waite, *op. cit.,* p. 222
229. Cirlot, *op. cit.,* p. 161
230. *Ibid.,* p. 162
231. *Ibid.*
232. *Ibid.,* p. 265
233. *Ibid.,* p. 163
234. Spence, *op. cit.,* p. 188
235. Cirlot, *op. cit.,* 183
236. Burckhardt, *op. cit.,* p. 135
237. Cirlot, *op. cit.,* p. 166
238. *Ibid.,* p. 167
239. *Ibid.*

240. Jung, *Psychology and Alchemy,* p. 381
241. Hall, *op. cit.,* p. XXVII
242. Waite, *op. cit.,* p. 108
243. John Layard, *Spiritual Disciplines, Papers from Eranos, 4* (New York: Bollingen Foundation, Inc., 1964), p. 149
244. *Ibid.,* p. 142
245. *Ibid.,* p. 118
246. *Ibid.,* p. 119
247. *Ibid.,* p. 123
248. *Ibid.,* p. 138
249. *Ibid.,* p. 142
250. Joseph Campbell, *The Mythic Image* (Princeton: Princeton University Press, 1975), p. 469
251. *Ibid.,* p. 467
252. Campbell, *The Masks of God, Occidental Mythology* p. 235
253. Hall, *op. cit.,* p. LIV
254. Campbell, *The Mythic Image,* p. 451
255. *Ibid.,* p. 29
256. Cirlot, p. 95
257. Campbell, *The Mythic Image,* p. 29
258. *Ibid.,* p. 465
259. *Ibid.,* p. 478
260. *Ibid.,* p. 16
261. *Ibid.*
262. *Ibid.,* p. 479
263. Cirlot, *op. cit.,* p. 105
264. Sir James Frazer, *The Golden Bough* (New York: Criterion Books, 1959), p. 87
265. *Ibid.*
266. *Ibid.,* p. 311
267. *Ibid.,* p. 82
268. *Ibid.,* p. 278
269. Cirlot, *op. cit.,* p. 48
270. Hall, *op. cit.,* p. XCII
271. Frazer, *op. cit.,* p. 567
272. Jung, *Psychology and Alchemy,* p. 358
273. Hermes Trismegistus, *Tractatus Aureus* (Leipzig, 1610)
274. Jung, *Mysterium Coniunctionis,* p. 219

275. *Ibid.*
276. Lindsay, *op. cit.,* p. 169
277. Larousse, *op. cit.,* p. 28
278. Cirlot, *op. cit.,* p. 363
279. Eric Partridge, *Origins: A Short Etymological Dictionary of Modern English* (New York: MacMillan, 1958), p. 638
280. Jung, *Alchemical Studies,* p. 225
281. Waite, *The Pictorial Key to the Tarot,* p. 147
282. Case, *op. cit.,* p. 186
283. *Ibid.,* p. 185
284. *Ibid.*
285. Cirlot, *op. cit.,* p. 350
286. *Ibid.,* p. 326
287. *Ibid.,* p. 324
288. *Ibid.,* p. 345
289. Case, *op. cit.,* p. 186
290. *Ibid.,* p. 131
291. *Ibid.*
292. Lindsay, *op. cit.,* p. 37
293. *Larousse, op. cit.,* p. 24
294. Jung, *Psychology and Alchemy,* p. 293
295. Waite, *The Pictorial Key to the Tarot,* p. 100
296. *Ibid.*
297. *Ibid.,* p. 88
298. *Ibid.,* p. 112
299. *Ibid.,* p. 115